CW00880211

AMIN RAJAN

Foreword by Rhiannon Chapman

1992
A ZERO
SUM
GAME

BUSINESS, KNOW-HOW, AND

TRAINING CHALLENGES IN

AN INTEGRATED EUROPE

INDUSTRIAL
SOCIETY
PRESS

First published 1990 by
The Industrial Society
Robert Hyde House
Bryanston Square
London W1H 7LN
Telephone: 01-262-2401

British Library Cataloguing in Publication Data
Rajan, Amin *1942–*
    A zero sum game : business know-how and training
challenges in an integrated Europe.
    1. Great Britain. Business firms
    I. Title
    338.70941

    ISBN 0–85290–594–7

Printed and bound in Great Britain by Billing & Sons Ltd, Worcester

To

Lyn, Nash, Anna,
Lisa, James and David

*for their love, support
and understanding.*

Despite all the singing and cheering Europe's companies are marching off to war. A war that will have its dead and wounded; a war ... from which not everyone will come back a winner.

Carlo De Benedetti
Chairman and Chief Executive
Olivetti

Contents

CONTENTS

CONTENTS

CONTENTS

List of figures

LIST OF FIGURES

List of tables

LIST OF TABLES

Foreword

At the inception of The European Community, a vivid cartoon was published of de Gaulle as an egg, poised on the edge of an omelette pan. He was depicted as asking, *'but what if I don't like being in an omelette and want to be an egg again?'*. Making the European omelette a reality is a delicate process, requiring a confidence and purposefulness not readily available in every domestic kitchen.

The irrevocability of Europe has not reached all hearts and minds even now; in very many respects, emotions and actions are still a long way from being fully integrated. Part of the problem, without any doubt, is the availability of good reference data which can provide the necessary guidance. To complete the omelette analogy, many crucial ingredients of the recipe are still not in place on the kitchen shelf.

For these reasons, this new work from Amin Rajan is particularly to be welcomed. Few people in Europe offer, as Professor Rajan can, a quality, informed overview of European business management and human resource issues. Labour markets are notoriously under-researched, and Europe is no exception. On the other hand, the critical competitive and restructuring pressures which challenge all businesses in the 1990s call for a set of responses which must be determined *now*. As Peter Drucker has said, *'Long-range planning is not about future decisions, but the future of present decisions'*.

Even the most committed Europeans can proceed only with the greatest caution into this brave new world, until we are equipped with a clearer focus upon which to determine our actions. There is no time to lose and timeliness, as the marketing gurus tell us, is key to competitiveness in today's customer-led markets. The ingredients of an effective, European business response are badly in need of the expert analysis which Amin Rajan provides in this important book.

Rhiannon Chapman,
Director, Personnel,
The International Stock Exchange

Acknowledgements

This book has benefited substantially from the co-operation of many organisations and individuals across Europe.

My foremost thanks are due to the Commission of the European Communities and CEDEFOP for funding some of the underlying research as well as facilitating contacts with various key individuals in all the member states. Certain sections in the book are now being used by the Commission in its various reports. However, the views presented here are my own: in no way do they represent the opinions of the Commission.

I would also like to thank the Organisation of Economic Co-operation and Development, the International Labour Office, the Nordic Council of Ministers, Training Agency and the Chartered Institute of Bankers for funding some of the research or for providing useful feed-back on it by involving me in their seminar programmes.

My special thanks go to six companies for giving financial support as well as an ideal platform to try out my ideas on business and human resource practioners: BP, British Telecom, Legal & General, Royal Insurance, Storehouse plc, and TSB Group. Indeed, it was their keen interest in my work that first gave me the idea to write this book. If this work succeeds in providing fresh insights, then its intellectual parentage rightly belongs to numerous individuals in these companies with whom I have had the privilege of working over the past two years.

I also feel especially privileged to have received advice, help and encouragement from my colleagues in the London Human Resource Group. Although they are many in number, I feel that I should mention each of them individually as a mark of genuine appreciation. They are: George Alford (Kleinwort Benson), Rodney Barker (Allen & Overy), David Bell (TSB Group), Alun Bowen (Peat Marwick McLintock), Rhiannon Chapman (The International Stock Exchange), Ron Collard (Coopers & Lybrand Deloitte), Chris Evans (Royal Insurance), Geoff Morgan (Lloyds Merchant Bank), Howard Paget (Barclays de Zoete Wedd), David Sharp (Bank of England), Brian Sheppard (BP), Chris Smith (Price Waterhouse), Sidney Smith (The First National Bank of Chicago), Geoff Tucker (Legal & General) and Roger Woodley (Securities and Investment Board).

At the Industrial Society, I would like to thank Gilles Desmons, Sheridan Maguire, Anna Smith and Sue Webb for their co-operation which served to give a clear steer to the book long before I started writing it. My very special thanks to Katherine Graham for her superb editorial help, provided with humour and aplomb.

I owe a special debt to Steve Davies at the TSB Group for excellent graphics. He has been instrumental in helping me to simplify various ideas into visual models.

Finally, every major venture has its unsung heroes. This one is no exception. First and foremost, this is a team effort. I am deeply grateful to Lyn Rajan, Nash Rajan and Lisa Rajan for their invaluable input throughout the research programme, including the eventual word processing and book setting. Also, their expertise in different areas greatly helped in inject clarity and rigour into the analysis

All in all, this book has incurred a heavy debt. If after all that, it has errors and shortcomings, then I alone am responsible for them.

Amin Rajan

List of abbreviations

B	Belgium		L	Luxembourg
DK	Denmark		NL	Netherlands
F	France		P	Portugal
GR	Greece		E	Spain
IRL	Ireland		UK	United Kingdom
I	Italy		D	West Germany

BIEP	Bureau d'Informations et de Privisions Economiquse (Paris)
CBI	Confederation of British Industries (London)
CEDEFOP	European Centre for the Development of Vocational Training (Berlin)
CENSIS	Centro Studi Investmenti Sociali (Rome)
CEREQ	Research Centre for Occupational and Training Analysis (Paris)
COMECON	Economic union of the Communist countries in Eastern Europe
EFTA	European Free Trade Area
GATT	General Agreement on Tariffs and Trade (Geneva)
GDP	Gross domestic product
ISIC	International Standard Industrial Classification
NCVQ	National Council for Vocational Qualifications (London)
NTI	National Training Initiative
OECD	Organisation for Economic Co-operation and Development (Paris)
TA	Taining Agency (Sheffield)
TECs	Training and Enterprise Councils
TVEI	Technical and Vocational Education Initiative
YTS	Youth Training Scheme

1

1.1   What is this book about?

It is about the European Community's ambitious programme for creating a single market by the end of 1992. It explains the programme, its rationale and its likely outcomes in a way that goes beyond anything that is currently available.

Much has been written about the programme but mainly in a general context. This book builds on this while venturing into detailed and unexplored issues in three critical and related areas: business, employment, and education and training. In the process, it highlights two overriding aspects:

• the scale of economic gains that are likely to flow from the programme

• the critical success factors that can enhance these gains.

1.2   What exactly will 1992 mean?

It will be the culmination of a long process initiated by the Treaty of Rome in 1957, which first formed the Community by dismantling some of the barriers to trade which, up until then, had existed between politically divided economies. Since then, trade and living standards have flourished in the member states.

However, the initial boost began to weaken, gradually in the early 1970s and markedly in the early 1980s, as global economic and technological changes made it imperative to eliminate the remaining barriers to trade.

It became clear that the economies of the member states could only regain their former dynamism if the 12 fragmented markets were combined into a single market with free movement of goods, services, capital and people. Empowered by the Single European Act 1987, the 1992 programme does just that. At present, it falls short of creating an economic union like, for example, the United States, because many outstanding issues remain unsolved in the harmonisation of national economic policies. Yet that does not detract from the programme's potential to transform the economic future of Europe.

But that is the theory. In practice, however, the programme also has the potential of turning into a zero sum game: akin to a game of poker where winners emerge but only at the expense of losers.

1.3   Why a zero sum game?

The programme could become a zero sum game for two reasons.

• Its initial impact will be felt in some 40 manufacturing and five service industries across the 12 member states. Over time, this impact will spread to other industries with whom these 45 key industries have buyer-seller relationships. Either way, the single market will intensify competition and, in the process, cause the rationalisation of capacity over a wide spectrum of activities. Bigger corporate units will come into being, with both the capacity to enjoy economies of scale and the flexibility to cater for the varied and changing needs of customers in diverse social, economic and cultural settings. In this new environment, business success will only accrue to those companies with the technology, work skills and know-how to provide customised products and services. On present reckoning, half the companies in Europe could well disappear by the year 2000, because they will lack these advantages.

• In any event, at least for the first half of this decade, the overall economic gains will be very modest, to say the least. They may improve over time as freer operation of market forces leads to greater efficiencies. But it could be a long haul: for many companies it will be a matter of the survival of the fittest. In the meantime unemployment will increase until European industry is lean and fit enough to reverse the tide.

1.4   Are there any other downsides?

Yes. Customisation will continue apace in Europe and elsewhere. On past form, this will require an ever-expanding reservoir of work skills and know-how which will be difficult to achieve. This is because, despite rising unemployment from restructuring, there are some worrying time bombs ticking away in the labour markets of the member states.

1.5   What are these time bombs?

There are six of them, all relating to specific gaps emerging in the labour market:

- **numbers gap,** arising from the excess of labour demand over labour supply, mainly as a result of the prospective contraction in the size of 16-24 age group due to demographic changes

- **skills gap,** arising from the increasing skills and know-how content of work at a time when many member states will be suffering from their failure to invest enough in education and training in the crucial decade of the 1980s when the world economy began to undergo major structural changes

- **gender gap,** arising from the fact that the newcomers to the labour market will be mothers returning to work at a time when the new jobs will be in occupations traditionally dominated by men

- **racial gap,** arising from the fact that ethnic minorities will form a growing proportion of the workforce at a time when the new jobs will be in the white collar occupations traditionally dominated by whites

- **revenue gap,** arising from increasing payroll costs owing directly to an ageing population requiring higher welfare budgets and indirectly to rising employers' national insurance contributions

- **productivity gap,** arising from increasing employment in service industries where regular productivity improvements are difficult to generate.

The numbers gap aside, all the other gaps are likely to emerge and widen over the rest of this decade thereby impairing cost-effective business growth through skills shortages, occupational mismatches and rising payroll costs.

1.6   Are there any solutions?

Yes. They will involve:

- **the European Commission,** in promoting greater labour mobility across the Community so that there is more efficient allocation of scarce resources

- **national governments,** in promoting higher participation rates in education and training, and equal opportunities for all employees, so that employers' myopic policies towards disadvantaged groups are tackled head-on

- **companies,** in adopting strategic measures that lead to more productive use of existing technology and human resources.

1.7   Will these solutions be enough?

No, in the short term they will serve merely to ease the emerging gaps. In the longer term, as customisation of products and services grows, a lot more will need to happen if the much needed capacity restructuring is to revitalise the Community's economies as they enter the know-how century.

1.8   Are additional actions needed?

Yes. Three sets of actions are needed, if the single market is to achieve what the Treaty of Rome did in its first highly successful decade.
   First, each member state will have to devise an education and training system that is at once:

- **comprehensive**, in terms using all the strands of education and training to their fullest extent

- **responsive,** in terms of constantly adapting to competitive and industrial changes

- **motivative,** in terms of encouraging individuals to engage in the process of lifetime learning, necessitated by the rising skills and know-how content of products and services

- **integrative,** in terms of creating the essential complementarity between all providers of education and training.

Second, individual companies will need to play a crucial role in helping to secure the above features. But that is not all. In order to obtain a competitive edge they will have to initiate or accelerate changes in areas such as work design, organisation design, technological usage, human resource allocation, skills and know-how development and training. These will be the stuff of the critical success factors.

Finally, to assist the overall process of skills and know-how development and deployment, individual governments will have to implement the proposed Social Dimension of the 1992 programme, which is designed to achieve an orderly management of the momentous changes that are likely to occur within each economy.

1.9 And if these actions are adopted?

Then it should be possible to devise a new vision of an integrated Europe that turns the zero sum into the positive sum game - one in which companies and individuals gain to varying degrees. This vision will shift the 'centre of economic gravity' from the Pacific Basin to Europe through improved competitiveness, underpinned by investment in new technologies, education and training on a scale far in excess of what is envisaged at present.

The vision is summarised in Figure 1.1 and described in detail in Chapter 18. It stands a high chance of being realised because of new trade opportunities arising from the geo-political changes in the EFTA countries of Western Europe and COMECON countries of Eastern Europe. In addition, trade opportunities will also flow from the single market. New trade from these three sources could help to promote a sustained round of higher economic growth, new investment and greater policy harmonisation.

It should also be possible to tackle any adverse side effects on the physical environment and disadvantaged groups: the former through proper environmental controls and the latter through the adoption of the proposed Charter for Social Rights which is designed to, among others, provide retraining and other forms of social protection, whilst restructuring occurs.

In a sense, this vision is implicit in the 1992 programme. But it begins to become credible only if the Community can home in on the issues surrounding the development, deployment and management of skills and know-how as they rapidly become prime instruments of business success in global trade in the next millennium.

Figure 1.1   A new vision for the integrated Europe

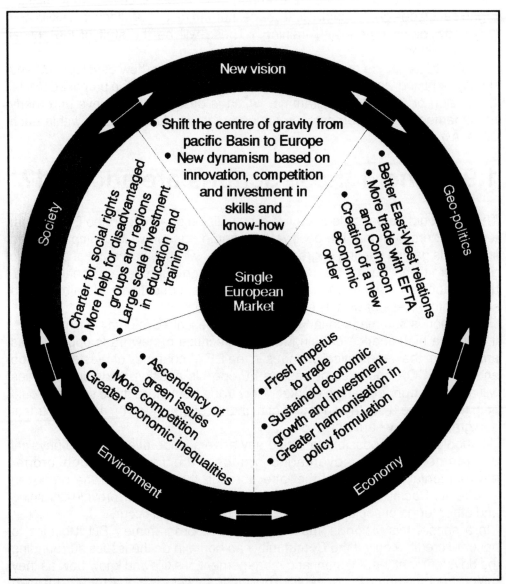

Source: CREATE Research Programme

PART A

Business challenges from the single market

The European Community's programme on the creation of the single market will have a major effect on certain industries in the first instance and then a knock-on effect on the others. Either way, its main point of impact will be the corporate sector which will, in turn, generate a ripple effect that will spread to other sectors of the economies of the member states. This part of the book thus aims to serve two functions:

- to provide essential details of the programme and its impact on the corporate sector

- to construct the foundation for analysing the wider issues associated with the programme.

These two functions are served by pursuing four critical questions:

- What does the programme involve and why is it so important?

- What will be the industrial impact of the programme?

- What do individual companies need to do to survive and prosper in the new competitive environment which will be created by the programme?

- What will be the wider implications of the necessary actions?

These questions are pursued in the next three chapters. Chapter 2 covers the first question and Chapters 3 and 4 cover the other three.

2

VISION OF A UNITED EUROPE

2.1   The Treaty of Rome

The Treaty of Rome has been an outstanding landmark of post-War Europe. Initially signed by six countries—Belgium, France, Luxembourg, Italy, the Netherlands and West Germany—it started the substantive process of drawing countries who had been at war with one another, on and off, for centuries into an economic union. Its stated goal was:

The Community shall have as its task, by establishing a common market and progressively approximating the economic policies of member states, to promote throughout the Community a harmonious development of economic activities, a continuous balanced expansion, an increase in stability, an accelerated standard of living and closer relations between the States belonging to it.

The Treaty was a bold step in two respects. First, it created an economic community as a way of eliminating age-old political and military rivalries that had devastated the European landscape in the past. Second, it created a common market covering three steps of a four-step process leading to the creation of an economic union. In sequence, the four steps in question involve the creation of:

- *a free trade area,* with no tariffs and quotas on trade between member states

- *a customs union*, which is a free trade area but now with a common level of tariffs on goods entering the union from outside

- *a common market*, in which there is a free movement of not only goods but also of factors of production such as labour, capital and enterprise

- *an economic union*, in which not only are the remaining non-tariff barriers removed but also there is harmonisation in monetary and fiscal policies of individual member states.

The Community's quantum leap to a common market led to a number of developments in the following decades. As the economic gains began to materialise, other countries also joined: Denmark, Ireland and the UK in the early 1970s, and Greece, Portugal and Spain in the early 1980s. Thus by 1986 the Community of Six had expanded to Twelve, with a population of some 320 million, outstripping the USSR, and a gross domestic product in excess of that of the USA.

As one would expect, the economic benefits have come mainly through growth in trade: intra-Community trade has increased some 30 fold over a 30 year period. The share of intra-Community trade in the gross domestic product of the member states (defined as total output) has doubled from six per cent in 1960 to 12 per cent in 1987; this at a time when the share of extra-Community trade has remained static at around nine per cent. In other words, trade between the member states has grown organically rather than at the expense of non-member countries. These are averages for the Community as a whole, with considerable inter-country variability, as shown in Figures 2.1 and 2.2.

Figure 2.1   Intra- and extra-Community trade as a percentage of GDP: 1960

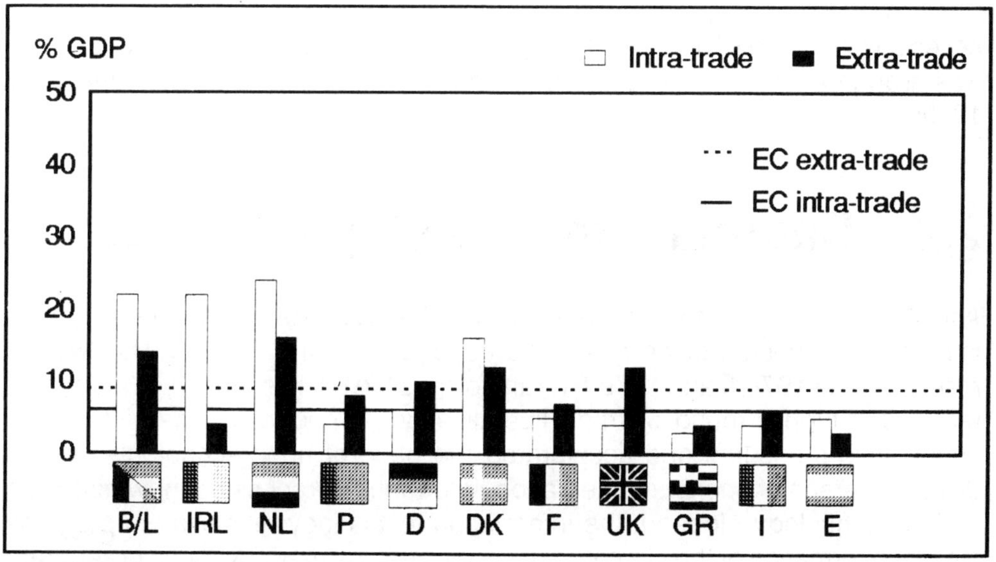

Source: EUROSTAT

Figure 2.2   Intra- and extra-Community trade as a percentage of GDP: 1987

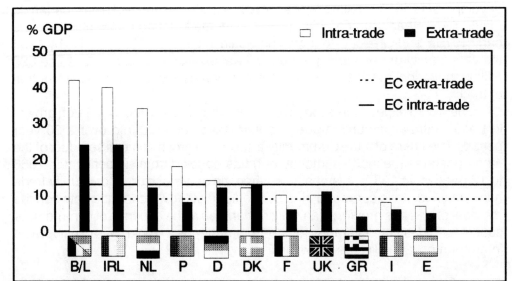

Source: EUROSTAT

In turn, this organic growth has helped to raise the rate of economic growth, especially in the first 15 years of the Community's existence. The average rate was around 2.5 per cent in the 1950s and more than double that by the early 1970s.

2.2   Rationale for the single market

Although progress in the aftermath of the formation of the Community was impressive, it could not be sustained beyond the early 1970s. The two 'oil recessions' of 1974-5 and 1979-81 transformed the world economy in a way that required a further round of trade liberalisation. Specifically, they intensified competitive pressures and accelerated the pace of new technologies in the disparate areas of energy conservation, information processing, new materials and biotechnology. Indeed, the information technology revolution in progress since the formation of the Community accelerated as new advances in separate areas of computing, electronics and telecommunications made it possible to integrate mechanical, electrical and hydraulic technologies. Under these developments, countries with large markets and large research and development (R&D) expenditures came to acquire a distinct competitive edge.

In this context, as a common market, the Community began to appear too fragmented and less dynamic. Outwardly, this was evidenced by the slow down in the annual rate of economic growth, as shown by Figure 2.3. Even after a sustained recovery since 1982, the Community's growth rate in the 1980s has averaged about half the rate achieved some 20 years earlier. This has been duly reflected in the area of employment: the proportion of people with jobs in the working age population has declined at a time when the Community's main competitors have been creating new jobs for those able to work (Figure 2.4). This deterioration in the Community's relative performance was diagnosed as symptomatic of a new economic malaise that came to be known as 'Eurosclerosis'.

Figure 2.3   Employment and GDP growth in the Community: 1961-89

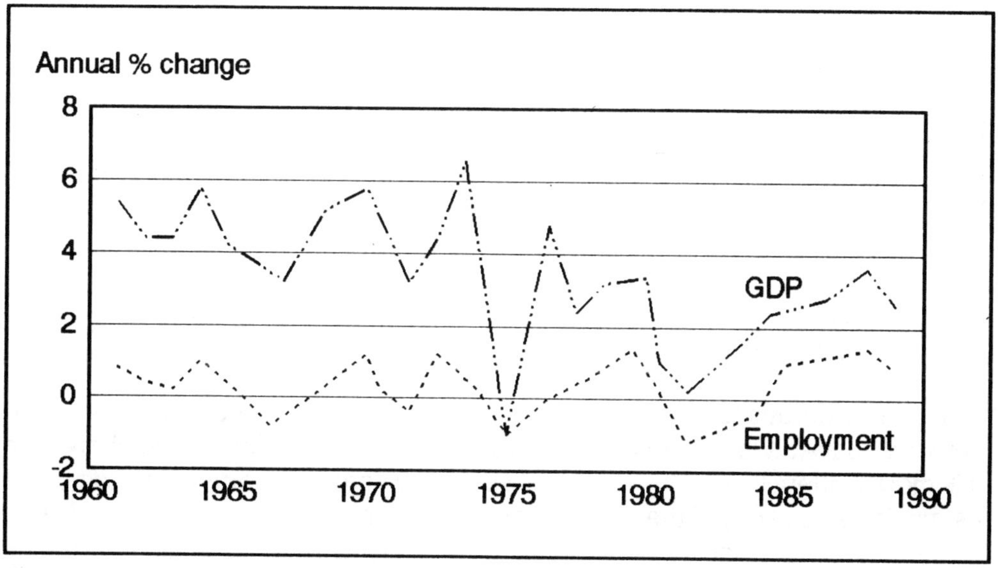

Source: Employment in Europe, 1989

Accordingly, since the early 1980s, there has been a growing belief that unless the Community makes a decisive shift towards an economic union its relative competitiveness will continue to decline. For example, until 1986, the prevailing non-tariff barriers between member states had largely contributed towards the

11

creation of 12 separate markets, ranging in size from 366,000 people in Luxembourg to over 60 million in West Germany. Worse still, even the largest German market was less than half the size of its Japanese counterpart and a quarter that of its United States counterpart. On its own, each member state could not hope to compete effectively with the giant resources of Japan and the United States.

Figure 2.4   Employment share of working-age population: 1968-88

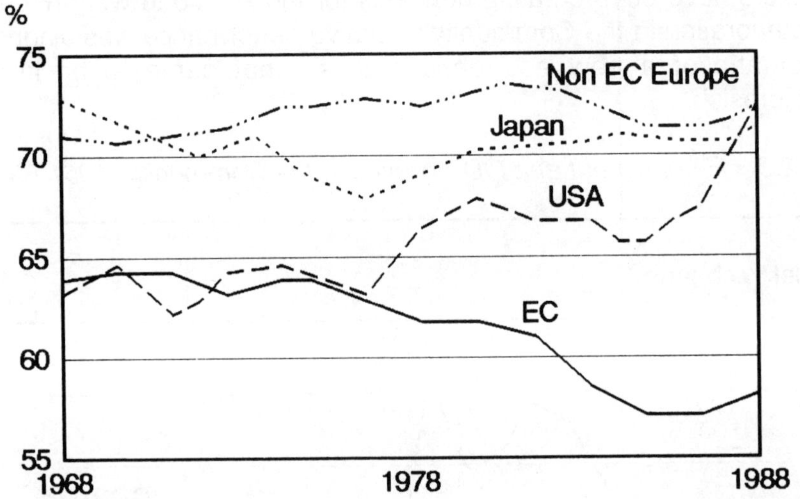

Source: EUROSTAT

Size considerations apart, the market fragmentation served to produce an outcome that was less than the sum of the effort that went into it. Nowhere was this more evident than in the area of R&D. Each year, the Community has spent as much as Japan, yet the results have been far less impressive as a whole, because the prevailing scientific compartmentalisation has resulted in wasteful duplication. Moreover, it has also ruled out the undertaking of high-risk, high-reward commercial projects over a range of manufacturing activities. Worse still, even when the individual country R&D effort has achieved new products, they have had to be adapted to meet the requirements of a host of differing national standards which have only raised costs that have been borne eventually by producers through lower output and by consumers through higher prices. As a result, even though many industries have been efficient they were disadvantaged in the Community when they ventured beyond their domestic market because of the added costs of adaptation and compliance.

As a result, the structure of the Community's industries came to reflect divided market and national attitudes. Even though many companies have operated throughout the Community in response to growth in trade, it has been all too difficult for them to rationalise their production activities. Even where this has been clearly possible - as in the case of pharmaceuticals, electronics and telecommunications - governments have sought to protect their home markets in deference to national or vested interests, thereby jeopardising their competitive potential.

All in all, whereas the creation of the common market has helped in generating new trade and wealth, potential gains from the first quantum leap became exhausted against the emergence of new forces in the global economy. The next leg of the Community's development can only come from the elimination of remaining barriers. The proposed creation of the single market by 31 December 1992 aims to do just that. However, under present plans, it will fall short of an economic union because harmonisation of macro-economic policies seems unlikely to occur before 1995.

2.3   What will the single market do?

Quite simply, it will sweep away the remaining barriers as a prelude to the establishment of a true economic union as defined in Section 2.1. It proposes to achieve this evolution in a step-by-step approach that will, initially, witness the dismantling of three kinds of barriers [1]:

- *Physical barriers:* currently, these mainly involve passport checks for people and customs documentation for goods as they cross national frontiers. Passport checks are to be eliminated on a progressive basis with due regard to continuing vigilance for criminals, drug traffickers and terrorists. Some countries, notably Benelux, France and West Germany, are already dismantling passport controls at key entry points. Similarly, on the goods side the welter of export-import documents which are processed at frontiers are to be eliminated through more simplified procedures.

- **_Technical barriers:_** these relate to regulations and standards that have evolved in each country in the past with respect to health, safety, protection and cultural values applying to various goods. For example, British-made chocolate has not been allowed to be sold in some member states because of conflicting definitions of chocolate, based on the cocoa content. Similarly, for years West German law has prohibited the sale within its borders of beers brewed in other member states because the additives they contain contravene the German 'purity laws'. Clearly, such regulations not only add extra costs because of the additional research, development and marketing efforts they involve, but they also distort production patterns because the same products are manufactured separately to separate standards for separate markets. Such technical barriers also apply to a range of services including capital movements, banking, insurance, telecommunications and transport, to the extent that they constitute formidable non-tariff obstacles to intra-Community trade. Under the current proposals, they will be eliminated through two avenues. First, national regulations applicable to production and marketing which concern health and safety will still be subject to the Community's harmonising legislation that will lay down certain mandatory requirements. Second, those national rules which do not concern such essential requirements will no longer be the subject of community legislation: instead, they will be automatically subject to national mutual recognition, enforceable before the European Court of Justice. This second avenue, in fact, will follow the precedent established by the now famous _Cassis de Dijon_ ruling in 1978 in which the Court held that products made and marketed according to the legal requirements in any one member state must be allowed to circulate freely in the rest of the Community. This ruling will apply across a wide and diverse field, covering physical products, intangible services and educational and training qualifications.

- **_Fiscal Barriers:_** at present the rates of indirect taxes such as VAT and excise duties vary considerably between the member states to the extent that even without physical and technical barriers they can cause significant price differences and distortions in trade patterns [2]. The proposed approach envisages a greater convergence in these rates in order to reduce tax-induced price differentials to the point where they do not cause significant distortions.

So much for the proposals. It is worth reiterating that they fall short of the creation of an economic union because many problems remain in the area of fiscal harmonisation. The Delors Plan makes new proposals for monetary harmonisation and outlines the key steps towards this, but does not offer a credible timetable. As a result, the present proposals are geared more towards the creation of a single market through the elimination of physical and technical barriers. The proposals are far-reaching, even though between them they fall short of creating an economic union. One the one hand, they will open up public procurement to competitive tender to all companies in the Community, thereby eliminating a major non-tariff barrier. On the other hand, they will secure greater inter-country movements through freedom of goods, freedom of services, freedom of capital and freedom of people.

2.4   The single market: The programme, process and perceptions

The programme has been outlined in the European Commission's 1985 White Paper which lists some three hundred Directives which have since been reduced to 279. It is expected that these will go through the necessary legislative process, leading to their full implementation by individual member states by the end of 1992.

The main thrust of these Directives was spelt out in eight basic points under the Single European Act which came into force in 1987.

These points extend beyond the creation of the single market and relate to wider issues that will eventually lead to economic union. The issues in question cover regional disparities, R&D, the role of the European Parliament, monetary union and fiscal harmonisation, to name the most important [3].

Under the Act, the legislative process leading to the creation of the single market in 1992 involves four parties: the European Commission in initiating legislation; the European Parliament in enacting it; the Council of Ministers (comprising ministers from member states) in approving it and issuing the Directives; and parliaments in individual member states in writing the Directives into national laws.

The Act also made a crucial amendment to the Treaty of Rome. As far as the measures relating to the single market are concerned, the Act has removed the legislative requirement of having a unanimous vote in the Council of Ministers and replaced it with the principle of qualified majority, under which each member state has a certain number of votes, as determined by the size of its population. However, in certain areas - including those covering employment issues - unanimous voting still remains a prerequisite.

So much for the programme and its associated legislation process. It would be fair to generalise that the concept of a single market has fired public imagination throughout the Community, albeit to varying degrees among different member states. This is despite the fact that, on present reckoning, it is unlikely to lead to an economic union in the foreseeable future because of the outstanding issues in the separate areas of fiscal and monetary harmonisation. An inter-governmental conference has been scheduled for the latter part of 1990 in order that these issues can be ironed out, so that economic union becomes a reality before the end of this decade. The momentous events in Eastern Europe in 1989-90 have lent an added urgency to the achievement of policy harmonisation, to ensure that a united Germany is firmly locked into the mainstream Community.

In this context, so bold have been the plans and pronouncements of the member states over the last two years that they have been charged with creating a 'Fortress Europe' by countries such as Japan and the United States. Stripped of the usual political rhetoric, the charge does not stand up to much examination. It was the European Community which pressured for a new round of talks on the liberalisation of international trade under the auspices of the General Agreement on Tariffs and Trade (GATT). This led to the convening of what is now known as the 'Uruguay Round'. The object behind the Community's push was to counter the growing protectionist sentiment in Washington as a result of the burgeoning American trade deficit in the mid-1980s. Indeed, it would be fair to say that lately the progress under the Uruguay Round has, if anything, hastened because the non-Community nations have increasingly come to realise that if GATT does not deliver a substantial measure of liberalisation, the Community will go its own way. In the event, there has been a clear parallel in pace and content between the 1992 programme and the Uruguay Round. The charge of Fortress Europe has been hardly audible since the summer of 1989.

2.5   The object of this book

This book has emerged from a number of research studies I have carried out for various organisations, including the European Commission. However, it is worth emphasising from the outset that none of the organisations bears any responsibility for the analysis and conclusions that follow. My studies examined three different aspects of the 1992 programme: business, employment, and education and training.

The analysis and assessment presented here relies on information emerging from many studies carried out by the Commission, other data sources and structured face-to-face interviews conducted by the author with a number of leading researchers and government officials from different member states concerned with the 1992 programme. In so far as some material is derived from one specific source, the source is identified in the beginning of the appropriate chapter (as in Part C).

The starting point of the research was, of course, the Cecchini Report published in 1988 [4]. It was the first and only document so far to have provided an assessment of the economic gains arising from the 1992 programme. Adopting a highly macro approach and using mathematical models, it estimated the gains in terms of additional gross domestic product, lower prices and extra jobs. Given their aggregative nature, the Cecchini results can only be treated as a *first instalment.* There are many detailed aspects of the programme that still remain to be assessed because they do not lend themselves to mathematical treatment of the sort adopted in that report. In any event, some of these aspects extend beyond the realm of conventional economic theories.

This book makes a much needed start towards dealing with various details. However, given their micro nature the issues are difficult to handle, partly because there are no good or recent data available on them, and partly because they represent enormous diversity, which does not always lend itself to ready generalisations. Given these limitations, the information that has been available up to the end of 1989 is presented here. If some of it appears out of date, that is because the latest information has not been available at the time of writing. In the circumstances, the book aims at least to provide a framework within which one can analyse new information as and when it is available.

Indeed, my basic aim is to provide ideas, information and a framework to enhance the understanding of the general public worldwide of the Community's momentous programme that has the potential to change radically the destiny of

Europe. On the one hand, the book invites the reader either to agree or to disagree with its analysis and if the latter, then to come up with alternative ideas, information and framework. Either way, its aim is to improve and advance the public's understanding of the 1992 programme on a scale that goes well beyond the Cecchini Report. This aim is pursued by adopting a four-point remit:

- to provide an assessment of the impact of the 1992 programme in three areas: business, employment, and education and training

- to identify the inter-relationships between these areas and their critical success factors

- to highlight the economic gains that are likely to arise from the 1992 programme

- to suggest ways by which the gains can be enhanced.

The remit has been pursued in a way which will serve to bring out the factors which will make or break the 1992 programme. For as we shall see in Part B and D, the projected gains from the programme will be, at best, rather modest. Worse still, because of certain political opposition, notable from the British Government, even these modest gains may not necessarily materialise. If the Community is to eliminate the curse of Eurosclerosis, companies, national governments and the European Commission need to do a lot more than they are currently. Much of this book is about analysing the current position in this context and suggesting constructive ways of moving forward.

2.6   Summary

This chapter has briefly outlined the evolution of the European Community since the signing of the Treaty of Rome in 1957. It has also described the rationale underlying the creation of the single market and the associated timetable and legislative process. It has then gone on to describe the main aims of this book. The main points emerging from the chapter are as follows:

- In the first 15 years of its existence, the Community reaped substantial economic benefits from increased trade between the member states, owing to the first round of elimination of tariffs on goods.

- However, by the mid-1970s, the initial dynamism was nearly exhausted. The Community's relative performance in world markets had begun to deteriorate. To make matters worse, the two 'oil' recessions of 1974-5 and 1979-81 had intensified global business competition and accelerated technological change on a scale that made it difficult to justify the existence of 12 separate markets in the Community. In order to improve its global competitiveness, there was an urgent need to exploit the economies of scale in production and have greater inter-country collaboration in R&D.

- These imperatives are now to be effected by creating a single market through the elimination of the remaining physical and technical barriers to trade in goods and services between the member states.   This new round of liberalisation envisages the incorporation of some 279 Community Directives in the national laws of the member states by 31 December 1992. On present reckoning, however, they will fall short of creating an economic union because there remain many outstanding issues in the harmonisation of monetary and fiscal policies.

- This book aims to provide a more detailed understanding of the programme, its operation, its impact and its downside in a way that goes well beyond the broad assessments that are available currently. The aim is pursued in the belief that the projected gains arising from the programme are likely to be modest, at best, and non-existent, at worst, unless individual companies, governments and the European Commission initiate certain critical actions.

3

INDUSTRIAL IMPACT

3.1 Introduction

As we saw in the last chapter, central to the 1992 programme is the achievement of four critical objectives: free movement of goods, free movement of services, free movement of capital and free movement of people. This chapter focuses on the first two freedoms which are to be secured through the elimination of physical and technical obstacles that have hitherto constituted the main non-tariff barriers. Its object is three-fold:

- to identify the industries that are most likely to be affected in the process

- to describe the nature of the forces that will be released as a result

- to assess the critical success factors for individual firms in the new competitive environment.

The chapter adopts a 'top-down' approach. First it provides an overview of the industries that are most likely to be affected once the single market is completed. As such, it focuses on the impact effect of the single market, so-called because it shows where the programme of directives will have its most immediate effect. It then proceeds to highlight the dynamic effect, so-called because it takes account of the knock-on responses both within and between industries, as generated by the impact effect.

The impact effect is presented in the next section and the dynamic effect in the one after. In both cases, the emphasis is on providing an overview of the industrial impact before subjecting it to a more detailed explanation in Chapter 4, using two case studies.

3.2   Impact effect

Many Directives outlined in the 1992 programme relate to individual industries in manufacturing and service sectors. By their very nature, these Directives will impact specifically on various industries and, in the process, affect their structure and performance. The extent of the impact will depend upon two factors: the scale of non-tariff barriers they attract at present; and the rate of import penetration of these industries in intra-Community trade.

In both contexts, the Cecchini Report provides a good indication of those industries most likely to be affected [1]. Its findings for manufacturing and service sectors are described below.

3.2.1   Manufacturing industries

Table 3.1 identifies the relevant industries under four groups using the International Standard Industrial Classification (ISIC) code. Tables 3.2 - 3.5 go on to provide a summary assessment of the likely impact resulting from the single market. For each group the assessment is primarily based on:

* **Scale of non-tariff barriers:** that is, how high are the current barriers? The higher they are the greater the possibility of increase in intra-Community trade through their elimination, and vice versa.

* **Penetration rate:**   that is, how far do the member states already have significant trade flows involving the relevant industries?   The higher the penetration rate the lower the potential for further growth in intra-Community trade, and vice versa.

Against the background of these two considerations, Tables 3.2 - 3.5 show that the programme will have a differential impact on the 40 industries that are most exposed to it. Three salient points emerge from the tables.

First, industries in Group 1 have a high degree of intra-Community import penetration, as well as already having a high degree of industrial concentration. However, they have yet to rise to the American and Japanese challenge in their own markets because of their relatively poor productivity. The creation of the single market will provide an opportunity for both industrial restructuring and cross-border co-operation in R & D which will serve to narrow the productivity gap. The medium term outlook of these industries can best be described as 'fair' because the gap is believed to be wide and the catch-up process will be long and sometimes painful in terms of its impact on employment.

Table 3.1   *Industrial groups directly affected by the 1992 programme*

Group 1		Group 4	
ICIS code:		*ICIS code:*	
330	Computers	247	Glass
344	Telecom equipment	248	Ceramics
372	Medical equipment	251	Industrial chemicals
		256	Other chemicals
		321	Agric. machinery
Group 2		322	Machine tools
		323	Textile machinery
ICIS code:		324	Food machinery
		325	Mining machinery
257	Pharmaceuticals	326	Transmissions
315	Boilermaking	327	Wood machinery
362	Railway equipment	345	Audiovisual
425	Wines and spirits	346	Consumer electricity
427	Brewing and malting	347	Electric lamps
428	Soft drinks	351	Motor vehicles
		364	Aerospace
		431	Wool
Group 3		432	Cotton
		438	Carpets
ICIS code:		451	Footwear
		453	Clothing
341	Cables	455	Household textiles
342	Electrical machinery	481	Rubber
361	Shipbuilding	491	Jewelry
417	Pasta	493	Photography
421	Chocolate	494	Toys

Source: 'Research on the cost of non-Europe', *Basic Findings,* Volume 2

It is hard to see how these industries can increase their employment levels over the next ten years, especially since American and Japanese competitors have also embarked on their own rationalisation programmes.

Table 3.2   Group 1: Competitively weak industries

A   Economic characteristics:

- High non-tariff barriers (public procurement and standards)

- High intra-EC import penetration rates and high degree of openness to third countries

- Little price disparity

- Strong growth in demand

- High technology content

- Moderate or substantial economies of scale

- High degree of concentration

- Relatively poor productivity of European firms compared with American or Japanese competitors

B   Effects of the single market:

- Restructuring

- Co-operation (on research and development)

- Improved competitiveness at world level

Internal market provides opportunity to become a force at world level.

Source: 'Employment in Europe, 1989' (European Commission, Brussels)

Second, industries in Group 2 and, to a lesser extent, Group 3 are likely to see rationalisation. This is because there are either substantial economies of scale (as in Group 2) or considerable surplus capacity at present (Group 3). The resulting rationalisation, however, is unlikely to be onerous in employment terms in the longer-term because there remains considerable potential for growth in intra-Community trade. But there is little doubt that in the first half of this decade Group 2 will see a rapid and sustained decline in employment.

Table 3.3   Group 2: Industries facing rationalisation

A   Economic characteristics:

• High non-tariff barriers (public procurement for sectors 315 and 362 and standards for sectors 257,425-8)

• Rather low intra-EC import penetration rates and little openness to third countries

• Wide price dispersion

• High degree of concentration

• Substantial economies of scale

B   Effects of the single market:

• Growth in intra-EC trade

• Restructuring (boilermaking and locomotive industries)

• Technical efficiency gains

• Narrowing of price disparities

Impact of the internal market likely to be most marked in this group, but adjustments will occur at different rates.

Source: 'Employment in Europe, 1989' (European Commission, Brussels)

Table 3.4   Group 3: Industries facing some changes

A   *Economic characteristics:*

Identical to those of group 2 except that price dispersion is low (less than 10 per cent) and extra-EC trade plays a greater role than intra-EC trade in the shipbuilding and electrical engineering industries.

B   *Effects of the single market:*

- Restructuring, leading to some rationalisation

- Technical and economic efficiency gains but much less marked than those for Group 2

Source: 'Employment in Europe, 1989' (European Commission, Brussels)

Table 3.5   Group 4: Industries affected indirectly

A   *Economic characteristics:*

- Moderate non-tariff barriers (standards and administrative barriers)

- High import penetration rates

- Price dispersion above 10 per cent

- Substantial economies of scale

B   *Effects of the single market:*

- Community's external trade policy more important than the single market

- But changes still likely, because of changes in distribution networks.

Source: 'Employment in Europe, 1989' (European Commission, Brussels)

Third, industries in Group 4 will also witness rationalisation, as a result of the knock-on effect. This is because the distribution channels that will be used by them will themselves undergo major rationalisation, owing to the progressive deregulation of the transport industry. As we shall see in the next chapter, the whole distribution sector is expected to change radically. In the process, it will forge vertical links - formal and informal - with its 'upstream' customers which happen to be many of the industries in Group 4. In order to devise and control the best distribution channels, many of the industries in this group will need to reorganise themselves through yet more industrial concentration. In the process, they will have to shed even more jobs.

3.2.2   Service industries

As in manufacturing, so in services: the 1992 programme will have a major impact. Both public and private services will be affected.

Public services will be affected as a result of the liberalisation of public procurement of goods and services which will be subject to open and competitive tendering across the Community. In the private sector, the service industries most likely to be affected include banking, insurance, finance, transport and communication. At present, each of them has the same characteristics as those in Tables 3.2 and 3.3: namely, low penetration and high non-tariff barriers. As a result, there is considerable potential for growth in intra-Community trade in these services after 1992. Equally, there is scope for rationalisation.

Overall, therefore, when it comes to the impact effect of the 1992 programme, the industries likely to be affected most are those in Tables 3.2 and 3.3 and the service industries mentioned in the previous paragraph. Much of the 1992 programme's thrust will be felt in them initially. It is time now to turn to the nature of the forces to be released when the most affected industries are exposed to the new competitive environment.

3.3   Dynamic effect

When it comes to the dynamic effect no detailed assessment is available at individual industry level. Some disaggregated growth forecasts are available for the period to 1993, as shown in Figure 3.1. But it is difficult to attempt quantification beyond that period because of the differences in industrial structure, customer-base, technological usage, costs and product quality between the individual member states. Therefore, all that one can offer is a tentative assessment that is substantially based on past experience.

Following the historical analysis given in Chapter 2, it seems prudent to view the creation of the single market as a culmination of two distinct waves of trade liberalisation in the Community since its inception: one lasting over the period 1958-80, and affecting mainly manufacturing industries subject to tariff barriers; and one lasting from 1985 to 1992 and affecting mainly manufacturing and service industries subject to non-tariff barriers. Thus it pays to know what has happened under the first wave, so as to be able to develop some insights into what is likely to happen under the second wave. In this context, a detailed analysis of the trade data suggests three outcomes:

- There has been a massive increase in intra-Community trade in manufactured goods: about ten-fold in the first wave and nearly twenty-fold since then.

- Despite these gains, certain member states have lost out. For example, the once prosperous French clothing industry lost its market share both in the Community and at home. In other words, at the level of individual industries the gains have taken the form of a zero sum game.

Figure 3.1   Sectorial output growth 1979-93 in the Community

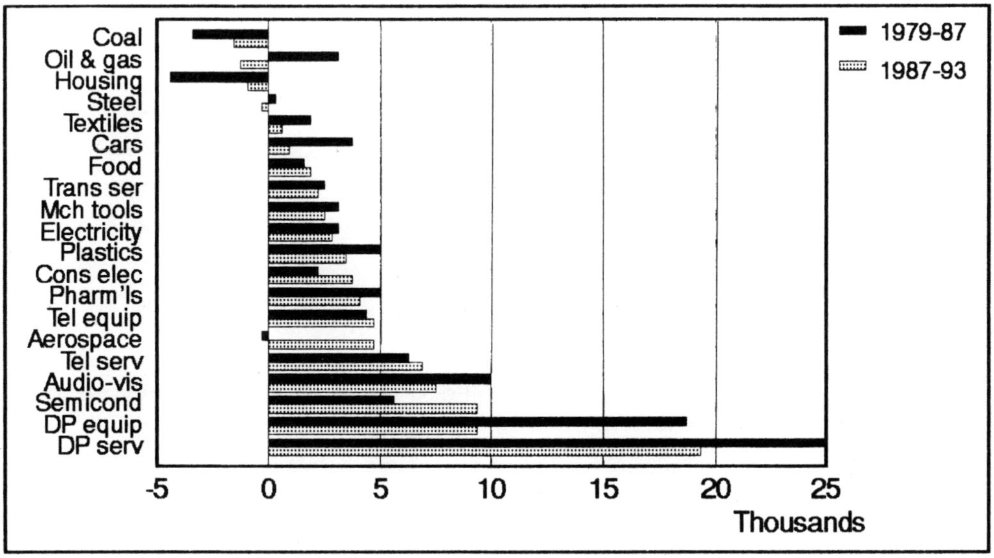

Source: Europe in 1993, Economic Outlook by Sector

- Indeed, the zero sum outcome has been particularly noticeable since the early 1970s when the Community's earlier dynamism had all but fizzled out, as we saw in Chapter 2. In retrospect, therefore, it seems as though countries like Denmark, Ireland and the UK joined the Community when the malaise of Eurosclerosis was beginning to take root. It is arguable whether they and other recent joiners such as Greece, Portugal and Spain have enjoyed the genuine benefits of even distribution of economic gains from the Community over the past two decades.

Why? Because, although operating at a macro level, trade liberalisation releases a number of forces that call for major competitive responses by individual companies. Unless these responses are there, even the giants of today can turn into the dinosaurs of tomorrow. This may sound tautological so let us elaborate. Figure 3.2 shows how macro aspects have fed into business and people aspects.

Figure 3.2   Impact of the single market

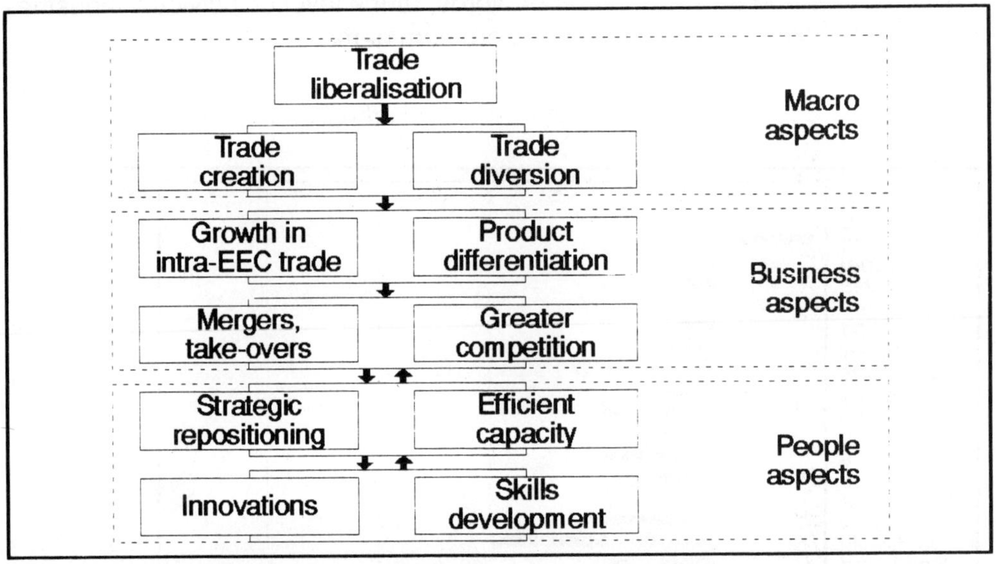

Source: CREATE Research Programme

3.3.1 Macro aspects

Under the first wave, the reduction of tariff barriers had a two-fold effect: trade creation and trade diversion. Trade creation came about as a result of the generation of new business opportunities that had previously been suppressed by tariffs. On the other hand, trade diversion came about as a result of individual member states finding it cheaper to trade with one another in preference to the non-member countries. For example, there was a substantial diversion of British trade from Commonwealth countries to the member states of the Community.

3.3.2 Business aspects

As we saw in Figures 2.1 and 2.2 in the previous chapter, there has been a marked increase in the importance of intra-Community trade between 1960 and 1987 due to both trade creation and trade diversion. More importantly this new trade was substantially in differentiated products with special characteristics that gave them a strong brand appeal in the eyes of the customers. In other words, the sort of products which catered for the specific needs and tastes of distinct market segments.

Such customisation required not only the proprietary ownership of various well-known brands (e.g. BMW cars) but also a unique store of know-how which helped to promote customisation in the first place. For many manufacturing firms, both of these proved difficult to develop in-house.

Corporate mergers and takeovers, therefore, provided a convenient vehicle. Beyond that, the removal of tariffs also took away the main prop for surplus capacity in individual member states. Mergers and takeovers, thus, also provided a vehicle for capacity restructuring. The cumulative effect of all these changes was increased competition.

3.3.3 People aspects

Against the background of gathering competition, successful companies began the substantive task of re-positioning themselves more strategically as well as creating efficient capacity. In practice, this meant having:

• a set of well-defined product, marketing, distribution and financial strategies;

- an innovative management that put a premium on sound industrial relations, skills development and technological progressivity. In other words, a type of management that developed and valued all its resources - human, physical and technological.

Indeed, for successful companies, there was a two-way relationship between people and business aspects: success was not just a matter of creating large business outfits that could weather competition but also of harnessing total organisational capability to the full.

As history testifies, many manufacturing companies failed in this process, even those who became significantly involved in mergers (e.g. Dunlop of UK and Pirelli of Italy). The absolute contraction in capacity, turnover and jobs in many British, French and Italian manufacturing firms, for example, bears witness to their seeming inability to adapt to the competitive forces unleashed by the first wave of liberalisation. There were, of course, other factors behind their relative failures. But these, too, required a competitive response, similar to the one dictated by the first wave then and the second wave now.

In terms of this historical analysis, it is clear that the second wave of liberalisation - culminating in the completion of the single market in 1992 - will release forces and outcomes that will not be too dissimilar from those witnessed by the Community over the past thirty years. Thus, the practical outcomes of the single market will be two-fold: there will be a step-increase in intra-Community trade in goods and services, especially customised ones, but the gains resulting from it will not be anything like uniformly distributed across the Community. These outcomes apply especially to those manufacturing and service industries identified in Section 3.2. However, over time, the same outcome will also apply to other industries which have strong input-output relationships with them. In other words, the dynamic effect will initially result in capacity restructuring in the industries most directly affected by the 1992 programme and, over time, in other industries at their 'upstream' end (suppliers) or 'downstream' end (customers).

The issue of uneven gains is an important one because the medium-term overall economic benefits from the 1992 programme are unlikely to be substantial. For example, the Cecchini Report suggests that, after an initial fall, the Community's GDP (i.e. total output of goods and services) would increase by a cumulative 4.5 per cent in the medium-term, *directly* due to the 1992 programme [1]. Welcome though the increase will be, the figure does not promise a step-change, once allowance is made for its unavoidable error margin.

However, at the level of individual companies in the industries affected, the changes could well mean survival or extinction. For them, 1992 could veritably be a zero sum game.

The foregoing analysis of the dynamic effect highlights two main points, both of which have significant implications for employment. First, it shows that capacity restructuring will be inevitable, both in order to phase out less efficient productive units and also to acquire the necessary know-how for customised products and services. Second, it shows that technological progressivity and development of skills and know-how will be crucial in ensuring survival in the new competitive environment. This is because in the single market there will be numerous customer segments distinguished by geography, personal taste, language, culture, tradition and history. For individual companies, success will require the provision of a varied range of products and services that take into account all these characteristics.

On the face of it, the proposition that the elimination of barriers will promote greater customisation seems paradoxical since the prevalence of these barriers has promoted the emergence of different customer segments over time. However, more immediately, the proposition applies to companies' output and not consumer demand. It argues that the single market will result in fewer producers who will attempt to serve the prevailing different customer segments simultaneously, in contrast to the current situation where numerous producers serve these segments on a more specialist basis. In other words, the growth in trade in customised products and services will reflect changes in the conditions of supply much more than in any changes in the conditions of demand, arising from greater social and cultural exchanges in the longer term.

Thus, for individual companies survival and success in the new competitive environment means having a productive capacity that is capable of generating all the advantages of economies of scale and yet is flexible enough to provide customisation.

This is exemplified by the vehicle manufacturing industry. Over time, it has come to have fewer producers world-wide. Yet each producer tends to have a wide range of models catering for different customer segments. More importantly, many of these models have come to be produced on the same assembly-line, using the most advanced computer-aided technologies that minimise the down-time for retooling between the production runs for different models. Indeed, as customer requirements have changed, the range of models has been expanded and their life cycle shortened, without a large scale corresponding change in productive capacity.

This example prompts two generalisations. First, as customer tasks and habits change in response to rising living standards, the demand they generate will increase; the more so in the single market, as social and cultural exchanges expand. Such customisation arising on the demand side will continue to occur, albeit gradually so that its effects will be felt in the longer term. Second, over the first half of this decade the impact of growth in intra-Community trade in customised products and services is more likely to be felt on the production side.

Accordingly, in order to succeed in the zero sum game individual companies will need to meet two conditions. First, they will have to invest in the modern technology which can switch between different product or service lines with minimum down-time so that production in smaller batches for different customer groups does not hinder the realisation of scale economies. Second, they will need an equally adaptable workforce with two vital attributes:

- multiple skills that can permit the effective performance of varied but specific work tasks under one job, irrespective of whether the tasks are sequentially related or not; and

- an expanding base of know-how that can accelerate progress in the distinct areas of research, development, production, delivery and after-sales service relating to an ever widening range of products and services.

Thus defined, the concept of know-how extends beyond the essential ability to perform specific tasks. Essentially, it underpins the ability to make requisite changes in any area of the conventional production-distribution cycle in response to changing customer behaviour. As living standards have improved in the past forty years or so, customers have become more sophisticated in their consumption patterns. In the single market context, the concept of know-how extends beyond the ability to perform specific tasks. It relates to the ability to make rapid changes in any area of the production-distribution cycle in response to changing customer requirements. In practice, it is about building new features into existing products and services, or creating new products and services with shorter shelf lives. In so far as this will be a continuous process, so will the corresponding process of skills and know-how development. Customisation will be paramount, but will require a wide and deep base of skills and know-how which is not easy to acquire. We return to this point in Part D. Many industries in the member states will be gripped by major structural change in the 1990s. In the next chapter we focus on two industries to provide further insights into this impending process of change.

3.4 Summary

This chapter has identified those manufacturing and service industries that are most likely to be affected by the completion of the single market. It has also attempted to describe the nature of the forces that will be released as the single market becomes a reality. Finally, it has provided an overview of the critical success factors needed to weather the fresh round of competition that will ensue. The main points emerging from the chapter are:

- The 1992 programme will have an impact on a number of manufacturing and service industries that currently have high non-tariff barriers and low import penetration. Directly, the programme will affect some forty industries in the manufacturing sector and about five in the service sector. Indirectly, it will also have a knock-on effect on other industries that have significant input-output links with those industries that will be directly affected.

- But this growth will occur mainly as a result of capacity rationalisation under which production will be concentrated within fewer companies who will then go on to serve wider markets with varied customer segments. As a result, new growth in trade will be in customised products and services. That will increasingly become intensive in skills and know-how.

- In this new environment, if individual companies are to survive they will have to reposition themselves more strategically by having well-defined product, marketing and distribution strategies. They will also need advanced technology, work skills and know-how that can provide economies of scale as well as flexibility and adaptability in meeting the changing customer needs.

- These requirements will be dictated exclusively by business imperatives. The overall economic gains arising from the 1992 programme are unlikely to be significant until the end of this decade. In the meantime, the accelerated process of industrial restructuring inspired by new competitive forces will ensure that the single market is a zero sum game for individual companies: winners will win only because the losers will lose, as the size of the 'cake' will not change much.

4

CASE STUDIES: IMPACT AND DYNAMIC EFFECTS

4.1 Introduction

The previous chapter has identified those industries in the manufacturing and service sectors that are likely to experience significant impact and dynamic effects, in a way that has clear implications for the quantity and quality of employment. Both the process of change and its human resource implications were couched in somewhat general terms because that chapter's objective was to provide an overview of the industrial impact of the 1992 programme.

In this chapter, we look at this process in greater detail in order to provide a more rigorous basis for assessing various employment aspects in Parts B and C. This has been done through a case study approach that focuses on two industries: insurance and wholesale distribution. They both serve to underline the concept of freedom of services, as envisaged by the 1992 programme. The choice of these industries has also been influenced by three other considerations.

First, they are both likely to undergo fundamental transformations. As such, they provide good examples of areas of extreme change that each member state will have to cope with as a result of the single market.

Second, they also constitute end points of a continuum, in the sense of being covered by the specific programme of Directives from the European Commission. At one end, the insurance industry has already been subjected to four Directives, as we shall see in the next section. Under them, by the end of 1992, it will have various freedoms, all of which will be underpinned by the principle of *home* country control. Thus, insurance companies operating in the member states will only be subject to the regulatory regime of the country of origin, irrespective of where they operate in the Community. In contrast, the wholesale distribution industry will not be covered by any specific directives. Yet it is likely to undergo major changes all the same because of its input-output links with the manufacturing, transport, communication and finance sectors, all of which have their own specific set of directives.

Third, the emphasis here on service industries is deliberate because much of the early work on the economics of 1992 has concentrated on manufacturing industries. It seems prudent to switch the focus, if only to emphasise that the 1992 programme is bound to have a major impact on service industries as well.

The case studies of the two chosen industries are presented separately in the next two sections.

4.2   Case study 1: Insurance

4.2.1   Background

The programme of the completion of the internal market in insurance by 1992 has three specific elements:

• freedom to open branches or establishments

• freedom to extend the range of services

• freedom to provide cross border services.

These three elements were first proposed in the Treaty of Rome (Articles 52 and 59). Prior to the Treaty, insurance had become increasingly regulated in this century, with the result that neither freedom of establishment nor freedom of services was the general rule in Europe before the Treaty began to take effect.

Even so, progress has been slow since then. It has been driven by three Directives:

• **The Re-insurance Directive:** adopted in 1964, this led to the abolition of the few restrictions that existed in relation to the re-insurance business.

• **The Non-Life Directive:** adopted in 1973, this led to the freedom of establishment in classes other than life insurance.

• **The Life Directive:** adopted in 1979, this led to the freedom of establishment in life insurance.

Between them, these three directives have provided a limited measure of liberalisation in the sense of affording freedom to establish branches that can do business in all classes of insurance in any member state. Although a move in the right direction, the directives constitute only a modest step because they do not permit cross-border selling of services. Furthermore, the branches and establishments in question are subject to regulatory regimes existing in the 'host' country and not 'home' country.

In the drive towards the progressive elimination of these limitations, a new non-life insurance Directive was adopted in 1988 which is likely to have come into effect in 1990. The Directive opens up the provision of cross-border services for large risks. Large risks are defined here as policy holders who, by virtue of their size, status or the nature of the risk, do not require special protection in the member state in which the risk is situated.

Once this Directive is implemented, the European Commission will follow it up with legislation to underwrite non-life risks for individuals across borders by 1992. There are now new proposals facilitating freedom of services in motor liability and life assurance. Their details need not concern us here since, when implemented, they are likely to be the first step towards full freedom for cross-border services. In the interim, there is likely to be some undermining of restrictive practices which have hitherto hindered insurance companies competing even on the basis of establishment in other member states (e.g. the strict control on policy wording and premium rates prevailing in West Germany).

4.2.2 Business impact of 1992

Figure 4.1 shows the relative position of the member states in terms of market structure and customer location. The UK's distinctive position in this context is noteworthy in that its insurance industry has a more competitive structure as well as a national and international customer orientation. These features stem from several factors related to its history, the tax system, the national culture and consumer habits, all of which have tended to create a highly sophisticated domestic market and a mature industry capable of doing business on a global basis.

The single market is expected to have a two-fold effect:

- it will initiate a chain reaction that will propel other European insurance industries in the direction of the UK, in terms of market structure and orientation

- it will encourage the large Continental insurers to venture into the UK market and the UK insurers into the Continental market.

Figure 4.1   Insurance: Market structure and environment

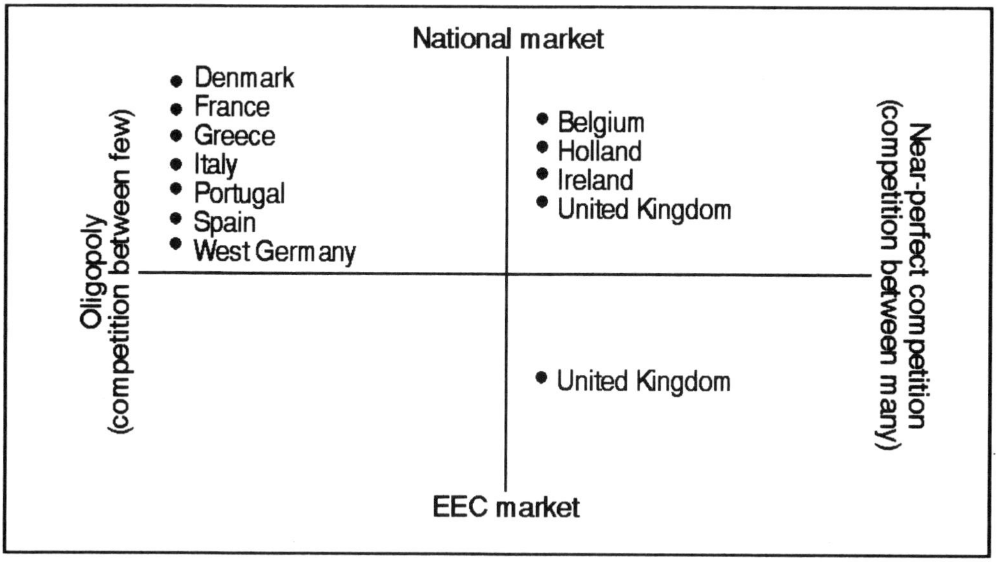

Source: CREATE Research Programme

Details of these effects have proved difficult to obtain because of the uncertainty factor but their central thrust can be readily identified in terms of focus and time profile.

As for focus, it is clear that there will be many changes that will have a direct bearing on the Community's insurance market. These changes are likely to be incremental and come in four overlapping but identifiable phases. As for their time profile, this is a matter of conjecture, as always. But there is a high probability that the insurance industry in France, the UK and West Germany will have entered the final phase by the latter half of this decade.

Figure 4.2 shows the phases and their approximate time profiles. The distinctive characteristics of each phase are as follows:

- ***Protective phase:*** as we saw in Figure 4.1, the insurance industry in a majority of member states has been in this phase until recently. Their regulatory regimes have effectively barred the new establishments from other countries and/or cross-border export of services. As a result, the individual industries have had a distinctive national orientation. Within national boundaries, however, there has been an emergence of large companies with the result that, on the whole, competition has been mainly confined to a few large players (i.e. oligopolies).

Figure 4.2   Insurance: Time profile of the single market

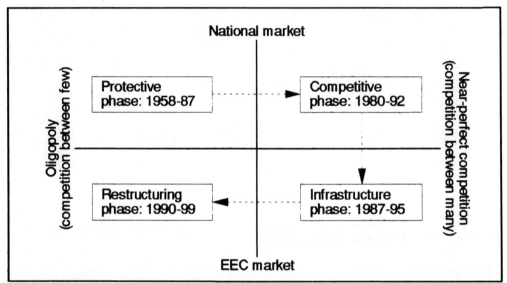

Source: CREATE Research Programme

- *Competitive phase:* the spectre of more cross-border trade in large industrial risks will increase competitive pressures in most of the member states. In this phase, individual insurers are more likely to become introspective rather than expansionist. On balance, they will be keener to re-examine their cost structures, staff effectiveness and technological usage in order to achieve competitive expense ratios prior to embarking on ambitious business strategies.

- *Infrastructure phase:* it is in this phase that we shall see significant signs of Community-wide increase in capacity. New collaborative ventures will be forged between insurers in one member state and intermediaries in others, as exemplified by the relationship between Gouda, a Netherlands insurance company, and Endsleigh, a British insurance retailer which is partly owned by Gouda. The object will be to forge vertical links that could provide incursions into uncharted territories, using well-known intermediaries in the new markets.

• **Restructuring phase:** with substantive vertical links established by the mid-nineties, two outcomes are likely to ensue: over-capacity and greater competition. As a result, the European insurance industry will enter a new phase, whose dominant thrust will be directed at restructuring through corporate mergers and acquisitions for which the scope is rather limited currently for a number of reasons. However, a decade from now, market forces will make them inevitable.

In the final analysis, for individual member states both the infrastructure phase and the restructuring phase will result in a two-way traffic: each member state's insurers will get into one another's markets, due to the pressures released by new competition. In all cases, the emphasis will be on selling customised services which appeal to the special needs of customers in diverse social, economic and cultural settings, as discussed in Section 3.3 in the previous chapter.

4.2.3   The role of information technology

So far, IT has played a significant role in the evolution of the insurance industry to varying degrees in each of the member states. In this context, the most innovative countries include France, Holland, Italy, the UK and West Germany. Some of them also happen to be the countries that are best placed - financially and organisationally - to enter one another's market. So, what role is IT likely to play in the successive phases?

In order to answer this question, it is essential to distinguish IT's three separate roles as far as the insurance industry is concerned.

• IT can be a process innovation, in the sense that it helps to automate work processes that previously were performed manually.

• IT can be a product innovation, in the sense that it can facilitate the creation of new and/or flexible products in a cost effective manner to the extent that such products cannot be produced economically, using time-honoured labour-intensive methods.

- IT can be an organisational innovation, in the sense that it permits new corporate structures that allow new distribution channels, decentralisation of work and flatter structures, on the one hand and continued central control on the other. In the French and UK insurance industries, for example, outstanding organisational innovation is evident in the delivery channels: retail functions have been passed on to intermediaries via IT-based networks, with the result that the insurers themselves now operate very different retail structures compared to a decade ago [1].

Thus, as we move towards the next century, IT will continue to act as all three kinds of innovation. But its dominant role will change.

- In the competitive phase, IT will be used more as a process innovation in order to achieve a lower expense ratio as perceptions of competition increase.

- In the infrastructure phase, IT will be used more as a process as well as a product innovation. This is because the new vertical linkages will be used to promote new/flexible products that will characterise increasingly the cross-border trade in customised products.

- In the restructuring phase, IT will be used increasingly as all three kinds of innovation simultaneously, but especially as an organisational innovation. This is because the restructuring of capacity will require substantial organisational changes as well as new distribution channels.

Within this overall pattern, we shall doubtless see a proliferation of electronic-based value added networks both within and between the member states. These will facilitate considerably business traffic between insurers, on the one hand, and their intermediaries on the other. As such, they will be part of that evolutionary process that will take the industry through the three phases described in Figure 4.2.

The networks will neither short-circuit the process that will lead to eventual restructuring nor by-pass it. The networks are expected to play a vital role in improving the commercial viability of industry in each member state. But this role will be facilitative, not causative: it will help to promote changes rather than cause them. For causes, we have to look at the changing regulatory regime and market environment.

Indeed, adoption of new technology will be only one of two preconditions for success. The other, and equally important, will be the availability of skills and expertise within individual insurance companies. As competition grows apace, non-life products will become more know-how intensive, in order that they can cater for specific circumstances of individual clients. Customisation will be an important attribute of cross-border trade in insurance services. This is because 1992 is likely to increase the range of choice for customers across the Community. Within a wider range, insurers are likely to target their marketing at specific client groups whose changing needs will require considerable flexibility in the product portfolios of individual insurers.

4.3   Case study 2: Wholesale distribution

4.3.1   Background

In the national accounts of the individual member states, wholesale distribution has been located as a distinct industry within a four-sphere cycle of activities associated with production and distribution of goods prior to consumption, as shown by the inner ring in Figure 4.3. The spheres are:

- *Production*, where goods are produced, irrespective of the country of origin.

- *Intermediate activities*, covering business services such as transport, finance and insurance, as used by wholesalers in order to facilitate the transfer and exchange of goods from producers to wholesalers.

- *Wholesaling*, involving provision of warehousing and resale services with regard to three district kinds of product: food; non-food (including household durable goods); and industrial products and raw materials. The first two kinds are usually sold to retailers and the third to companies.

- *Retailing*, involving the sale of goods to households.

  As the outer segments of Figure 4.3 also show, there is a similar cycle for services but it has only two spheres: production and retailing. In many cases, the spheres are not distinguishable. Examples of services in this context include: banking, insurance, travel, catering, entertainment and hairdressing.

Figure 4.3   Conventional view of wholesale distribution

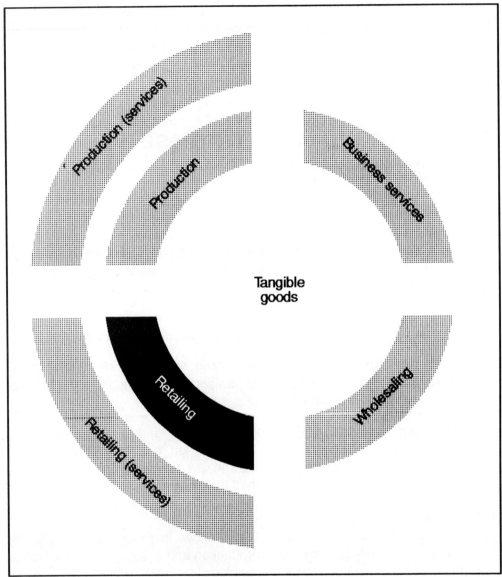

Source: CREATE Research Programme

Thus placed, wholesaling has a clearly defined set of activities in principle in the national accounts. Yet, in practice, these activities have proved increasingly difficult to measure over the past twenty years, because of the emergence of a new economic sector, directly as the result of weakening demarcations between the four sequential spheres described above.

Often referred to as the quaternary sector, this new entity is an essential feature of the so-called Second Industrial Revolution [2]. It is distinct from the three conventional sectors that characterised a modern economy until the first 'oil shock' in 1973: primary, secondary and tertiary. The distinctiveness becomes obvious against the background of six developments occurring in wholesale distribution in the last decade in the member states, as shown in Figure 4.4. Summarised below, they are:

- *Externalisation:* the shake-out in the manufacturing sector in response to the 1974-5 and 1979-81 world-wide economic recessions led to the externalisation of the wholesale function, which was previously performed in-house as a subsidiary activity in many manufacturing companies. This proved mutually beneficial in that it increased the business volume in wholesale distribution, thereby providing the potential for economies of scale, and it enabled manufacturing firms to enjoy these economies of scale at one remove. Under externalisation, the scope of wholesale distribution has increasingly expanded to include warehousing; transport and logistics; insurance; repair, maintenance and recovery; engineering services; marketing; and merchandising and promotion.

- *Verticalisation:* business growth in turn enabled wholesalers to widen the scope of their activities by diversifying into ancillary functions such as transport, export-import and retailing, thereby encompassing a larger segment of the distribution cycle into their business mix. Higher growth also enabled wholesalers to forge closer links with their suppliers as a way of securing economies of scale in buying, finance and distribution.

- *Specialisation:* diversification was more evident in product lines catering for the household market. Alongside that, there was also significant specialisation relating to industrial products and raw materials usually bought by the corporate sector. This form of specialisation was promoted by the growing complexity of the technical and distributional characteristics of the items in question.

Figure 4.4   Wholesale distribution in the new quaternary sector

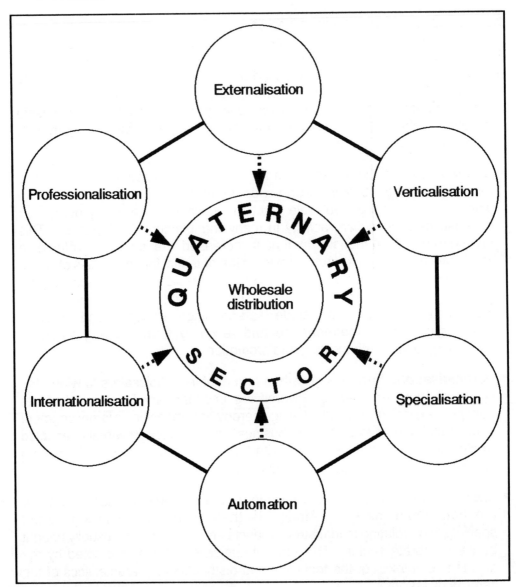

Source: CREATE Research Programme

- **Automation:** expansion in the scale and complexity of the operations could only be achieved cost effectively with the use of information technology. It has been used in order processing, vehicle booking, warehouse management, stock control, dispatch, proof of goods delivery, invoicing, financial reporting, budgeting, market research and rapid communication with 'upstream' suppliers and 'downstream' retailers. Those wholesalers who have diversified into retailing have also introduced elaborate electronic point of sale terminals at check-outs. Whatever their product range, wholesalers have been receptive to the new technology, as the concept of 'just-in-time' has spread from manufacturing into distribution.

- **Internationalisation:** economies of scale and scope - both in buying and selling - have enabled wholesalers to expand their supplier and customer base on an international scale, in pursuit of low-cost supplies and high-margin sales. This is corroborated by two indicators: growth in intra-Community trade in semi- and finished- manufacturers; and the exceptional growth in the Community's trade with Far Eastern suppliers who as yet do not have their own well-defined selling points in the Community [2].

- **Professionalisation:** all the above developments have witnessed a dramatic increase in the know-how component of all wholesale functions. The industry has, as a result, witnessed an increase in the share of professional occupations such as management, information systems specialists, technologists, technicians, business planners, marketing specialists and logistics experts.

These developments are indeed occurring in varying degrees over a range of service industries which increasingly comprise the new quaternary sector. The industries in question are: financial services, business services, communication services, retail trades, and wholesale distribution. They are at the leading-edge of six developments heralding the onset of the second industrial revolution:

- large scale use of information technology

- globalisation in buying and selling

- product and market diversification

- growing industrial concentration

- rapid product innovation

- and rapid emergence of know-how as a prime resource.

In the light of these on-going developments, the wholesale distribution sector in every member state is undergoing a change, albeit at varying rates. With the completion of the single market in 1992, the pace of change is likely to accelerate both directly and indirectly. Directly, due to the proposed deregulation of road and air transport which will reduce costs and stimulate competition amongst wholesalers across the Community. Indirectly, due to the fresh stimulus to intra-Community trade in general emanating from the dismantling of various technical and administrative barriers. So what are the prospects for wholesale distribution in the single market in the 1990s?

4.3.2   Business impact of 1992

Currently, there are significant inter-country divergences in market structure, business environment and technological usage in the wholesale distribution sector in individual member states. At the same time, there is little doubt that these differences are weakening under the combined impact of the six developments discussed in the previous sub-section. The single market will doubtless provide fresh impetus towards greater convergence.

Overall, the divergence-convergence dichotomy will continue into the future. Following the past pattern, it will be an evolutionary process. Despite its continuous nature, it is possible to identify some overlapping but nevertheless distinct phases towards greater convergences. Of course, the pace of evolution will vary between individual member states, such that individual wholesale distribution sectors will be in different phases at a given point in time. It is possible to identify the nature of prospective evolution and the individual phases within it in the 1990s, after the creation of the single market. In this context, the starting point here is Figure 4.3 which presents the demarcations in the conventional cycle of activities. It is highly probable that the wholesale distribution sectors in individual member states will go through three sequential phases, as follows.

- **Internal restructuring phase:** this phase will see the continuation of two distinct developments, both of which have already been occurring since about the middle of the last decade in many member states (see Figure 4.5). First, there will be further weakening of demarcations between retailing and wholesaling particularly in household lines involving food and non-food products. Second, alongside this diversification, there will be the emergence of large wholesalers, specialising in industrial products and raw materials. In other words, the wholesale distribution sector will continue to become polarised between specialist and generalist wholesalers, for reasons identified in the last sub-section. Within the polarity, the implied vertical diversification will mainly occur in non-specialist lines in order to serve a wider customer-base.

- *Transitional phase:* retailing of goods and services, which had been carried out hitherto as separate activities, will increasingly overlap in response to the diversification occurring into the goods sub-sector (Figure 4.6). Under this scenario, many mainstream retailers of household lines will offer financial, travel, entertainment, catering and dry-cleaning services through their outlets. Thus, the conventional downstream retail sector will see the emergence of many generalist retailers. As a part of this process, some of those wholesalers who have diversified into the retailing of household goods will also be drawn into generalist retailing, as a competitive response. This form of horizontal diversification will occur in order to enjoy economies of scale in distribution and economies of scope in product and service range.

- *Greater integration phase:* under this phase large wholesalers and retailers will begin to diversify into intermediate business services such as transport, insurance and export-import (Figure 4.7). This sort of vertical diversification will be facilitated by the new competitive pressures released by the single market. Thus the single market will entail considerable rationalisation of capacity on the one hand; and acceleration of the other six developments identified in the previous sub-section, on the other. The diversification will take one of two forms: creating outright ownership of productive capacity in these services through organic or acquisitional growth or forming vertical links through collaborative ventures - formal or informal - with established business service firms. The object will be to enjoy further economies of scale and scope associated with vertical diversification.

Figure 4.5   Internal restructuring phase

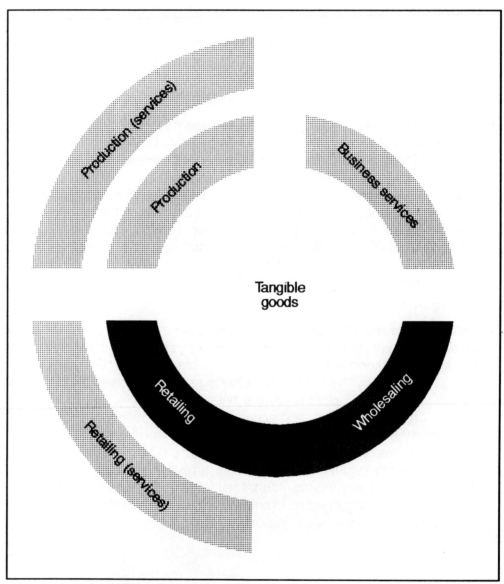

Source: CREATE Research Programme

Figure 4.6   Transitional

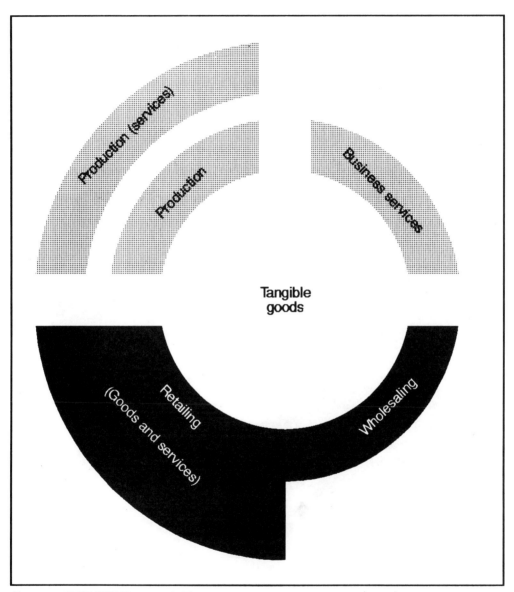

Source: CREATE Research Programme

Figure 4.7   Integration phase

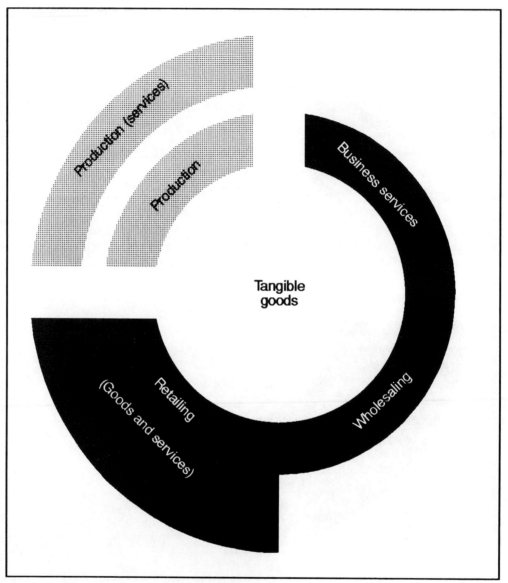

Source: CREATE Research Programme

4.3.3 The role of information technology

In the three phases outlined above, IT and 1992 are likely to play separate but significant roles. Taking them in turn, IT will play a major role as one or more of three types of innovation:

- as a process innovation, automating all routine operations (e.g. cash balancing, stock control, logistics);

- as a product innovation, facilitating the creation of new services (e.g. charge cards, travel booking);

- as an organisational innovation, facilitating the establishment of larger but fewer stores, the removal of managerial levels and greater centralisation of common services (e.g. pricing, marketing and distribution).

Figure 4.8 outlines the nature of the prospective changes that are likely to occur under each of the phases discussed above. For each phase, the relevant changes are bounded by two kinds of innovation, which are likely to constitute the dominant thrust of IT in the phase in question. For example, in the internal restructuring phase, IT will be used principally as an organisational and as a process innovation. In the next phase, it will constitute process-product innovation; and in the final phase a product-organisation innovation.

It is clear from the list of changes associated with each phase that wholesale distribution will continue to undergo major changes, whose collective thrust will increasingly push the sector into the quaternary sector. The single market will accentuate this trend because manufacturers will be looking for more efficient channels of distribution and logistics as a part of their own rationalisation process. At the very least, the prospective changes will transform the sector in terms of product and service mix; market environment; industrial structure; technological usage; international orientation; industrial concentration; and horizontal and vertical linkages.

Figure 4.8   Information technology and structural change

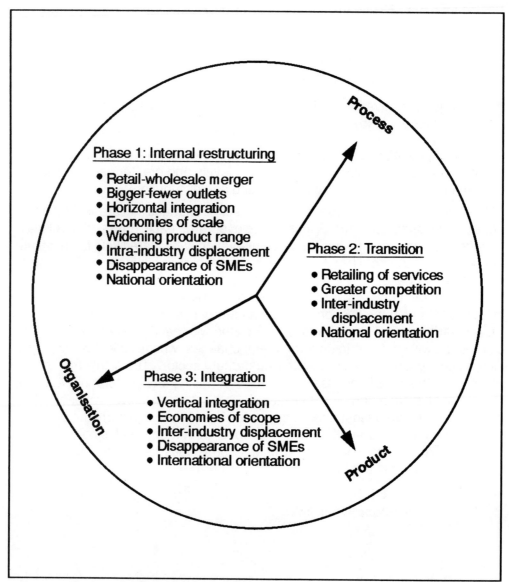

Source: CREATE Research Programme

4.4   Summary

Building on the overview presented in the last chapter, this chapter has provided further details about the nature of the dynamic effect associated with the 1992 programme.

It has done so by using a case study approach that provides a selective focus on two industries that are likely to undergo major changes in their structure, product mix, technology and distribution channels, namely, insurance and wholesale distribution. The salient points emerging from the case studies are as follows:

- The programme has a clear potential for affecting some industries directly and others through a knock-on effect because of the web of supplier-customer relationship between them. Insurance constitutes a good example of an industry where the direct effect will be profound. At the other extreme, wholesale distribution provides a good example of an industry where the knock-on effect will be equally profound.

- Between them, the two case studies exemplify developments that are likely to occur over significant segments of manufacturing and services alike. Specifically, they show that the programme will promote industrial restructuring and emergence of larger business units with the ability to exploit the economies of scale in production and distribution; and the economies of scope in product and services range.

- The restructuring process will have other inter-related features as well. On the output side, it will witness greater customisation of goods and services, with special emphasis on creating value added for customers through specific product features or through widening of product range. On the input side, it will require a more intensive and extensive use of information technology in three distinct areas: automation of routine work processes; creation of new products, services and distribution channels; and re-organisation of work, involving fewer hierarchies and geographical decentralisations.

- The restructuring process will, therefore, have a broad-based impact which will enhance the role of work skills and know-how.

PART B

Labour market challenges from the single market

Part A has examined the business challenges associated with the single market. We now move on to consider the employment challenges.

The economies of the member states have been undergoing major structural changes largely due to the world-wide recessions of 1973-4 and 1979-81. In turn, they have affected the evolution of both quantity and quality of labour demand over time. There have also been changes occurring independently in the labour supply due to demographic and social developments. As a result, the labour markets of individual member states have been experiencing various imbalances for the past two decades. Given their deep-seated causes, in all likelyhood, the imbalances would prevail over the rest of this decade, irrespective of the single market. Thus, when assessing the employment challenges of the single market, it is essential to be familiar with the historical developments.

Accordingly, this Part first identifies the likely employment impact of the single market (Chapter 5). It then examines the past and prospective trends in labour supply (Chapter 6) and labour demand (Chapter 7). Having done that, it places the challenges from the single market in a wider context (Chapter 7) and suggests actions that need to be taken to ensure that both the historical and the new imbalances can be minimised (Chapter 8).

In the four Chapters under this Part, the emphasis is on broad trends and solutions, given their pre-occupation with all the member states. This serves to provide a good overview before focusing on the experiences of individual member states in Part C.

5

EMPLOYMENT IMPACT: AN OVERVIEW

5.1   Introduction

Chapters 3 and 4 have provided an assessment of the direct and indirect impact of the 1992 programme on various industries by considering the changes that are likely to occur in the conditions of supply. This chapter considers their employment implications. But in an important sense it goes even further by assessing the employment impact of the likely changes in the level of demand inspired by cost reductions associated with the elimination of various barriers. As such, it provides an overall assessment of employment impact. However, it is worth bearing in mind that such an assessment is the final outcome of two distinct sets of *net* effects as shown below:

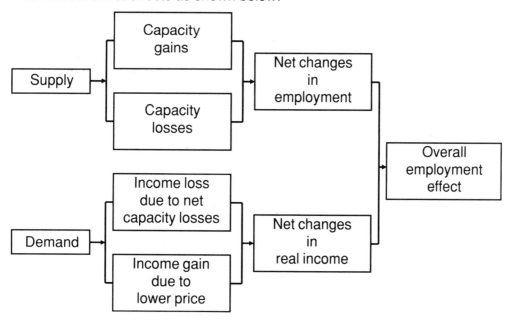

On the supply side, the process of industrial restructuring will lead to capacity rationalisation which will involve capacity increases for some companies and losses for others. This is the first set of net effects. On the demand side, there are also likely to be two offsetting effects: change in income arising from rationalisation which is likely to be negative; and the increase in the spending power of all incomes due to the reduction in costs and prices associated with the use of more efficient capacity and the elimination of barriers. The rest of this chapter considers these elements separately, highlighting regional and technological dimensions where relevant.

5.2   Restructuring effect

Chapter 3 has identified five groups of industries which are likely to be affected directly by the 1992 programme, the first four in the manufacturing sector and the last one in the service sector. There are no Community-wide estimates available on the last (services) group but available data on manufacturing industries (given in Tables B1 and B2 in the Appendix) show that Groups 2, 3 and 4 have already been subject to employment contractions since 1983. More significantly perhaps, the size of annual contractions in recent years has been larger than those experienced in the period 1975-83, which also included the severe 1979-81 recession. Group 1, on the other hand, shows a variable pattern. Overall, though, there is little doubt that the contractions evident since 1983 will persist well into this decade.

There are two points worthy of note regarding prospective contractions: one relating to the avenues through which they will occur and one relating to their knock-on effect.

The first of these is discussed below and the second in Section 5.4. The contraction in employment will occur through one or more of the following four avenues of restructuring:

* **Mergers and acquisitions:** in the past, these have had the effect of reducing employment as and when the resulting duplicated capacity and functions have been phased out. Since 1983 there has been a new wave of mergers and acquisitions, notably involving companies within and between the member states (see Figure 5.1). Its pace is likely to accelerate over the next five years or so. In the Community context, however, the extent of reduction under the

current wave will depend on, among other things, the stance of monetary and fiscal policies prevailing in the member states concerned. Under a favourable stance, there would be better chances for creating new jobs and/or redeployment opportunities within the companies concerned. However, the balance of possibilities will be towards reductions in jobs because most of the mergers and acquisitions will be oriented towards the elimination of surplus capacity in the single market.

- **Internal restructuring:** many multinational companies have production capacity in more than one state because of prevailing technical barriers or public procurement regulations. Such companies will embark on a substantial programme of rationalisation leading to fewer but larger production and distribution sites in order to enjoy the economies of scale. By their very nature, such companies are multinational in their market orientation. Capacity rationalisation will improve their competitiveness in other global markets where they also operate. Thus, employment reductions associated with rationalisation may be, at least to a certain extent, moderated by the renewed ability to compete better outside Europe.

Figure 5.1   Mergers and acquisitions involving EC-based companies

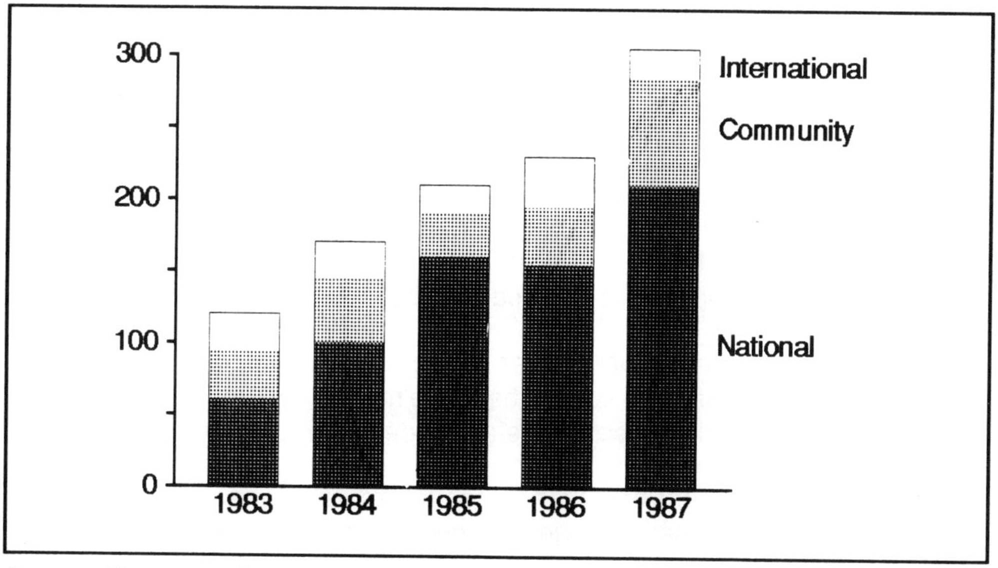

Source: European Commission

- *Improved efficiency:* some companies may have neither the European nor the global orientation associated with the two avenues described above. The 1992 programme may encourage them to become more competitive in order to survive. Such companies may well shed inefficient capacity or simply upgrade it, with different implications for employment: job reductions if the capacity is shed, and skills enhancement if it is upgraded.

- *Corporate deaths:* some companies will fail to survive in the new competitive climate and hence disappear altogether.

From the foregoing analysis, it is clear that different avenues will have different kinds of employment effect. It is difficult to quantify them individually. As for their collective impact, there is little doubt that it will be negative, at least initially. For, through these four avenues, the Community's corporate landscape is set to change dramatically.

For example, Sir John Harvey Jones (former chairman of Britain's Imperial Chemical Industries) provided a prediction at a *Financial Times* conference in October 1988 that by the year 2000 more than half of Europe's factories would close and half its companies would either disappear or be taken over. At the same conference the Chairman of ABB, the Swiss-Swedish engineering group, predicted that of all European companies affected by the 1992 programme 'one third would see themselves as winners and two thirds as losers at the outset'.

In order to understand the logic of this proposition, it is worth considering some examples.

- At present, there are fifty tractor manufacturers in Western Europe, scrambling for a market of about 200,000 tractor sales a year. In USA, there are only four tractor manufacturers with annual sales of about the same number [1]. The multiplicity of European manufacturers has occurred as a result of different technical standards to the extent that it is difficult for some producers to manufacture a tractor without significant engineering alterations.

- Domestic appliances provide an even more striking example. In USA, there are four manufacturers who supply the entire market. In Western Europe, for a market of roughly similar size there are three hundred producers [2].

- The imbalance is evident in heavy engineering as well. For example, there are ten manufacturers of electricity generating equipment in the member states, but only two in USA. There are 16 producers of railway stock in the member states but only two in the US. Finally, there are eleven manufacturers of telephone exchanges in the member states but only four in USA [3].

These examples are illustrative and not definitive. They serve to underline the significant potential that now exists for the rationalisation of capacity across various sectors. There are no comparable data available on service industries but informed opinion suggests that there, too, there is a notable efficiency gap between the member states on the one hand, and the United States and Japan, on the other.

The elimination of various physical and technical barriers will no doubt go a long way towards reducing, if not eliminating, the efficiency gap through industrial restructuring. Irrespective of the stance of macroeconomic policy, this outcome is expected to occur because of the intensification of market forces.

In the new environment, the emphasis will be on having more efficient capacity that will generate maximum possible value added, whilst divesting or sub-contracting those activities which have low value added. Similar considerations will lead to greater specialisation in the input-output linkages that characterise commercial relationships between companies. The trend towards customisation will doubtless reinforce the search for higher value added. Together they will demand a superior repertoire of work skills and know-how, as described in Chapter 3.

Thus, two outcomes will emerge from restructuring: a lower level of employment but greater emphasis on its quality. The fact that these outcomes are couched here in qualitative terms should not detract from the fact they are only the visible end of a major rationalisation process which will create winners at the expense of losers. This is because there is nothing in the 1992 programme which will directly and substantially increase the overall level of demand to the extent that the 'size of the cake' itself may be expanding whilst shares of individual companies are changing. For the rest of the decade, the single market has all the attributes of a zero sum game. We return to this point in Chapter 14.

5.3 Regional effect: Fear of 'social dumping'

The regional aspect of restructuring is almost impossible to analyse since no studies have yet been carried out on the comparative advantage of different regions. In any event a region's advantage is usually expressed in terms of historical factors, to the extent that the impact of the 1992 programme can only be satisfactorily studied after the single market has been in operation for a while. However, it is still possible to offer a tentative assessment based on two offsetting influences arising from the programme.

The first of these relates to the range of factors which have, over the years, influenced the comparative advantage of different regions. These are given in Table 5.1. The fact that some regions are more prosperous than others is a reflection of their relative advantage in terms of the identified factors. Thus, under the major rationalisation now in progress, the regions that are more favoured at present will become even more so. This applies particularly to the Benelux countries, northern France, the south-east of Britain and the Ruhr. In the new competitive environment, a prosperous region will continue to prosper because companies will be interested in least-cost location, when *all* considerations are taken into account. By this argument prevailing regional disparities will worsen, assuming there are no other policy changes in addition to those proposed in the 1992 programme.

Table 5.1   Factors influencing the location of firms

Market potential

- local market demand, growth potential

- potential for economies of scale.

Macro-economic context/economic policy

- growth rate of the economy, its capacity to absorb shocks

- exchange rates, credit rates, taxation (income/company taxes)

- industrial policy: research and development, subsidies, energy policy

- commercial policy: import constraints, non-tariff barriers.

Labour market

- labour costs
- qualification of the workforce
- labour market legislation: working-time, redundancy legislation
- social climate: industrial relations, flexibility, trade union activity.

Geographical situation

- proximity of clients, suppliers
- transport costs (and communications).

Infrastructure

- energy costs (electricity, gas, water)
- industrial sites (costs and expansion potential)
- services (banks, insurance, ...)
- educational institutions (universities, research institutions, etc.).

Type of activity

- product life-cycle
- labour intensity.

Other factors

- social, cultural and language factors
- quality of living environment.

Source: 'Employment in Europe, 1989' (European Commission, Brussels)

There is, however, the prospect of a countervailing influence on the horizon. This arises from the possibility of *social dumping*, defined here as the use of inferior levels of pay, working conditions and social standards in order to improve market shares and competitiveness on the part of individual companies. For example, in industries where labour costs are an important element of operating costs, many companies will be tempted to relocate to the southern member states, notably Greece, Italy, Portugal and Spain which have the lowest unit labour costs (Figure 5.2), high overall unemployment and high youth unemployment (Figure 5.3). In particular, under social dumping the lower unit wage costs and cheaper social security systems of the less advanced regions may act as an inducement to inward investment from other member states.

At present, the risk of social dumping is apparent rather than real. Although some inward investment has occurred in Ireland, Portugal and Spain, there is as yet no evidence to suggest that new employers follow the local rates of pay and terms and conditions of work. Instead, there appears to be an amalgam of practices prevailing in home and host countries. In any event, there is less risk of social dumping occurring if the Social Dimension of the 1992 programme is

Figure 5.2 Labour costs and unit labour costs in the member states: 1987

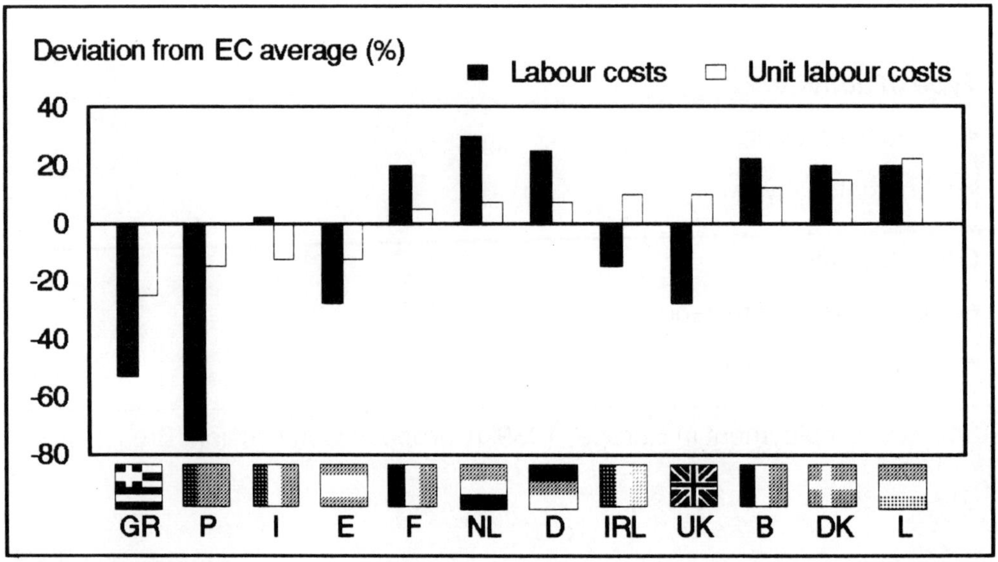

Source: EUROSTAT

adopted—a point that we return to in Chapter 17. Two caveats are worth making. First, if the risk becomes real there is the possibility of a backlash: better terms and conditions of work in other countries (notably the northern member states) could come under pressure. Socially this would be a retrograde step, but the point is worth making in the economic context of the regional redistribution of industries after 1992. Second, it is arguable whether some of the low-cost locations in the southern member states have the necessary training and skills infrastructure to accommodate a large-scale inward migration of new firms. Doubtless, in less-skilled activities this constraint is less obvious. But in the age of rapid customisation of products and services such infrastructures will feature prominently in location decisions.

On present reckoning, the first of the two offsetting influences is likely to be more significant at least over the rest of this decade. The implication is that the existing regional disparities may well worsen as the result of the single market. This observation underlines the importance of the Social Dimension, as discussed in Chapter 17.

Figure 5.3 Youth unemployment and total unemployment: May 1989

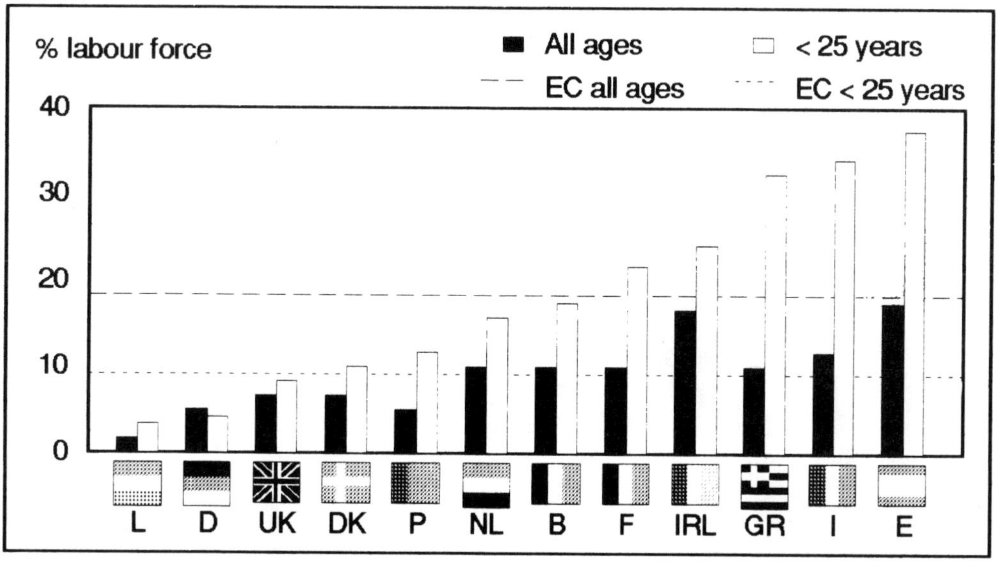

Source: EUROSTAT

5.4 J-curve effect

The assessment in the previous two sections has focused on the likely developments on the supply side. Now we consider the demand side.

In this context, within individual member states, there are likely to be two developments. The first of these will relate to change in incomes brought about directly by the rationalisation of capacity. The second will relate to the increase in consumers' spending power as the removal of physical and technical barriers - and the consequent rationalisation - reduces industrial costs and prices. The two developments could have a beneficial influence on real spending power within the Community.

Table 5.2 *Cumulative impact of the single market on gross domestic product and employment*

(Percentage on a cumulative basis)

| | | 1989-95 | | | | | |
		Year 1	Year 2	Year 3	Year 4	Year 5	Year 6
France:	GDP	1.1	2.0	2.9	3.7	4.4	5.1
	Employment	-0.3	0.0	0.3	0.7	1.2	1.6
Italy:	GDP	1.4	3.2	4.5	5.2	5.4	5.5
	Employment	-0.6	-0.2	0.3	0.7	1.1	1.4
UK:	GDP	0.8	2.4	3.3	3.6	3.8	4.0
	Employment	-0.6	-0.1	0.7	1.1	1.3	1.4
West Germany:	GDP	1.2	2.0	2.6	2.9	3.5	4.2
	Employment	-0.3	0.1	0.5	0.8	1.2	1.7
Europe - 12:	GDP	1.1	2.3	3.2	3.6	4.1	4.5
	Employment	-0.4	0.0	0.5	0.8	1.2	1.5

Source: Paulo Cecchini,' Research on the "Cost of non-Europe", Basic Findings, Volume 2 ' (Commission of the European Communities, Brussels, 1988)

Thus, when the demand-side effects are set alongside the supply-side effects, it becomes possible to present the overall impact of the 1992 programme on the gross domestic product (ie. total output) and employment in each member state. The relevant estimates show that the 1992 programme will have the effect of raising the GDP by 4.5 per cent on a cumulative basis in the first six years, starting from 1989 (Table 5.2).

For the four member states for which disaggregated forecasts are available, it is clear that France will experience the highest increase and the UK the lowest. When it comes to overall employment, the relativity in gains and losses are also similar.

As for their time profile, it is clear that in each case the evolution of employment is expected to follow the familiar J-curve effect, with employment first contracting in the rationalisation phase and then expanding as efficiency gains and real income gains occur. As Figure 5.4 shows, the extent of contraction would depend upon whether those Directives leading to the completion of the single market are implemented simultaneously or progressively. At the moment, the latter seems the most likely possibility - a point to which we return in Chapter 14.

Figure 5.5   Effect of the single market on employment: Alternative scenarios

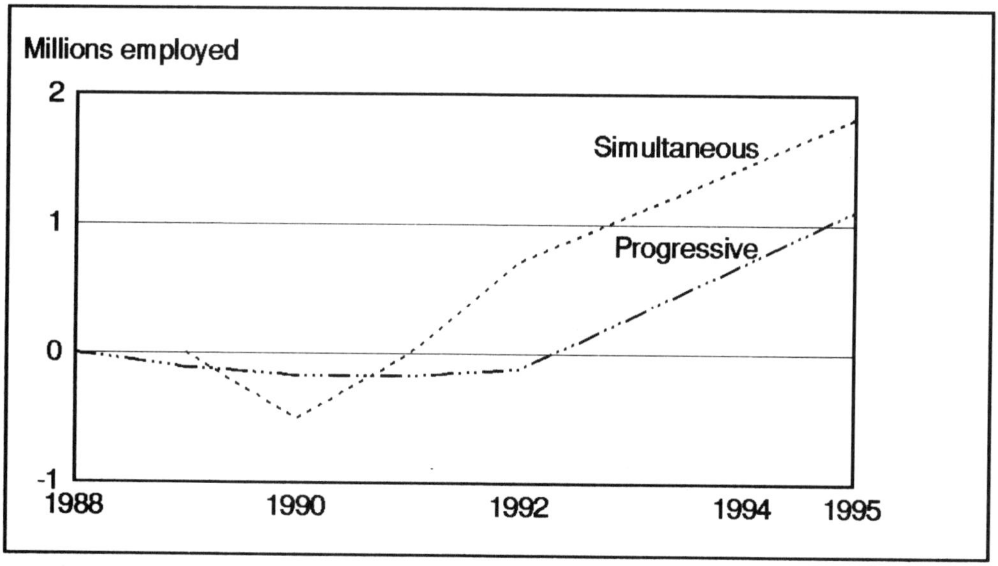

Source: Studies on the Economics of Integration

For now, it is worth noting that most industries identified in Table 3.1 are already experiencing major industrial restructuring. That this process should generate such small gains looks paradoxical until it is realised that the estimates in Table 5.2 are the outcomes of two sets of offsetting developments which themselves are subject to further offsets as described in Section 5.1. These double offsets corroborate the view that bold and imaginative though the 1992 programme is, the gains arising from it at least until the middle of this decade will be in the nature of a game of poker where winners win only because losers lose.

In this zero sum game, the offsets may well be even larger than our qualitative assessment suggests because since the 1960s the Community's economies have become more labour intensive, as evidenced by Figure 5.5. For example, in the period 1961-73, GDP growth rates of over 4.5 per cent were needed to generate any increase in employment. In the period 1980-9, that threshold has dropped to only two per cent. The implied increase in labour intensity over time has become an inherent feature of the economies of the member states as they have become more services orientated. For the foreseeable future, this upward trend is expected to continue and, in the process, it will serve to conceal the 'real' employment impact of the 1992 programme. It also raises some worrying issues in the area of labour productivity to which we return in Chapters 7, 15 and 18.

Figure 5.6   Employment and GDP growth in the Community: 1960-89

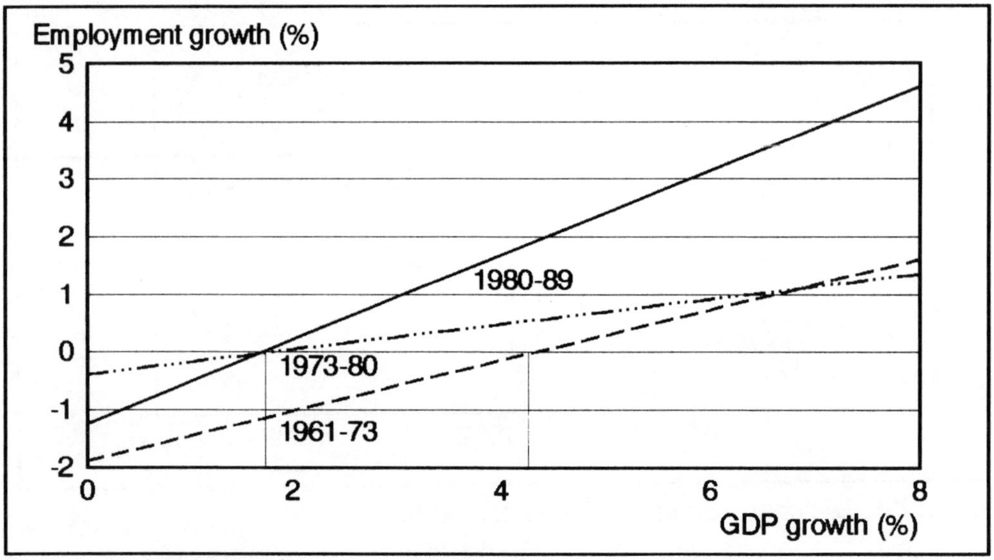

Source: Employment in Europe, 1989

5.5 Summary

This chapter has provided an assessment of the overall employment impact of the 1992 programme. It has shown that estimates of the likely impact are essentially expressed in net terms. This is because there are certain offsetting elements arising from changing conditions of supply in the industries affected and from changing conditions of demand in the wider economies in which the industries operate. The salient points emerging from the chapter are as follows.

- On the supply side, the process of industrial restructuring will lead to capacity rationalisation. The size of its impact on jobs will depend upon which of the following four avenues are used: mergers and acquisitions, internal restructuring, improved efficiency and corporate deaths.

- The first and fourth avenues will cause job losses because the companies concerned will be mainly European-orientated. As such, they will be more subject to greater competition. The second avenue may cause some job gains because the companies concerned will mainly have a global orientation. As such, they may be able to use their increased efficiency in Europe to compete better elsewhere. The third avenue may cause job losses if it involves capacity cuts, or skills enhancement if it involves capacity upgrading.

- Overall, the 1992 programme will involve far-reaching rationalisation. The process has already started in earnest. In the regional context, it will serve to widen regional disparities in income and jobs: the weaker regions will suffer disproportionately, even after allowing for the risk of 'social dumping'.

- On the demand side, the 1992 programme will have an expansionary influence when allowance is made for the increase in consumers' spending power resulting from price reductions caused by the single market.

- When supply-side and demand-side changes are taken into account, there will be, at best, a rather modest improvement in gross domestic product and employment. Accordingly, in the medium term, the single market's impact will be felt substantially through industrial restructuring which will take the form of a zero sum game: winners will win only because losers will lose.

6

LABOUR FORCE TRENDS: A SUPPLY-SIDE APPROACH

6.1   Background and issues

Since the 1960s, the demographic trends in nearly all the Western industrialised countries have had two notable features: a continuing decline in the fertility rate and a continuing increase in the longevity rate.

The drop in the fertility rate has occurred under the combined impact of improvements in the technology of birth-control, such as the pill and the intrauterine device (IUD) and women's increasing career aspirations. As a result, the average family size and the time spent on child-rearing have declined, leading to two inter-related outcomes:

- in the short-term it has caused a step-increase in the participation rate of women in the labour force, especially since the early 1970s; and

- in the longer-term, it has caused a step-decline in the number of young persons in the age group 15-24. This phenomenon has become evident particularly since 1985 and is likely to trough around the middle of this decade.

The increase in the longevity rate has been almost continuous and has been substantially dictated by the ongoing improvements in health, welfare and living conditions of the elderly, all occurring as part of improvements in living standards associated with economic growth.

The two outcomes in turn have begun to generate three-fold implications for the labour force:

- changing age structure, leading to an ageing workforce

- changing sex structure, leading to more female workers

- rising dependency ratio, leading to more retirees per employed worker.

There have been various empirical studies on the impact of demographic developments [1; 2; 3; 4]. Their focus tends to be on the implications for health and pensions expenditure. In so far as they consider the impact on labour supply, this is either couched in generalised terms [3; 4] or substantially based on *a priori* reasoning [1; 3]. Certainly, they shed little light on how demographic changes will affect the projected economic gains resulting from the creation of the single market. Nor do they provide a comparative picture of prospective labour supply trends in different countries, against the background of differing developments in their respective labour markets.

This chapter begins a modest attempt at an analysis of past and prospective trends in the labour force of individual member states. The inter-relationship between these trends on the one hand, and the single market on the other, is considered in the next chapter, after doing a similar comparative evaluation of the prospective trends in labour demand.

Before that, however, it is essential to explain the definitional link between population and labour force, since the latter is the best proxy indicator of labour supply. For a given country, labour force estimates are derived by first multiplying its total population of each sex and each age group by the corresponding labour market participation rate derived from the regular labour force survey, and then summing up results over all sex and age groups. The resulting estimate is an aggregate of three distinct categories of labour force: employed persons, self-employed persons and unemployed persons. As such the estimate constitutes the closest approximation to total supply of labour. This is a wider definition in that it includes everyone within a certain statutory age range (usually 16-65) who is willing and able to participate in economic activity through the medium of paid work. There is, of course, a narrower definition which defines labour force in terms of only those in employment and self-employment: as such, it includes those who are in paid work.

As always, there are no hard and fast rules about the relative merits of either definition. It all depends on the context in which they are being used. Given that our interest is a more general one, in this chapter, we use both definitions while pursuing the following two pertinent questions:

- What have been the trends in the labour force in the recent past and what factors have influenced them?

- What are the most likely trends in the labour force in the foreseeable future and what factors will influence them?

6.2   Recent trends and causal factors

Using the wider definition, Table 6.1 gives the estimates of labour force size for 1975 and 1985 for the nine member states for whom the latest data are available. It also gives the estimates of absolute numerical change between these years (third column) and then *decomposes* the change into its two components: changes in population and changes in participation rates (fourth and fifth columns). Corresponding estimates based on percentage change are given in the accompanying Table 6.2. Analysis of the data in the two tables prompts the following salient points about the trends in the period 1975-85:

- *Uneven growth between countries and gender:* the collective male labour force of the nine countries grew by 3.136 million (equivalent to 4.6 per cent). The pattern of growth was, however, far from even. At one extreme, Italy, the Netherlands, Ireland and Denmark had the fastest relative (percentage) growth rates, at the other extreme, Luxembourg and Belgium had negative growth rates. As for the female labour force, all countries experienced growth but at a highly variable rates; with the Netherlands, Italy, Denmark and Ireland recording the most pronounced increases.

- *Favourable population impact across the countries and gender:* in all countries and for both sexes, population growth helped to increase the labour force. In other words, there was a notable increase in the number of people of working age.

- *Differential participation rate between countries and gender:* the male participation rate declined in all countries in the tables except France, Italy and Denmark. In contrast, the female participation rate increased in all countries, especially in the Netherlands, Italy, Denmark and Luxembourg. The differential growth pattern between the sexes reflects the changes in the industrial structure due to the two 'oil recessions' of 1974-5 and 1979-81.

Table 6.1   Change in total labour force of nine countries: 1975-85

(Thousands)

Country	Labour force		Change 1975-85	Part of change due to:	
				Population	Participation rates
	1975	1985			
Males					
B	2,518.4	2,476.3	-42.1	163.1	-205.2
DK	1,404.9	1,514.3	109.4	81.6	27.9
F	13,886.8	14,261.5	374.7	1,157.5	-782.7
IRL	848.3	909.8	61.5	122.7	-61.1
I	13,669.9	15,123.8	1,453.9	1,112.6	341.4
L	104.6	101.1	-3.5	4.8	-8.3
NL	3,495.4	3,786.3	290.9	515.3	-224.4
UK	16,090.8	16,258.8	168.0	824.8	-656.9
D	16,725.3	17,448.7	723.4	1,541.1	-817.7
Europe - 9	68,744.4	71,880.6	3,136.2	5,523.5	-2,387.0
Females					
B	1,204.3	1,500.9	296.6	100.9	195.8
DK	904.2	1,271.0	366.8	63.5	303.3
F	8,332.8	10,290.0	1,957.2	979.3	978.0
IRL	306.5	416.6	110.1	58.0	52.1
I	4,972.4	7,846.1	2,873.7	552.3	2,321.4
L	40.1	53.2	13.1	4.9	8.3
NL	1,136.1	2,013.6	877.5	253.8	623.7
UK	9,860.5	11,417.7	1,557.2	606.8	950.4
D	9438.6	11,234.1	1,795.5	654.2	1,142.3
Europe - 9	36,195.5	46,043.2	9,847.7	3,273.7	6,575.3
Total M+F	104,939.9	117,923.8	12,983.9	8,797.2	4,188.3

Source: Demographic and labour force analysis, based on Eurostat data banks

Under them there was a contraction in manufacturing employment and expansion in services employment in most of the member states. The contraction impacted disproportionately on male employees and the expansion on female employees. The higher participation rate for females is also indicative of their rising career aspirations, associated with the emergence of the dual-career family.

Thus the overall increase of 12.4 per cent in the labour force of the nine countries is a net outcome of three tendencies: population growth (8.4 per cent), growth in female participation rate (18.2 per cent); and decline in male participation rate (-3.5 per cent). As a result, the labour force grew faster than the population.

Estimates of labour force based on the narrow definition are given in Table 6.3 (in absolute terms) and Table 6.4 (in percentages). Here, the impact of the changing industrial structure is even more pronounced. The employed male labour force contracted by 0.9 per cent in the period 1975-85: the favourable population impact being more than offset by the unfavourable drop in the participation rate. In contrast, the female employed labour force increased by 17.3 per cent, as a result of positive growth in population and participation rates.

On either definition, however, it is clear that the size of the labour force has increased in the recent past. Generally speaking, it has been helped by growth in both population and female participation rates, which together have served to offset the decline in the male participation rate. It is equally clear that population growth has not been helped much by migration (see Table 6.5). Thus, the trends in the labour force in the recent past have come about as a result of population and industrial forces that have substantially and directly emanated from within individual member states. Indirectly, of course, industrial forces also have their origins in the two global recessions.

Table 6.2   Change between 1975-85 as percentage of the labour force in 1975 for nine countries

Country	Percentage change	Part of change due to:	
		Population	Participation rates
B	-1.7	6.5	-8.1
DK	7.8	5.8	2.0
F	2.7	8.3	5.6
IRL	7.3	14.5	-7.2
I	10.6	8.1	2.5
L	-3.3	4.6	-7.9
NL	8.3	14.7	-6.4
UK	1.0	5.1	-4.1
D	4.3	9.2	-4.9
Europe - 9	4.6	8.0	-3.5
Females			
B	24.6	8.4	16.3
DK	40.6	7.0	33.5
F	23.5	11.8	11.7
IRL	35.9	18.9	17.0
I	57.8	11.1	46.7
L	32.7	12.1	20.6
NL	77.2	22.3	54.9
UK	15.8	6.2	9.6
D	19.0	6.9	12.1
Europe - 9	27.2	9.0	18.2
Total M+F	12.4	8.4	4.0

Source: Demographic and labour force analysis, based on Eurostat data banks

Table 6.3   Change in employed labour force of nine countries: 1975-85

(Thousands)

Country	Population in employment		Change 1975-85	Part of change due to:	
				Population	Employment rates
	1975	1985			
Males					
B	2,408.7	2,292.7	-116.0	152.0	-268.0
DK	1,304.6	1,417.9	113.3	77.7	35.6
F	13,495.9	12,986.5	-509.4	1,080.8	-1,590.2
IRL	763.5	750.6	-12.9	99.2	-112.1
I	13,263.8	14,092.9	829.1	980.6	-151.6
L	104.1	98.9	-5.2	4.7	-10.0
NL	3,375.4	3,412.5	37.1	472.2	-435.2
UK	15,410.6	14,323.5	-1,087.0	686.6	-1,783.6
D	16,238.4	16,414.2	175.8	1,429.4	-1,253.6
Europe - 9	66,365.0	65,789.7	-575.2	4,983.4	-5,568.7
Females					
B	1,138.3	1,233.3	94.9	80.9	14.0
DK	844.6	1,150.5	305.9	59.2	246.1
F	7,963.4	8,973.5	1,010.0	872.5	137.5
IRL	279.5	336.1	56.6	46.0	10.6
I	4,716.9	6,624.9	1,908.0	412.5	1,495.4
L	39.3	50.9	11.6	4.7	6.9
NL	1,103.9	1,763.9	660.0	221.6	438.4
UK	9,343.2	10,159.8	816.6	517.6	299.0
D	9,139.1	10,272.8	1,133.6	587.3	546.4
Europe - 9	34,568.2	40,565.7	5,997.2	2,802.3	3,194.3
Total M+F	10,0933.4	106,355.4	5,421.9	7,796.3	-2,374.4

Source: Demographic and labour force analysis, based on Eurostat data banks

Table 6.4   Change between 1975-85 as a percentage of numbers in
employment in 1975 in nine countries

Country	Total change	Part of change due to:	
		Population structure	Employment rates
Males			
B	-4.8	6.3	-11.1
DK	8.7	6.0	2.7
F	-3.8	8.0	-11.8
IRL	-1.7	13.0	-14.7
I	6.3	7.4	-1.1
L	-5.0	4.5	-9.6
NL	1.1	14.0	-12.9
UK	-7.1	4.5	-11.6
D	1.1	8.8	-7.7
Europe - 9	-0.9	7.5	-8.4
Females			
B	8.3	7.1	1.2
DK	36.2	7.1	29.1
F	12.7	11.0	1.7
IRL	20.2	16.4	3.8
I	40.4	8.7	31.7
L	29.4	11.9	17.5
NL	59.8	20.1	39.7
UK	8.7	5.5	3.2
D	12.4	6.4	6.0
Europe - 9	17.3	8.1	9.2
Total M+F	5.4	7.7	-2.4

Source: Demographic and labour force analysis, based on Eurostat data banks

Table 6.5   Change in labour force and its sources: 1975-85

(Thousands)

Country	Labour force		Part of change due to:		
			Migration	'Native' population	Participation rates
	1975	1985			
Males					
B	2,518.4	2,476.3	-4.0	167.1	-205.2
DK	1,404.9	1,514.3	3.1	78.5	27.9
F	13,886.8	14,261.5	-4.2	1,161.7	-782.7
IRL	848.3	909.8	-12.3	135.0	-61.1
I	13,669.9	15,123.8	80.6	1,031.9	341.4
L	104.6	101.1	1.1	3.7	-8.3
NL	3,495.4	3,786.3	58.8	456.4	-224.4
UK	16,090.8	16,258.8	-233.6	1,058.4	-656.9
D	16,725.3	17,448.7	-55.7	1,596.8	-817.7
Europe - 9	68,744.4	71,880.6	-166.2	5,689.5	-2,387.0
Females					
B	1,204.3	1,500.9	0.9	100.0	195.8
DK	904.2	1,271.0	3.3	60.2	303.3
F	8,332.8	10,290.1	170.4	808.9	978.0
IRL	306.5	416.6	-16.2	74.2	52.1
I	4,972.4	7,846.1	134.3	418.0	2,321.4
L	40.1	53.2	4.0	0.9	8.3
NL	1,136.1	2,013.6	50.8	203.0	623.7
UK	9,860.5	11,417.7	-23.0	629.8	950.4
D	9,438.6	11,235.1	110.2	544.0	1,142.3
Europe - 9	36,195.5	46,044.3	434.7	2,839.0	6,575.3
Total M+F	104,939.7	117,924.9	286.4	8,528.6	4,188.3

Source: Demographic and labour force analysis, based on Eurostat data banks

6.3   Future trends and causal factors

6.3.1   Eurostat forecasts

Prediction of future trends in the labour force is largely a matter of forecasting population changes and participation rates. The former is less difficult because, for example, all those who are born after 1974 will gradually begin to enter the labour market on reaching the age of about 16, at which compulsory education ceases in most of the member states. In other words, they will begin to appear in the labour market from around 1990. This form of lead-time greatly assists the task of predicting the impact of population changes on the labour force. For forecast periods longer than 16 years, there is a need to make assumptions about future fertility rates. This task, too, is far from onerous.

However, problems arise in predicting the two other components of labour

Table 6.6   *Projected labour force of the Community assuming participation rates at 1985 level*

(Thousands)

Country	1985	1990	1995	2000	2025
B	3,977	4,010	3,968	3,879	3,155
DK	2,775	2,855	2,890	2,853	2,455
F	24,553	25,309	25,934	26,319	24,505
G	4,036	4,131	4,225	4,287	4,327
IRL	1,326	1,424	1,528	1,632	1,880
I	22,970	23,743	24,140	23,965	19,906
L	154	157	156	156	140
NL	5,800	6,150	6,311	6,312	5,563
P	4,654	4,968	5,227	5,417	5,188
E	13,980	14,735	15,353	15,713	15,409
UK	27,676	28,325	28,362	28,535	27,939
D	28,684	29,181	28,677	27,805	21,192
Europe - 12	140,585	144,988	146,771	146,873	131,659

Source: Demographic and labour force analysis, based on Eurostat data banks

force: migration and participation rates. A complex question is used by Eurostat to assess these components [for details, see reference 5]. In a nutshell, the method ignores the migration aspects and further assumes that participation rates in future will be the same as those prevailing in 1985. The resulting estimates for the period 1985-2025 for each member state are given in Tables 6.6 and 6.7. The total for the whole Community is summarised graphically in Figure 6.1. The analysis of these estimates show that:

- *Peak in the year 2000:* the Community's total labour force will peak in the year 2000 and thereafter show a steady but marked decline to the year 2025. The decline will occur in both sex groups, but more notably in men.

- *Ageing labour force:* with the contraction in the age group 16-24, the population structure will be increasingly dominated by prime age workers (25-44) and older workers (45-64). Thus alongside the overall contraction, the average age of the labour force will increase noticeably.

- *Uneven pattern of decline in time and between countries:* the decline will become especially noticeable after the year 2000: until then, the labour force will continue to increase in most countries, with the notable exceptions of Italy and West Germany. Even after 2000, Greece and Ireland will continue to experience an increase; at a time when all other countries will experience a decline of varying degrees, with Italy and West Germany bearing the brunt of this.

Overall, therefore, the Community will experience a growth of nearly 2 million in its collective labour force in this decade, followed by a headlong contraction of some 15 million in the first 25 years of the next century. In a historical context, this uneven pattern is doubly significant. First, the projected growth of 2 million in the 1990s will be the slowest of any decade since the last War. It implies a considerable deceleration in the underlying rate of growth that has underpinned the unprecedented post-War economic prosperity in Europe. Second, the subsequent contraction of 15 million is a phenomenon that also has no peace-time parallels in the living memory.

It is, therefore, understandable that many forecasters have treated the identified future trends as constituting the so-called demographic time bomb. Indeed, the implied crisis has a global orientation because similar trends are also expected in the USA, Canada, Japan and the Scandinavian countries (see

Figures 6.2 and 6.3, for example).

Table 6.7   Community labour force, by age and sex: 1985 - 2025 *

(Thousands)

	1985	1990	1995	2000	2025
Males					
16-24	15,957	15,390	13,591	12,311	10,868
25-44	42,608	45,750	47,692	48,247	38,125
45-64	27,423	27,745	29,077	30,281	38,102
65+	1,003	1,158	1,289	1,321	1,611
Total	86,991	90,043	91,649	92,160	88,706
Females					
16-24	12,954	12,377	10,854	9,823	8,626
25-44	26,084	28,025	28,946	28,929	22,695
45-64	14,056	13,983	14,720	15,369	15,925
65+	503	559	602	592	705
Total	53,597	54,944	55,122	54,713	47,951
Total M+F					
16-24	28,911	27,767	24,445	22,134	19,494
25-44	68,692	73,775	76,638	77,176	60,820
45-64	41,479	41,728	43,797	45,650	49,027
65+	1,506	1,717	1,891	1,913	2,316
Total	140,588	144,987	146,771	146,873	131,657

* Covers Europe - 12. All estimates assume participation rates continue at
the 1985 level.

Source: Demographic and labour force analysis, based on Eurostat data banks

Figure 6.1   Net entrants to the EC labour force per annum: 1961-2025

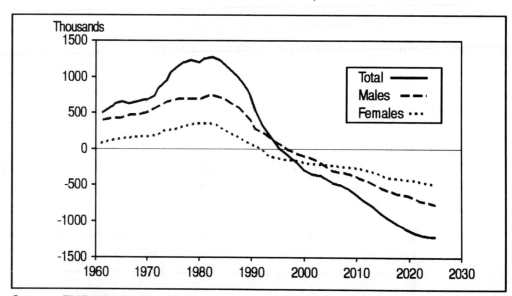

Source: EUROSTAT: Demographic and Labour Force Analysis, 1988

Figure 6.2   Key demographic trends in the USA: 1985-2000

- The population & the workforce will grow more slowly than at any time since the 1930s

- The average age of the workforce will rise; the pool of young workers entering the labour market will shrink

- More women will enter the workforce

- Minorities will represent the largest share of the increase in the population & the workforce since the First World War

- In the period 1985-2000, there will be 25 million (20 per cent) net new workers

- 4/5 of which = non whites (20 per cent), white women (40 per cent), & immigrants (20 per cent)

Source: Hudson Institute, Workforce 2000, 1987

Figure 6.3   Age group 16-24: Labour force projections, 1990-2000

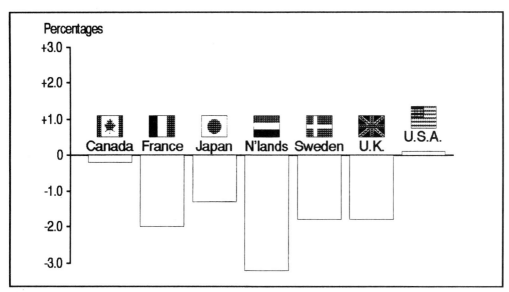

Source: OECD, 'Employment Outlook', *September 1988*

6.3.2   Caveats

At the same time, it is essential not to be too alarmist because the Eurostat forecasts are based on two critical assumptions: no significant net migration into the Community and constant participation rates for men and women at their respective 1985 levels.

Taking these assumptions in turn, it is most unlikely that the migratory balance will remain at zero [6], largely because of the massive differential in fertility rates between the Community on the one hand and some of the surrounding non-member countries on the other. This is exemplified in Table 6.8. The prosperous economies of the north are likely to exercise various 'pull' factors. Under their combined impact, the Community may conceivably end up with higher inward migration than has been the case in this decade [for further details, see references 7 and 8].

Table 6.8 *Fertility rates in Mediterranean countries, 1985*

France	1.8	Algeria	7.0
Italy	1.6	Morocco	5.9
Spain	2.0	Tunisia	4.9

Source: 'Tous les pays du monde 1985', Population et Societes, 226, (INED, July-August 1985)

Figure 6.4   *Female participation rates: 1987-2000*

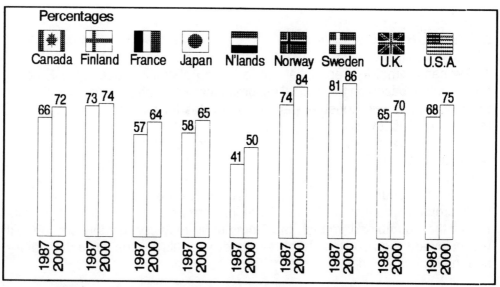

Source: OECD, 'Employment Outlook', *September 1988*

As for the assumption on participation rates, the Eurostat forecasts by no means constitute the only scenario. Recent forecasts from the OECD (given in Figure 6.4 and Table 6.9) show that by the year 2000:

- the female participation rate is expected to rise in all countries for whom the forecasts are available

- the decline in male participation rate experienced in the recent past is likely to either slow down or even reverse (notably in the Netherlands and the UK) in the future.

Although these estimates do not cover all the member states, they do show that the assumption of static participation rates, implicit in the Eurostat forecasts, is not necessarily shared by the OECD. More fundamentally, the Eurostat forecasts implicitly disregard the importance of enduring social developments that have promoted rising social aspirations on the part of women and the consequent emergence of dual-career family [9; 10]. It would seem realistic to treat the Eurostat forecasts as constituting the 'worst-case' and not the 'central-case' scenario. Clearly, they err on the side of pessimism.

This does not mean that the impending demographic crisis is merely a matter of assumptions on migration and participation rates: far from it. What it does mean is that there will be a change in the size of the labour force directly and labour supply indirectly. But at this stage its seriousness is difficult to assess without making certain assumptions, which could well turn out to be rather pessimistic, in retrospect.

Table 6.9   Labour participation rates for males and females: 1973-2000

(percentages)

	Age groups	1973		1987		1990		2000	
		M	F	M	F	M	F	M	F
France	15-24	57	45	46	39	47	39	43	36
	25-54	97	54	96	71	96	75	95	80
	55-64	72	37	48	32	45	30	43	29
	Total	86	51	78	57	78	60	78	64
Netherlands	15-24	59	51	49	48	52	50	48	48
	25-54	95	26	91	46	91	51	93	59
	55-64	77	15	41	10	41	10	48	15
	Total	84	31	74	41	76	45	79	50
United Kingdom	15-24	78	62	82	72	81	72	81	74
	25-54	96	59	93	69	93	71	93	75
	55-64	88	40	67	35	68	37	68	39
	Total	93	57	88	65	88	66	89	70
United States	15-24	75	55	73	65	74	66	75	70
	25-54	94	52	93	72	93	74	92	81
	55-64	77	41	67	42	65	43	63	45
	Total	89	53	87	68	87	70	86	75
Sweden	15-24	68	60	66	67	65	65	63	64
	25-54	94	69	95	90	95	92	95	95
	55-64	83	46	75	64	76	66	78	75
	Total	87	63	86	81	86	83	87	86

The labour force participation rate is defined as the labour force for all ages over 15 divided by the total population aged 15-64.

Source: 'Employment outlook' (OECD, September 1988, Paris)

6.4 Summary

This chapter has highlighted past and prospective trends in the labour force of those member states for whom data are available. This has been done so as to facilitate an analysis of the impact of the 1992 programme on various labour market imbalances that are considered in the next chapter. The main points emerging from this chapter are as follows:

• In the period 1975-85, the total labour force of the Community increased by around 12 per cent.

• This increase was the net outcome of three factors: increase in the population of working age; increase in the female participation rate; and decrease in the male participation rate. There was no uniformity in the pattern of evolution in these three factors between individual member states.

• The overall variabilities in the growth rates in working population are due to social and cultural forces unique to each member state. Variabilities in participation rates were partly due to two forces.

• First, there was a radical shift in the industrial structure caused by the 'oil' recessions of 1974-75 and 1979-81 which led to a contraction in male-based manufacturing occupations and an increase in female-based services occupations. Second, the rise in female participation was further assisted by women's rising career aspirations associated with the emergence of dual career families.

• In the period 1985-2025, the Community's overall labour force will see a modest growth of 2 million in this decade, followed by a contraction of 15 million in the ensuing 25 years.

• Neither of these have historical parallels. They imply a major reversal in the buoyant growth pattern since 1945 which has served to underpin the unprecedented economic prosperity. The concept of 'demographic crisis' is, therefore, not a misnomer. Equally, it is not immutable.

continued...

- The prospective growth rates will vary significantly between individual member states. At one extreme, Greece and Ireland are expected to have a net increase in their labour force by 2025: at the other, Italy and West Germany are expected to have a net decrease. In all member states, men and women are expected to be equally affected.

- However, these forecasts are based on the assumptions that participation rates (for men and women) and migration rates will remain constant at their 1985 levels.

- The assumed constancy is dictated by the fact that these factors are difficult to forecast into the future. As a result, the forecasts merely reflect projected changes in the population of working age.

- In that sense, they are a 'worst-case' scenario. There are credible alternative scenarios that envisage higher migration and participation rates.

- As a result, the impending demographic crisis need not necessarily be severe. In other words, some contraction will occur in the size of the labour force, but its severity is open to debate.

7

LABOUR FORCE TRENDS: A DEMAND-SIDE APPROACH

7.1   Issues: The six time bombs

The previous chapter has shown that, notwithstanding their overall pessimistic underlying assumptions, the Eurostat forecasts foreshadow a demographic crisis in the sense of a reduction in potential labour supply in most of the member states between now and the year 2025. The implied reduction has little relevance in the labour market context, *per se*. This is because the projected reduction in supply has to be set alongside the projected growth in demand in order to ascertain whether the supply-side changes imply major imbalances in the labour market. Such a comparison of supply and demand trends is essential since, as we saw in Chapter 5, the single market is likely to cause unemployment especially to the mid-1990s. Furthermore, a comprehensive analysis would also involve examining any resulting imbalances in both a static as well as a dynamic context.

  The static context applies when the quantity and quality of demand is directly set alongside the corresponding supply at a given point in time or over a short time period. The dynamic context applies when the supply-side changes cause a chain reaction elsewhere in the economy which then creates a knock-on (lagged) effect on demand. In order to quantify these static and dynamic imbalances associated with supply-side changes, one needs a large-scale econometric model with well-defined parameters on population and labour market. No member state has such a capability at present.

  Worse still, at present there are no long-term forecasts available on quality and quantity of labour demand in individual member states. Those that are available either cover a short time horizon [1] or have bench-marks in the distant past such that they do not take into account the significant changes in individual labour markets since 1986 [2]. Even when they appear to, they do not have details on how the single market will affect labour demand. Perforce, here, we have had to rely on indirect and anecdotal information on the one hand and informed views on the other. Information emerging from these disparate sources is brought together by pursuing six questions in the two defined contexts. These questions relate to prospective trends in supply and demand in the 1990s only because beyond that period any analysis is necessarily speculative, in the light of two important developments. First, the expected arrival of fifth generation computers, relying heavily on artificial intelligence and knowledge-based expert systems with considerable potential for displacing qualified manpower. Second, the recent events in Eastern Europe, leading to greater migration between the Community on the one hand and the newly emerging liberal democracies on the other. The relevant questions are presented below. They will affect both supply and demand.

7.1.1   Static context

- What will the numbers gap be when the numerical supply and demand projections are brought together?

- What will the skills gap be when the qualitative supply and demand projections are brought together?

- What will the gender gap be when the gender features of supply and demand projections are brought together?

- What will the racial gap be when the ethnic features of supply and demand are brought together?

7.1.2   Dynamic context

- Will the demographic crisis create a revenue gap by affecting health and social security budgets directly and employers' payroll costs indirectly?

- Will the ageing labour force create a productivity gap owing to occupational, sectoral and spatial immobility on the one hand, and industrial restructuring on the other?

Collectively, these questions have the attributes of individual time bombs, once it is appreciated that the importance of know-how and skills will be rising at a time when there will be an absolute contraction in the size of the age group 16-24, which has hitherto provided the main input into the education and training systems. But how lethal are these time bombs when taken *individually* ? In order to answer the question, each of them is taken one at a time in this chapter. In the process, four important aspects of the Community's labour market are highlighted:

- prospective demand trends, in the absence of the single market

- the nature of prospective imbalances, if any

- the impact of the single market on the identified imbalances

- the type of challenges facing individual employers and governments in the member states.

7.2   Static context

7.2.1   Time bomb 1: Numbers gap

Currently, there are no labour demand forecasts available for individual member states which could be set alongside the supply forecasts within a consistent framework. We thus have to rely on 'second order' estimates which can serve the *minimum* purpose of providing *prima facie* signs of imbalances. Such estimates are derived from simple extrapolations of demand trends since 1982, as indicated by the OECD data of total civilian employment (including the employees and the self-employed). The starting date in this context is 1982 because by then the worst of the recession was over in most member states. The result of the extrapolations are further corroborated by evidence on individual countries emanating from two recent studies [1; 2].

On the simplifying assumption that there will be no major changes in the structure of economies of the individual member states, extrapolations can be used to provide indications of the direction of growth in demand in terms of three possible outcomes in the 1990s: positive, static and negative. The assumption is then relaxed to take into account the effect of the single market.

Analysis of the latest figures [3] suggests prospective demand outcomes for each member state, as shown in Table 7.1. The corresponding supply outcomes suggested by Table 6.6 are also given alongside. The last column in Table 7.1 therefore provides a tentative indication of whether these projections imply:

- excess demand

- excess supply

- proximate balance.

Table 7.1   State of the labour market: 1990-2000

	Demand			Supply			Labour Market		
	+	0	-	+	0	-	D+	0	S+
Belgium		●				●	●		
Denmark	●				●		●		
W.Germany	●					●	●		
France	●			●				●	
Greece	●			●				●	
Ireland			●	●					●
Italy	●			●				●	
Luxembourg	●				●		●		
Netherlands	●			●				●	
Portugal	●			●				●	
Spain			●	●					●
UK	●			●				●	

Source: see text

The results in the table show that in the 1990s the individual member states might well fall into one of these categories:

- **Excess demand:** Belgium, Denmark, Luxembourg and West Germany

- **Proximate balance:** France, Greece, Italy, the Netherlands, Portugal and the UK

- **Excess supply:** Ireland and Spain

Thus, our *elementary* analysis shows that at present there are no obvious signs of a widespread numerical gap emerging between demand and supply in the 1990s. This conclusion is reinforced when allowance is made for the fact that the supply trends in Table 7.1 are based on the 'worst case' scenario that assumes that participation and migration rates will remain constant at their respective 1985 levels.

7.2.2   Time bomb 2: Skills gap

Forecasts of skills requirements are not available for individual member states, but it is possible to form a Community-wide view of occupational requirements in terms of:

- quantitative changes, indicated by increases or decreases in their numerical size

- qualitative changes, indicated by increases or decreases in their skills content that reflect re-skilling or de-skilling of work performed in the occupation concerned.

The assessment emerging from four studies [1; 2; 4; 5; 6; 7] is summarised in Figure 7.1. It presents the quantitative and qualitative changes that are likely to occur in the 1990s in many of the member states. The results indicate four likely trends as indicated by the following groups:

- **Group 1: qualitative and quantitative growth;** many occupations, especially covering services functions, are likely to grow in numbers and skills content (north-east quadrant).

- *Group 2: quantitative decline but qualitative growth;* some occupations are likely to increase in terms of their skills content but decrease in terms of their numerical size (south-east quadrant).

- *Group 3: quantitative growth but qualitative decline;* some occupations will increase in numerical size but contract in terms of their skills content (north-west quadrant). Some of these are similar to those in Group 2 (e.g. secretarial and clerical services) except that they involve part-time (P/T) work.

- *Group 4: quantitative and qualitative decline;* these occupations will be the victims of continuing automation and the labour shake-out in manufacturing industries.

When the four groups are considered together, they suggest two noteworthy points. First, the average education, training and skills content of the occupational structure is likely to increase in a large majority of the member states. Second, the next generation of new jobs will occur in Group 1 which are qualifications-based white collar occupations, and in Group 2 which covers many

Figure 7.1 Quantitative and qualitative changes in occupational structure

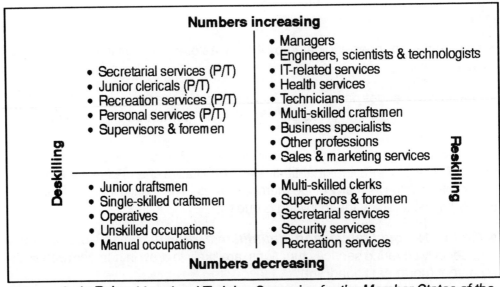

Source: Amin Rajan, *Vocational Training Scenarios for the Member States of the European Community, 1988*

part-time and low level occupations. Indeed, under the combined impact of new technologies and industrial change it is most likely that all over the Community Group 1 will emerge as the fastest growing, thereby raising the average skills content of the workforce.

This observation turns into a matter of concern, however, when it is set alongside two key supply trends, shown in Table 6.7.

First, the age group 16-24 will contract relatively and absolutely. This is the group through which the education and training systems have traditionally transmitted skills and know-how into the labour market. Second, the largest numerical and relative growth in supply will occur in the older age group (45-64). But it is worth remembering that in the 1990s this group will largely comprise those with one or more of the following characteristics:

• received minimal schooling in their formative years in the period 1930-45

• exposed to a high incidence of unemployment because of association with manufacturing industries

• received minimal training at work, in an age when training was not regarded as a high profile activity

• suffered skills obsolescence because of structural changes (male) and child rearing (female).

When these observations are set alongside the widely accepted view that the average skills content of work will be rising in the next decade, there is every likelihood of a skills gap emerging in the next decade. A series of recent CEDEFOP studies also lend strong corroborative evidence to this conclusion [1; 4; 6; 7]. Evidence on the rising importance of know-how and work skills emerging from these studies is rather qualitative. But that does not detract from the clarity of its overall message because recent quantitative evidence on the United States labour market bears close parallels. The American evidence shows that the 'skills rating' of new jobs in the period to the year 2000 will be, on the whole, higher than that of existing jobs (Figure 7.2).

Figure 7.2   United States: Skills rating of current and new jobs

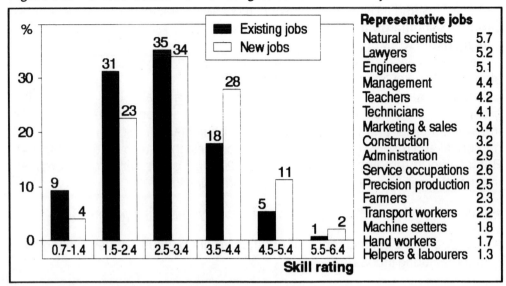

Source: Hudson Institute, *Workforce 2000, 1987*

As Part C will show, there will be a skills crisis in many member states. But there is a danger of confusing symptom with cause. In the 1990s, there will be a skills gap because of the cumulative neglect of training in the crucial decade of the 1980s. In so far as the contraction in school leaver population will worsen the gap, that will not happen for another 15 years or so. By then there will be fewer experienced workers who will have engaged in continuous work experience and training. After all, the emerging skills gap is in intermediate and higher level occupations, shown in Figure 7.1, where the average employee age is typically over 30. For the next five years or so, the gap will occur even without the projected contraction in the school leaver population because it has its origins in long-standing inadequate skills development within companies in many member states.

7.2.3   Time bomb 3: Gender gap

The 'worst-case' scenario, assuming constant participation rates, envisages a slight fall in the size of the female labour force and an increase in the size of the male labour force in the 1990s, as we saw in Table 6.7. However, alternative forecasts suggest a very significant increase in the size of the female labour force, as was shown in Figure 6.9. In fact, there is a strong possibility that the Community could end up in a situation similar to the USA (Figure 6.2) in that women could become a dominant component of the growth in the labour force [3].

Under this scenario, there is a strong possibility of a gender gap emerging. This is because although some of the new jobs will be part-time and therefore suit the circumstances of women with family responsibilities, many new jobs will be full-time and in occupations traditionally dominated by men (north-east quadrant in Figure 7.1). Those women with the necessary qualifications for these jobs would still require considerable retraining because the skills content of jobs will continue to rise, thereby promoting skills obsolescence amongst women who have been absent from the labour market during the period of accelerated technological and structural change.

Skills obsolescence will be one factor promoting the gender gap. The other is the tradition under which professional jobs have become the preserve of male workers. Thus, the perpetuation of current employer practices could turn out to be a major contributor to the gap, unless the Community's proposed Social Charter eradicates these prejudices.

7.2.4   Time bomb 4: Racial gap

There are no statistics available on the share of ethnic minorities in the growth in the future labour force in member states. Some indirect evidence suggests that their share could grow substantially and follow the pattern predicted for the USA (Figure 6.2). This is for two reasons. At a time when the fertility rate of the indigenous population has declined in various member states, the rates for minorities have remained unchanged. Also, minorities tend to have a large element of young people, who have a higher rate of reproduction.

For example, in the UK, under the combined effect of these two factors, the non-white population is expected to account for 500,000 out of the total projected population increase of 600,000 over the period 1986-91. Similar estimates are not readily available for other member states but there is every likelihood of a strong growth in the non-white component of the labour force in most member states.

In the circumstances, there is likely to be a racial gap in the sense that the non-white population will have a less than fair share of new jobs; partly because of employer prejudices and partly because of the low participation rates of non-whites in higher education.

7.3   Dynamic context

7.3.1   Time bomb 5: Revenue gap

The ageing of the population will create acute financial problems for social security systems in the member states as a result of the additional expenditure on health and pensions which will inevitably occur if current benefit rates remain unchanged. This additional expenditure, in turn, will raise corporate payroll costs and reduce profitability. This is because hitherto a large part of it has been borne by employers through their national insurance contributions [8]. As a result, employers will be confronted with some painful choices, for which they are singularly ill-prepared. Let us elaborate on this argument.

Table 7.2 gives estimates on dependency ratio, expressed here as number of non-economically active persons aged 60 and over per thousand of economically active population. The ratio provides an internationally standardised measure of demographic crisis in different member states. From the table it is clear that:

- the ratio has risen substantially since 1950

- the ratio will rise in all the member states except Ireland and the UK, at least over the rest of this century

- the rise will be substantial for Greece, Italy, Spain and West Germany.

The fiscal impact of the rise in the past is evident in Table 7.3, which shows that the share of the compulsory social security contribution in GDP has risen in all the member states. On a Community-wide basis, the increase in this share has been about 50 per cent (27 per cent in 1965 and 40 per cent in 1986).

The rise is largely due to the head-long growth in state spending on social security in general and pensions in particular.

Table 7.2   Number of non-active people aged 60 and over in comparison to active population

(per thousand)

	1950	1980	2000	2025
Belgium	311	424	468	671
France	235	361	386	560
Greece	153	366	494	559
Ireland	200	304	257	342
Italy	196	416	515	685
Luxenbourg	219	388	470	734
The Netherlands	210	364	401	756
Portugal	158	263	313	428
Spain	179	376	452	544
UK	242	348	344	460
West Germany	222	385	469	701

Source: Calculations based on data and projections in Population Active 1950-2025 (ILO, Geneva, 1986)

Table 7.3   Evolution of fiscal pressure

(compulsory contributions as % of GDP)

	1965	1975	1986
Belgium	30.8	41.1	45.5
France	35.0	37.4	44.2
Greece	20.6	24.6	36.7
Ireland	26.0	31.5	40.2
Italy	23.6	25.1	36.2
Luxembourg	30.4	39.3	42.4
The Netherlands	33.2	43.7	45.5
Portugal	18.4	24.7	32.4
Spain	14.7	19.6	30.4
UK	30.6	35.4	39.0
West Germany	31.6	35.7	37.5
EEC Average	27.1	33.3	40.0

Source: 'Statistiques des recettes publiques des pays members de l'OCED' (OECD, Paris, 1988)

For example, in the period 1965-85, pensions rose as follows:

	per cent of GDP	
	1965	1985
Denmark	8	13
West Germany	10	12
France	8	13
Italy	8	16

Some of this growth was due in part to the 'real increase' in response to rising aspirations of the elderly, and some to an increase in the dependency ratio.

When we look to the future, the picture is equally worrying, as Tables 7.4 and 7.5 show for health and pension expenditures respectively. However, in order to put the problem into a more realistic context, allowance has to be made for the reduction in education expenditure and family benefits, as a result of the reduction in the fertility rates. When that is done, it is clear that total social expenditure will rise by 35 per cent in real terms in the period 1980-2040, assuming that the base year's benefit rates remain unchanged (see Figure 7.3).

Table 7.4 Future evolution of health expenditure if real benefits per capita increase at the same rate as during 1975-84

	1980 = 100		Annual rate of increase (%)
	1980	2040	
Belgium	100	1,101	4.1
Denmark	100	195	1.2
France	100	1,986	4.8
West Germany	100	220	1.5
Italy	100	503	2.6
The Netherlands	100	185	0.5
UK	100	262	1.3
Sweden	100	433	2.2
USA	100	435	1.5
Japan	100	1,725	4.2

Source: 'Demographic ageing: Consequences for social policy' (Paris, OECD, 1988)

Table 7.5 *Influence of population development on pension expenditure, 1980-2040*

(1980 = 100)

	1980	2000	2025	2040
Belgium	100	104	131	136
Denmark	100	99	123	124
France	100	122	169	172
West Germany	100	122	138	126
Italy	100	114	141	134
The Netherlands	100	127	160	160
UK	100	98	128	130
USA	100	119	205	215
Japan	100	180	215	229

Source: 'Demographic ageing: Consequences for social policy' (Paris, OECD, 1988)

Figure 7.3 *Social expenditure due to demographic changes: 1980-2040*

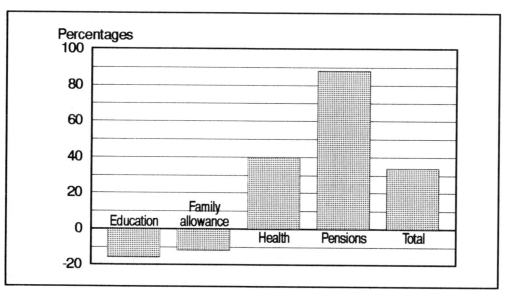

Source: *Statistiques des recettes publiques de pays members de l'OECD, OECD, Paris, 1988*

However, the projected growth already looks highly conservative in the light of the increases in the real value of benefits since 1980. Research in progress by this author shows that at current rates of benefits, employers in France, Italy, the UK and West Germany can expect to have their social security contribution rise by between 15 and 40 per cent in real terms in the 1990s, as a direct result of demographic changes.

From the foregoing analysis it is clear that the individual member states will be faced with two choices:

• either increase - quite massively - compulsory social security contributions

• or reduce *per capita* social security expenditure.

Given their numerical strength, older people will become a political force to be reckoned with in future, if the American experience is any guide [8], and governments will find it even more difficult to resist their 'legitimate' demands, if the past is any guide. On the other hand, a substantial increase in compulsory contributions can raise payroll costs and affect international business competitiveness. At present, individual member states appear to be adopting both these options. As a result, unit labour costs have been rising. The rise will become pronounced after 1995 when the demographic crisis will begin to bite in earnest. As a result, employers will have three choices:

• resort to greater substitution of technology for labour, particularly for less skilled occupations

• restructure work, in order to raise productivity and reduce employment

• absorb cost increases and face the decline in competitiveness.

At present, awareness of the demographic crisis is seemingly low amongst the corporate community in almost all the member states. This is also borne out by detailed studies which show that personnel managers have a higher awareness than line managers who have the principal responsibility for employees [9]. Even amongst the companies where awareness is high, little thought has been given to the revenue gap and its implications. Indeed, few companies now appear to have specific plans to deal with the demographic crisis in general or the revenue gap in particular. The implication is that corporate costs will rise and undermine profitability in the short run and physical investment in the long run. Alternatively demand for labour could fall and with it will fall output and profits, in the absence of capital substitution and work restructuring.

7.3.2   Time bomb 6: Productivity gap

Over the next decade, the outlook for sustained productivity improvement looks uncertain in most of the member states. The uncertainty stems partly from the emerging demographic changes and partly from on-going industrial changes.

Taking them in turn, there are currently two schools of thought about the impact of an ageing labour force on productivity improvement, as follows:

- **School A:** ageing workers are less adaptable because the ageing process affects the capacity and willingness to innovate by impairing sectoral, occupational and spatial mobility. As a result, productivity growth will slow down in future. Before long, this process will adversely affect economic growth.

- **School B:** ageing workers are only less mobile in spatial terms. This is more than compensated for by the continuous process of know-how development, associated with prolonged work experience and learning-by-doing. As know-how emerges as a prime resource in the 1990s, the 'cult of youth' will weaken because the requisite know-how will be specific to a firm's products, markets, technology and working methods. In other words, know-how that is based on learning-by-doing will be more valuable than that acquired by the young person in the formal education sector. Far from inhibiting innovation, the know-how of the older workers will accelerate it by breaking down sectoral and occupational boundaries. The all-too-obvious emergence of the multi-skilled craftsperson or clerk moving between industries is but an outward manifestation of the new generation of older workers who have undergone continuous self-enlightenment during their working lives. This school of thought accepts that many older workers are disadvantaged, as described in Sub-Section 7.2.2. However, there are others who are not and they comprise the majority of older workers who retained their jobs during successive phases of industrial restructuring in the past.

It is difficult to know which school of thought will have more validity in the uncertain economic climate of the 1990s. However, a recent study [10] on knowledge-based and skills-intensive occupations has shown that:

- there is evidence in support of School B, especially in the areas of service occupations

- employers' preference for younger workers owes more to employer inertia and attitudes, and less to such workers' work performance

- employers' resistance to older workers also stems from employers' seeming lack of inter-personal skills in motivating, managing, developing and deploying older workers.

It is therefore difficult to accept the proposition that an ageing labour force will automatically open up a productivity gap. However, the same cannot be said about the other potential contributor, namely industrial changes.

As Figure 7.4 exemplifies, service industries are emerging as the largest employers in the member states. This process of tertiarisation has been evident since the first 'oil' crisis in 1973. It is welcomed in the sense that it has led to the creation of new jobs right across the Community, especially at a time when manufacturing employment has been contracting substantially.

This process of job generation, however, has proved a mixed blessing in a fundamental respect: growth in labour productivity in services has been very low compared to that in manufacturing. This is best illustrated by taking the

Figure 7.4   Share of service industries in civilian employment: 1975-86

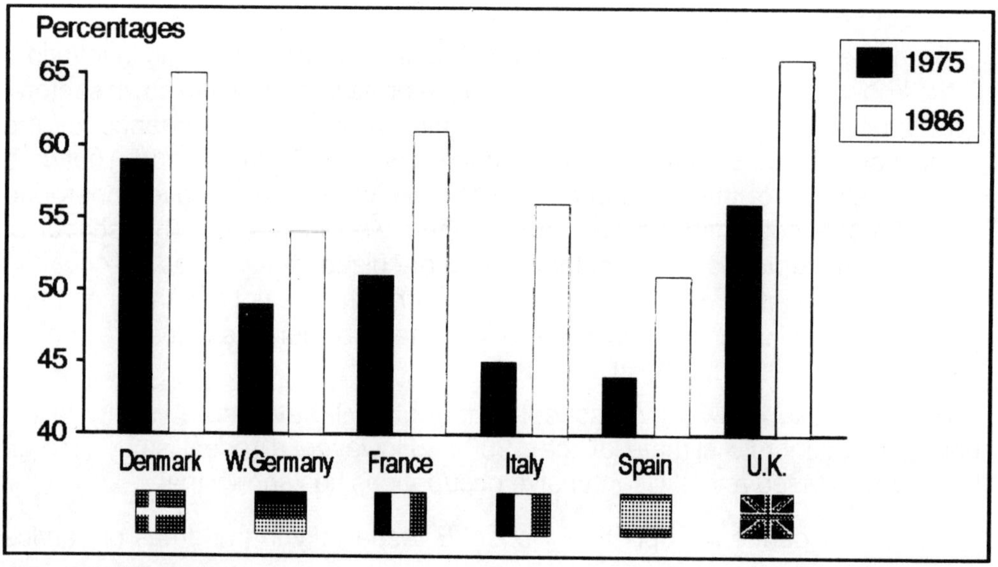

Source: EUROSTAT

102

example of the most tertiarised economy, the USA. As Figure 7.5 shows, there has been a big differential in the productivity performance of its three broad sectors. The poor performance of the services sector is largely due to its high labour intensity and low technological usage. Of course, individual service industries like banking and insurance have been exceptionally innovative but they are small compared to other industries like retail distribution, health, education and public services which continue to rely on labour-intensive methods despite the significant automation of many of their routine operations.

The lower productivity potential of services is not a problem *per se*, because in a highly tertiarised economy it is still possible to achieve high and sustained economic growth by utilising all unused labour — ie. by an extensive use of the available factors of production. However, against the background of major demographic changes the option of extensive use of labour is not an easy one. Unless intensive use is promoted through productivity-enhancing working methods or new technologies, all the member states could well suffer a productivity gap directly and economic growth gap indirectly.

Figure 7.5   Productivity growth in the USA

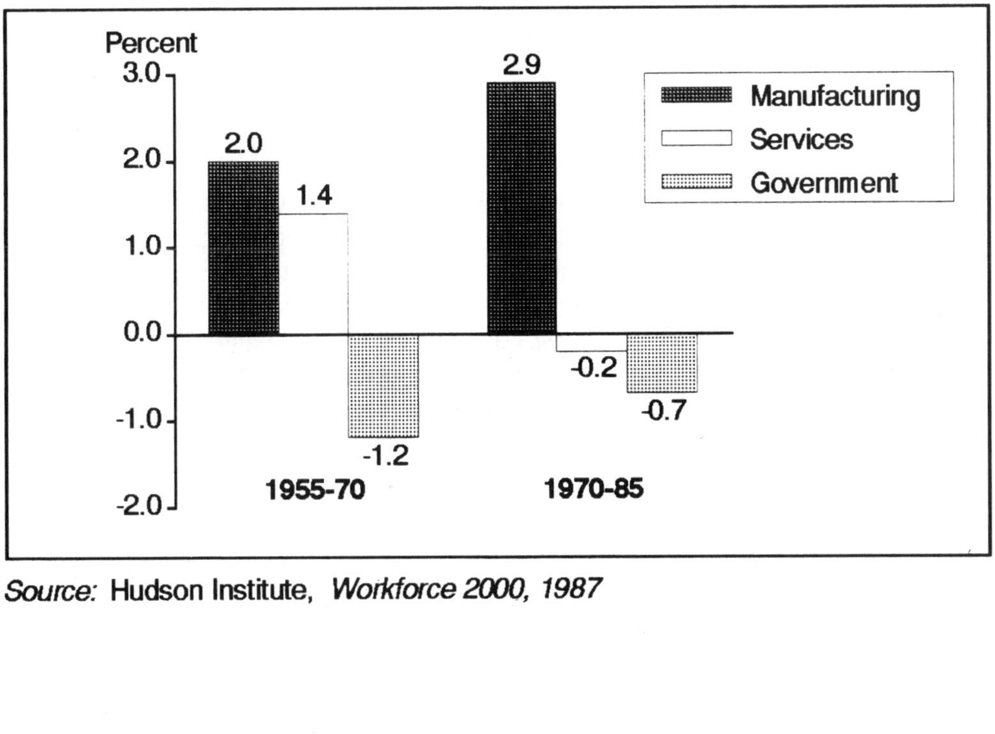

Source: Hudson Institute, *Workforce 2000, 1987*

103

7.4 Single market and the time bombs

The previous two sectors have examined the six emerging gaps against the background of long-standing developments occurring within individual member states. It is now time to look at the impact of the single market on the identified gaps.

As we saw in Chapters 3, 4 and 5, the single market will promote growth in customised products in manufacturing and service industries. Such products will rely increasingly on know-how and new skills because of their special appeal to certain customer groups and technological usage. Furthermore, for individual companies, business success will involve creating a special market niche. But in the age of customisation, niche players can only survive and prosper if they have the necessary know-how. Thus, dictated by technology, deregulation, gathering competition and diversification, the pace of change in the 1990s could well be so rapid that it will be the individual employer who will be best placed to identify the repertoire of skills it needs and to supply it in-house as far as possible by providing quality training.

As we saw in Chapter 5, some informal forecasts from the Community's leading industrialists suggest that in the next ten years anything up to half the factories in the Community could close and half its companies could either disappear or be taken over. The process of rationalisation is already evident in the accelerating pace of corporate mergers and acquisitions.

Thus, there is every likelihood that the single market will reinforce the factors that have promoted the importance of know-how and work skills in business success over the past two decades. As a result, the single market will serve to widen the skills gap directly and the gender and racial gaps indirectly, given that women and ethnic minorities may well be disadvantaged in relation to the new generation of jobs, if current employer policies and practices are allowed to persist. On the other hand, if the single market does result in higher unemployment due to industrial restructuring, then it is hard to see how the numbers gap can be at all serious especially since it is not expected to be notable even without the single market.

As far as the revenue and productivity gaps are concerned, the single market is likely to narrow the former and widen the latter.

Taking them in turn, the higher economic growth that is likely to result from the single market will generate additional tax revenue that will help to contain at least some of the pressures on social security contributions. Whether the additional tax revenue will be used to subsidise social expenditure will depend upon the rules relating to the funding of social expenditure in individual member states. At the least, however, the additional revenue will serve to contain the pressure on employers' contributions to social security funds.

Finally, the single market is expected to worsen the productivity gap because it will accentuate the trend towards service sector employment in most of the member states, as intra-Community trade in services receives a fresh impetus. Indeed, the productivity gap has already become evident over the past two decades, as shown by the observed changes in the relationship between economic growth and employment. For example, as we saw in Chapter 5, currently a growth rate of 2 per cent generates 1 per cent more jobs: 15 years ago the same rate was consistent with a static level of employment. There has been a secular change in the employment content of growth that was not deemed possible as recently as three years ago. There are many causes and they centre around the relative shift in the activity base — from manufacturing to services and from blue collar to white collar jobs. However, against the background of high and rising levels of unemployment, the productivity gap has not been a source of concern. But in the 1990s it will become one, because under the existing education and training policies it is hard to see how the newly unemployed workers can be absorbed into service industries without extensive retraining and geographical mobility. Over time, therefore, output growth in services could well slow down, thereby slowing down overall economic growth. In the longer term, the gap can only be narrowed by a combination of measures that improves service sector productivity growth and the skills of unemployed workers, making them more employable in the service industries.

7.5 Summary

This chapter has highlighted the trends in labour demand in order to evaluate the extent to which there will be imbalances in the labour markets of individual member states in response to two emerging developments: the demographic crisis and the single market. These imbalances are discussed here both in a static as well as a dynamic context: static in the sense of attempting a direct comparison between quantitative and qualitative trends in demand and supply over a *given period;* and dynamic, in the sense of identifying a wider chain reaction. The salient points emerging from the chapter are as follows:

• In the static context, the demographic crisis could potentially give rise to four kinds of gap, numbers, skills, gender and racial, the last three being closely inter-related.

• The *numbers gap* is associated with imbalances arising from the numerical excess of labour demand over supply. Four member states are likely to suffer such a gap: Belgium, Denmark, Luxembourg and West Germany. On the other hand, Ireland and Spain are likely to experience excess supply. The remaining member states are unlikely to be affected significantly either way.

• The *skills gap* is associated with skills shortages emerging from the rising skills content of work, the concentration of new jobs into knowledge-based and skills-intensive occupations and the predominance of many under-trained persons among older workers who will comprise the largest labour market group. The skills gap is expected to occur in all the member states in varying degrees.

• The *gender gap* is associated with the twin phenomena under which women will comprise a significant component of growth in the labour force at a time when new jobs will be concentrated in hitherto male-dominated occupations. The gender gap is likely to emerge in all the member states.

• The *racial gap*, too, is associated with the twin phenomena under which ethnic minorities will comprise a significant component of growth in the labour force at a time when new jobs will be concentrated in hitherto indigenous

continued ...

(white-dominated) occupations. This gap, too, is likely to occur in all the member states.

- In the dynamic context, emerging demographic changes could potentially give rise to two other kinds of gap: revenue and productivity.

- The *revenue gap* is associated with rising social security costs as an ageing population makes progressively greater demands for health and pension expenditure. Through higher social security contributions, this will have the effect of raising payroll costs and undermine profitability, investment, output and economic growth. The revenue gap will occur in all the member states. Of all the gaps, this is the one to which employers appear to be most oblivious.

- The *productivity gap* is associated with two phenomena: an ageing population hindering efficiency improvements through reduced sectoral, occupational and spatial mobility; and headlong growth in service industries where the productivity growth is restricted because of the white collar and/or labour-intensive nature of work. There is little hard evidence to support the first phenomenon. The second phenomenon is more serious, however. There is a real risk that productivity growth will slow down in all the member states as more and more people work in service industries. With it could slow down the rate of growth in the economies and their tax revenues.

- As far as the single market is concerned, it will have a mixed and offsetting impact on the gaps outlined above. On the one hand, it will serve to widen the skills gap across the Community and the skills content of work at a time when employers are not likely to be doing enough to develop the requisite skills in-house. In turn, the skills gap will widen gender, racial and productivity gaps.

- On the other hand, the single market will ease the numbers gap because of higher unemployment arising from industrial restructuring. Indeed, the Community's unemployment is likely to persist in the 10-17 million range in this decade. Finally, the single market will help the revenue gap because it will generate more tax revenue through higher economic growth.

8

MACRO AND MICRO LEVEL SOLUTIONS

8.1   Issues

The previous chapter has identified and evaluated various gaps in the labour markets of the member states, as a result of the emerging demographic changes in the 1990s on the one hand and the creation of the single market on the other. This chapter now suggests various practical solutions whose adoption can go a long way towards narrowing those prospective gaps.

It is as well to emphasise at the outset that in so far as some of the solutions discussed here relate to changes in the broad areas of education and training, their detailed discussion is deferred to Part C. As a result, they intentionally receive only a passing reference.

Furthermore, the areas identified for action are the ones where immediate response would be at once desirable and practical. In all cases, the emphasis is on identifying solutions that can assist in narrowing the identified gaps by adopting two sets of actions. The first set aims at certain short-term measures that can ease recruitment difficulties through the use of new sources of recruitment. The second set aims at long-term measures that can limit the scale of recruitment through the use of productivity-enhancing working methods. As always, the distinction between the two sets, of course, is not so clear cut in practice: realistically, certain measures belong to both sets.

The approach adopted here is top-down, going from macro level, starting with the Community, and then progressing down to the level of individual governments and companies.

This is done by pursuing three distinct questions:

• How will the single market itself serve to narrow the gaps through greater spatial, sectoral and occupational mobility, both within and between the member states?

- What actions can be taken at the level of individual governments?

- What actions can be taken at the level of individual employers?

8.2   Community-level solutions

8.2.1   Rationale for labour mobility

The main actions that the European Commission can take relate to the creation of a single European labour market in which there is greater labour mobility between geographical areas, industries and occupations through the principle of freedom of people. The concept of a transnational labour market is important in a social as well as an economic context. In the social context, it will serve to emphasise the breakdown of age-old barriers between the member states. In the economic context, it will provide a much needed mechanism for allocating scarce skills more efficiently across the Community by diverting them to areas, industries and occupations where they can generate the maximum possible economic gains.

This allocation issue is vital for two reasons, one relating to efficiency and one to scarcity.

Taking them in turn, there is some evidence of educational 'overkill' in member states such as Denmark, France, the UK and West Germany [1]. Against the background of the severe economic recessions in 1974-5 and 1979-81, many employers have tended to recruit the most qualified candidates available in their local labour market, irrespective of the educational needs of the jobs concerned. We return to this point in Chapter 15 but it is worth pointing out here that this seeming inefficiency in the labour usage has come about partly due to high unemployment and partly due to the lack of information on job opportunities outside the high unemployment areas. The overkill has occurred particularly in lower level occupations in manufacturing and services alike. It was believed to be widespread in the early 1980s at the trough of the recession. Since then, although its incidence has declined, it has become institutionalised in many localities, as employers have rigidly stuck to the new qualifications requirements.

These apparent inefficiencies are all the more worrying, occurring as they have alongside the notable scarcities of qualified manpower and skills shortages in other parts of the Community [1]. No rigorous evidence on this point is available for the past decade because it is not a phenomenon that has been systematically studied owing to the prevalence of various barriers to mobility. However, with the creation of the single market, new studies have been able to identify surpluses and scarcities at the national level, as evidenced by the examples of two countries: West Germany and France.

According to the Institute of Labour Markets and Vocational Research (Institut fur Arbeitsmarkt und Berufsorschung), in 1980 there was in West Germany a total of 1,501,000 university graduates, 874,000 of whom will still be employed in the year 2000. There will be an additional demand for 627,000 graduates by the end of the century because of retirements in the interim. But in the year 2000, the new supply of the graduates will be 2,109,000. If the 627,000 graduates for whom demand is identified are subtracted from the new supply figure, then by the year 2000, the country will have 1,482,000 university graduates for whom extra jobs will have to be found [2]. For this to happen, the West German economy has to grow at a phenomenal rate: a prospect which has only a slim chance, even after taking into account the economic boost arising from the possible unification with East Germany. There is, thus, a probability of graduate surpluses in West Germany. At the other extreme, France will need to more than double its stock of graduates, from 1,111,000 in 1982 to 2,616,000 in the year 2000. As we shall see in Part C, changes have been initiated in the education system to meet the new target. But their impact is not likely to be enough and graduate shortages may well become a major feature of the French labour market in the latter part of this decade [3].

8.2.2   Current proposals for a single labour market

In order to hasten the pace of inter- and intra- country mobility, the European Commission has proposed a number of measures under two general headings: creation of conditions that guarantee genuine freedom of movement of persons and occupational mobility; and coping with structural changes associated with the single market. The associated details are described in a recent report [4]. Among various proposed measures, three are particularly noteworthy. But as we shall see below, in each case the proposed measures appear to fall short of requirements, thereby calling for additional action.

The first of these measures aims to promote the mutual recognition of educational achievements by establishing the comparability of qualifications relating to vocational training and higher education between the member states. Since 1975, there has been a series of measures which led to the mutual recognition of qualifications for six medical professions: doctors, nurses, dentists, veterinary surgeons, midwives and pharmacists. More recently, measures have also been initiated that will lead to the mutual recognition of vocational training qualifications in various trades in six industries: hotel and catering, motor vehicle repairs, construction, electrical engineering, agriculture, horticulture, forestry, textiles and clothing.

However, progress so far has been painfully slow. At the present rate, no substantial recognition will be possible for graduates and professional-based occupations until the year 2000. These are the very occupations that are likely to grow rapidly, as we saw in Figure 7.1 in the previous chapter. Furthermore, these occupations also lend themselves to national and international transfers because their labour market has the potential for becoming truly international, as industrial regrouping and restructuring continue apace. Accordingly, the European Commission will need to speed up its plans for a wider system of mutual recognition. As its own report shows, labour mobility between the member states has been conspicuous by its absence so far [4].

The second of the significant measures relates to the plans for the issue of so-called vocational training passports, which is, in a sense, an adjunct of the mutual recognition principle. It involves issuing special training cards to individuals on the basis of their acquired work experience and work-based training. The object is to provide output-based certificates of competency: so-called, because the certificate will provide evidence of what an individual is capable of doing, irrespective of the formal educational and training qualifications s/he possesses.

Here, too, progress has been excessively slow so far, largely because various member states wish to persist with their long-established input-based systems that assess competency on the basis of formal qualifications acquired. Countries such as Italy and West Germany prefer the input system because, amongst others, it is deemed to be more objective. In contrast, the UK is moving towards an output-based system under the auspices of the National Council for Vocational Qualifications (NCVQ). There is, thus, a major impasse to overcome.

The third and final measure relates to the inter-country exchange of information on vacancies. Currently, this occurs under the so-called SEDOC — European System for the International Clearing of Vacancies and Applications for Employment. It involves the exchange of information in two distinct but related areas: living and working conditions; and unfilled vacancies. Although in operation for well over a decade, the system has yet to live up to its promise. The information exchange under it has been neither frequent nor systematic [4].

Plans are afoot to revitalise it by transforming it into what is provisionally called the European Labour Market Network. Relying heavily on the use of new communications technology, the proposed network will aim to:

- match vacancies and job seekers

- provide information relating to the location of new business activities

- match training facilities to business needs

- promote greater awareness of labour market developments in all the member states.

For the foreseeable future, however, the system is unlikely to provide a major 'clearing system', not because of any inadvertent oversight on the part of its designers but because of some seemingly intractable definitional problems. This becomes obvious when one compares standard occupational job titles between and within the member states. In all cases they are unreliable, being highly 'user-friendly' in some cases or subjective in others. At any rate, the titles do not correctly describe the functional content of work associated with them; nor do they take into account the on-going changes into functional content due to technology or overt work redesign. Moreover, most employers have their own classification which is far removed from the standard classification.

Accordingly, in order to ensure greater success, the Network will have to adopt a more comprehensive definition of jobs that describes them in terms of three attributes: specific functions performed under them; generic skills (including linguistic competencies) needed to perform these functions; and their relevant education and training qualifications, expressed in terms of both the host country's and other member states' education systems.

8.2.3 Prospects for a single labour market

A recent report on the social dimension of the single market [4] has argued that greater spatial mobility will occur through five avenues:

- increased integration of the economies of the member states through further growth in intra-community trade

- opening up of public contracts

- changing perceptions of labour markets on the part of individual employers

- various Community programmes, designed to promote mobility within the European scientific community e.g. SCIENCE, ESPRIT, RACE, as described in Chapter 17

- reform of structural funds, leading to a more dynamic regional policy and more even economic development between regions.

Collectively all these measures and avenues will constitute an essential catalyst to a phenomenon that has been notably inconspicuous since the formation of the Community: the Commission's own estimates on spatial mobility shows how insignificant it has been so far [4]. But it would seem unrealistic to expect dramatic changes in the rate of spatial mobility within and between member states in the foreseeable future. In fact, what is most likely to speed up is the occupational and sectoral mobility within individual member states.

This is for two reasons: one economic, one social. Taking them in turn, although the specific measures and awareness will undoubtedly promote spatial mobility, their influence in the beginning is likely to be overwhelmed by changes in the occupational structure inspired jointly by industrial restructuring and new technologies. The social reason relates to the rapid emergence of the notion of the dual-career family. The two reasons are developed in detail below.

8.2.4   Dynamics of occupational change

Throughout the Community, structural changes are having a two-fold effect: creation of new industries and new occupations associated with them; and expansion in the functional content of work, vertical and horizontal, within existing industries and occupations. Either way, new occupations are being created whilst the functional content of existing occupations is changing. Crude estimates derived from our research would seem to suggest that no more than

10 per cent of the changes in the community's occupational structures in the last decade are due to the emergence of new occupations. The precise estimate is clearly a matter of conjecture. But the substantive point is that an overwhelming proportion of occupational changes are due to changing functional content of existing occupations, which has involved reclassification of jobs and individuals. Research done for this book makes it possible to project this process into the future in order to assess the likely changes in this decade.

The projected changes are shown in Figure 8.1. The process started in the north-west quadrant. Most of the member states are now in the south-west quadrant. As a result of the single market, companies will strive to develop new skills to underpin prospective growth in product customisation in the next decade, thereby moving them into the south-east quadrant. This process will then continue such that by the turn of the century, three outcomes are most likely:

- Current divisions between occupations will erode, as a growing number of functions come to be performed under each of them.

- As a result, in the case of certain broad occupational groups, it will be possible for individual employees to progress upwards from one group to another, as their repertoire of work-skills expands. This will apply particularly to many craft-based occupations in the manufacturing and clerical-based occupations in the service industries.

- New occupations will emerge (north-east quadrant) under the combined impact of work restructuring and in-house development of new skills. These occupations will cover individuals with multiple skills, straddling a number of disciplines.

From the point of view of intra-Community spatial mobility, the second outcome will gradually emerge as the biggest micro-level barrier, for two reasons. First, it will create fresh career progression for employees in those member states who are able to participate in the dynamics of this four-stage process in Figure 8.1. These employees will have more career opportunities in their own countries than before. Second, to the extent that there will be inter-country differences in the speed and content of these processes, the functional and skills content of identical occupations will be different between member states at a given point in time. As a result, the mutual recognition of diplomas, as proposed by the Commission, will inevitably fall short of establishing occupational comparability, at least in the eyes of employers.

Figure 8.1   The dynamics of changing occupational balance

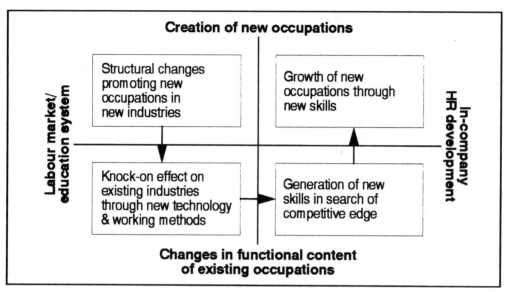

Source: CREATE Research Programme

In this context, the spread of the UK-style NCVQ is a welcome development, in that it identifies the nature of competences reached by individuals, irrespective of the qualifications they may or may not hold. This will undoubtedly permit intra-occupational and intra-industry mobility first within a country and then within the Community. However, the process is likely to be slow because not many employers are as yet familiar with the NCVQ approach in the UK, let alone elsewhere. Accordingly, there is a need for a large-scale programme of dissemination within the corporate sector in all the member states about the merits of NCVQ. Otherwise there is a serious risk that the structural changes in the wake of the single market will promote intra-country rather than intra-Community mobility.

8.2.5   Emergence of the dual-career family

As a result of the rising participation of women in the workforce, the notion of dual-career families is firmly taking root across the Community. As we saw in Figure 6.4 in Chapter 6, the female participation rate is expected to increase in many member states over this decade. This may serve to mitigate against intra-Community mobility because suitable job opportunities will have to exist in the host country for both partners in a family.

Indeed, the problem appears all the more acute because of the fact that the partners of skilled workers have high career aspirations. In addition, they have high educational aspirations for their children. In France, the UK and West Germany, for example, both these factors have mitigated against inter-regional mobility on a notable scale in the 1980s.

The barriers associated with the emergence of dual-career families are subjective and psychological. As such, they are highly enduring and difficult to overcome by policy action. In the final analysis, they will be influenced by each family's own personal circumstances as well as by its perceptions of the overall attractiveness of any region or country within the Community.

In the light of the foregoing analysis, it seems unlikely that there will be intra-Community mobility on a scale that will notably ease the numbers and skills gap, even if there were significant pockets of scarcity co-existing with surpluses. Instead, what is more likely to happen is greater intra-country mobility between industries and occupations, as a result of on-going structural changes that will now be influenced by the creation of the single market. But as the American evidence shows, over time greater labour mobility is likely to occur between the member states. The Commission can at least have some influence on its pace, if it generates a fresh momentum behind the three solutions discussed in Sub-Section 8.2.2.

8.3　Government-level solutions

There are three specific areas in which individual governments can help to ease the prospective gaps.

8.3.1　Higher participation rate in education

As we shall see in Chapter 16, there is considerable scope for promoting a higher participation rate amongst the two age groups through which the education system has traditionally transferred skills and know-how to the labour market: teenagers (15-19 age group) and young adults (20-24 age group). For both these groups, the rates vary considerably within the community but that does not detract from the fact that there is still considerable potential for raising them in almost every member state. It is clear that although numerically there would be fewer young people in the Community in the 1990s, their quantitative decline could be more than compensated for by higher participation rates in the post-compulsory education sectors. Any qualitative improvement could help to narrow the skills gap.

In countries like France, Italy and the UK new initiatives have been forthcoming in this context, as shown by a CEDEFOP report [5]. However, there is little doubt that much more could be done in these and other member states. The current participation rates are far too low in relation to the know-how requirements of the single market.

8.3.2　Extensive retraining of disadvantaged groups

The identified labour market gaps in the 1990s can be substantially narrowed if member states also embark on extensive retraining of the two groups of workers who are currently disadvantaged but could prove a vital resource in the 1990s: married women and the unemployed.

At present, both groups remain on the fringe of labour markets right across the Community, partly due to employer attitudes but mainly due to their over-exposure to skills obsolescence or irrelevance in the face of rapid structural and technological change. As the pace of change accelerates in response to the fresh competitive pressures generated by the single market, these two groups will be increasingly relegated to part-time or tenuous jobs that offer little training and career enhancement. Many of them could become long-term unemployed.

In order to avoid the prospective waste of this valuable resource, there is a strong case for expanding the education and training programmes for them. Notable attempts have been made in most of the member states [details are given in reference 1]. But these fall short of requirements. In the tight labour market of the 1990s the so-called free rider problem will be all too evident: employers with exemplary practices towards recruitment, training and development of the disadvantaged groups will end up as the unwitting recruitment pool for others without such practices. Exemplary employers' investment in training will therefore not generate adequate return because of the practice of 'poaching' by others.

On strict economic grounds alone there is a strong case for an extensive publicly-provided training provision which can generate positive 'externalities' for all employers, both in terms of providing the necessary skills and containing inflationary wage pressures normally associated with poaching. On social grounds, too, the benefits could be significant in terms of offering individuals interesting careers and social esteem.

8.3.3   Equal opportunities policies

For disadvantaged workers, retraining is valuable. But in itself it is not enough because part of their disadvantage stems from prejudices that prevail in the employer community. In countries like France, Italy, the UK and West Germany there are laws which promulgate equal opportunities at the workplace for women and ethnic minorities. Yet despite having the requisite qualifications, these groups continue to be over-represented in lower level occupations and under-represented in intermediate and higher level occupations [6].

Labour market pressures in the 1990s would obviously serve to undermine these attitudes. But they are unlikely to eradicate the seeming discrimination which already exacts a high economic cost across the Community. There is an urgent need for the member states to enforce equal opportunities through a proactive policy. If left to market forces, the slave trade would still be with us today!

8.4   Employer-level solutions

The macro level actions outlined in the last two sections can take a long time to work through because they are designed to overcome age-old structural, institutional, social and attitudinal problems. Because of their very nature, they can operate only over time. However, the same cannot be said about the solutions that are open to employers. Not only have they many solutions to choose from, but also some of the solutions can operate very rapidly.

According to our research, there are about eleven solutions that employers can adopt in order to overcome the six gaps highlighted in Chapter 7. For ease of presentation they are classified here in a four quadrant model. Using a variant of a scheme devised at the Institute of Manpower Studies [7], the model distinguishes and juxtaposes two continuums:

- **Internal-external:** some solutions are internal in the sense that they involve making changes that are internal to individual companies and are therefore within their sphere of influence. Some solutions are external in the sense that they involve responding to changes in the outside labour market.

- **Strategic-tactical:** some solutions can produce a lasting change towards narrowing the gap; some are merely short-term palliatives.

The options open to the employers to cope with the decline in school leavers in the individual member states are outlined in Figure 8.2. They may be generalised into four categories:

- **Throwing money at the problem:** the solutions in the north-east quadrant involve cost escalation because of competitive price bidding in the labour market.

- **Using internal labour market (ILM):** the solutions in the south-west quadrant mean making better use of existing staff; or promoting them rapidly into shortage occupations; or using companies' own ILM as recruitment points both internally and, where relevant, internationally. The last course can enable a firm to direct its recruitment efforts beyond its local labour market.

- **Changing recruitment criteria and using recruitment targeted at other worker groups:** the solutions in the north-east quadrant involve changing recruitment criteria, in terms of both entry requirements and worker groups; the latter leading to the substitution of women, disabled workers, older workers and ethnic minorities for younger workers, wherever possible. These four substitution groups also tend to have a high incidence of unemployment. So the solutions here also involve recruiting those who are out of work.

Figure 8.2   Responses to decline in school leaver population

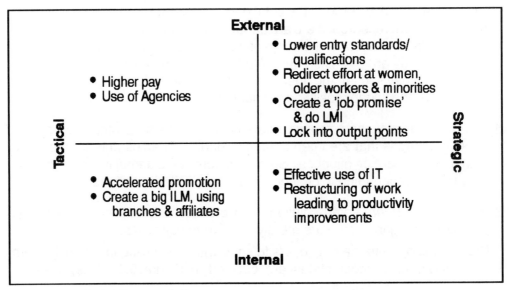

Source: *CREATE Research Programme*

Additionally, two other solutions are listed in this quadrant.   One involves creating a job promise and the other involves carrying out labour market research.   In practice, the first of these requires tailoring jobs to suit the needs of potential workers in the locality. The second requires employers to lock into various output points by establishing closer links with schools and colleges in a way that ensures that young people in them become aware of job possibilities and, as a result, have less incentive to drift voluntarily into unemployment.

- ***Adopting lasting solutions:***   solutions in the south-east quadrant are designed to solve the gap on a lasting basis, by restructuring work and making more intensive use of technology.

Solutions in Figure 8.2 are primarily targeted at solving the numbers gap. But they also have the added merit in tackling, to a certain extent, the gender, racial, revenue and productivity gaps.   As for the skills gap, the solutions are approximately similar, as shown in Figure 8.3.

The main difference here is in the south-east quadrant which now also includes emphasis on:

• training and development

• use of productivity enhancing working methods.

Figure 8.3   Responses to skills shortages

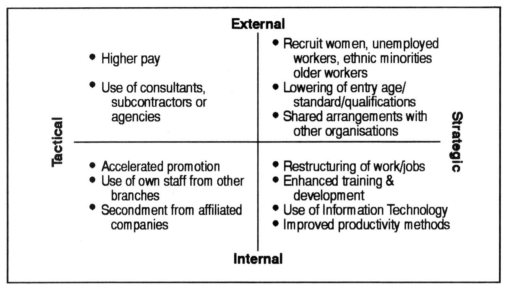

Source: CREATE Research Programme

When Figures 8.2 and 8.3 are considered together two salient points emerge. First, if employers choose to exercise 'external' solutions, these will only help to *ease* recruitment, in the sense that they will be able to afford recruitment costs or recruit from a wider potential pool. On the other hand, if they opt for the 'internal' solutions, these will serve to *limit* the scale of recruitment because the main thrust of internal factors is directed at improving labour utilisation. For social reasons, external solutions may be more appealing: for economic reasons internal solutions may be more desirable. Second, the solutions in the different quadrants are not mutually exclusive. For example, it may be possible to rely on higher pay as a vehicle of achieving the restructuring of work or higher productivity. Thus, individual employers will have to devise a combination of solutions that will best meet their own circumstances.

Our research shows that companies in many member states are being far from proactive in identifying their future needs and producing plans for meeting them. This seeming lack of proactivity is partly due to the lack of awareness of their future skills needs and partly due to the knowledge that there are multiple options in meeting these needs as and when they actually arise. That is not to say that when confronted with their needs most employers will adopt strategic options that constitute lasting solutions (given in the south-east quadrant in Figures 8.2 and 8.3). After all, some of these desirable solutions have long lead-times in their implementation: to overcome the likely skills shortages in the 1990s employers need to act now, if they are to achieve cost effective business growth in the single market. At present, there are few, if any, indications of employers' proactivity in this context.

8.5   Summary

This chapter has identified various solutions that can be adopted in order to ease prospective gaps in the Community's labour market in the 1990s. This chapter has restricted itself to actions outside the field of education and training since that is covered more fully in Part C. The identified solutions may be implemented at three levels: European Commission, individual governments and individual employers.

- At the Commission level, the introduction of the mutual recognition of qualifications and the training 'passport' constitute a step in the right direction, as does the creation of a new information network on vacancies. Indirectly, too, the 1992 programme is creating a number of avenues through which sectoral, occupational and spatial mobility can improve, thereby easing some of the gaps. However, progress thus far has been slow and fresh momentum is needed.

- Be that as it may, there is a strong indication that the Commission-related solutions will promote inter-sectoral and inter-occupational mobility within individual member states rather than between them. Spatial mobility has been constrained in the past by social as much as economic factors. The non-economic factors will take time to weaken. So, the impact of the Community-related solutions will be limited in the early years of the 1990s. Over time, of course, they will generate a beneficial impact.

- At the governmental level, three actions are needed:
  - promotion of higher participation rate in education, in order to compensate for the quantitative contraction in the labour force by qualitative improvement;
  - extensive retraining of disadvantaged workers, such as married women and ethnic minorities, who will otherwise remain at the fringe of the labour market because of their higher exposure to skills obsolescence.

continued...

- promotion of equal opportunities policies to ensure that disadvantaged workers do not continue to suffer discrimination because of the long-standing prejudices held by many employers. These prejudices have no economic or social logic in the turbulent labour markets of the 1990s. Yet market forces alone will not curb them. Purposeful action will be needed on the part of governments. Certainly, their current efforts fall short of requirements.

- At the employer level, there are a number of solutions. Some involve merely responding to pressures in the external labour market, others mean making changes to a firm's own internal labour market. Some amount to palliatives designed to provide a temporary relief; others constitute strategic changes that could ease labour market gaps on a lasting basis.

- These solutions are not mutually exclusive: they offer a menu of options. However, if the Community's employers are to implement strategic solutions then they need to act now because some of these solutions have a long lead-time in implementation.

- At present there are no significant signs that the Community's employers understand the nature and significance of the six gaps nor will they will act in time to narrow them. Indeed, the six gaps are like individual time bombs, waiting to explode.

PART C

Education and training challenges

Part B has identified various supply-side and demand-side developments in the Community's labour markets. It used an approach that aggregated the member states as if they were either fairly homogeneous or capable of simple aggregation. In real life, of course, neither of these suppositions are valid. In fact the extent of detail presented in Part B was substantially influenced by the availability of internationally comparable data.

This Part of the book continues with the same approach but with one notable difference: it discusses the results of a number of research studies carried out by this author on individual member states. As a result, it conveys the reality of at least some aspects of individual labour markets.

It starts with those economic and social trends arising from Part B which pose notable education and training challenges (Chapter 9). It then goes on to provide an overview of the implications of these trends in three counties: Denmark, Ireland and West Germany (Chapter 9). This overview paves the way for a more detailed focus on three other member states: France, Italy and the UK (Chapters 10, 11 and 12 respectively). The perspectives on individual countries take account of several factors; many of which do not relate to the single market either directly or indirectly. Thus, having covered them, this Part goes on to focus on the single market and sets out the challenges which it is likely to pose (Chapter 13).

9

DEVELOPMENTS IN THE COMMUNITY'S LABOUR MARKETS

9.1   General trends

9.1.1   Prospective demographic and social trends

As we saw in Chapters 6 and 7, under the combined impact of falling birth rates and increasing longevity, three major developments are expected to occur in an overwhelming majority of the member states over the next decade:

- **Fewer school leavers:**   numerically, there will be fewer school leavers coming into the labour market or going into higher education. The output from the higher education sector will decline, unless the participation rate for higher education increases. Figure 9.1 provides some examples. It also shows that the problem is not specific to the Community: other industrialised economies are also expected to suffer a similar decline. The implication is two-fold: the Community will have fewer young entrants to the labour markets and there will be fewer younger students enrolling for higher educational courses, in the absence of an increase in the participation rate.

- **More older workers:** the age structure of the workforce is likely to move in favour of older workers (see Figures 9.2 and 9.3 for some examples). A majority of these workers will have had no more than basic schooling in their early formative years. Thus, historical inadequacies of the education and training systems in member states such as Belgium, France, Greece, Ireland, Italy, Portugal, Spain and the UK will be felt even more acutely in the future, via the dominant worker groups.

- *Rising female participation rate:* in all the member states, the share of women in the workforce will increase. As well as providing some examples, Figure 6.4 (in Chapter 6) showed that this phenomenon, too, has parallels in other advanced industrialised countries. Furthermore, the expected increase in the participation rate will be mainly due to more women returning to work after having a family. The implication is that many new entrants to the labour market will either have had no more than basic schooling because of the historical inadequacies of the education and training systems or be subject to skills obsolescence due to enforced absence from the labour market, at a time when technology and competitive pressures will be rapidly changing the skills content of work.

Figure 9.1   Age group 16-24: Labour force projections, 1990-2000

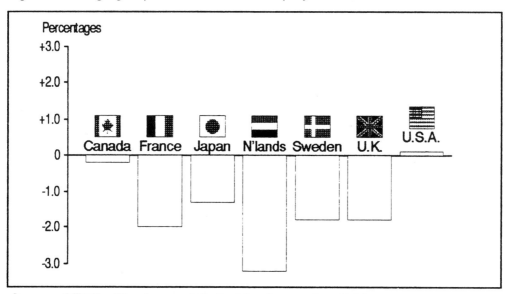

Source: OECD, 'Employment Outlook', September 1988

9.1.2   Labour market trends

In the training context, prospective demographic trends would not seem so awesome but for the fact that they will occur against a background of historical labour market trends which have already opened up significant skills and training 'gaps' in all the member states [1].

The OECD data (given in the 1989 edition of *Employment Outlook*) summarise these trends for each of the member states over the period 1966-86. Although the rate of evolution varies between countries, their directions are roughly similar across the Community. There are four generalised tendencies:

- *Ascendancy of services:* the industrial structure of employment has changed in all the member states in favour of service industries and occupations. There has been a relative and absolute contraction in employment in primary and production sectors. Furthermore, in many service industries, industrial structure remains fragmented with the result that industry-wide training provision is at best inadequate and at worst non-existent.

- *Ascendancy of female employment:* the share of female employment has increased in all the member states. Much of this increase is concentrated in the service industries and occupations where the possibilities for part-time work for the 'second bread-winner' in the family are the highest.

Figure 9.2   Age group 25-54: Labour force projections, 1990-2000

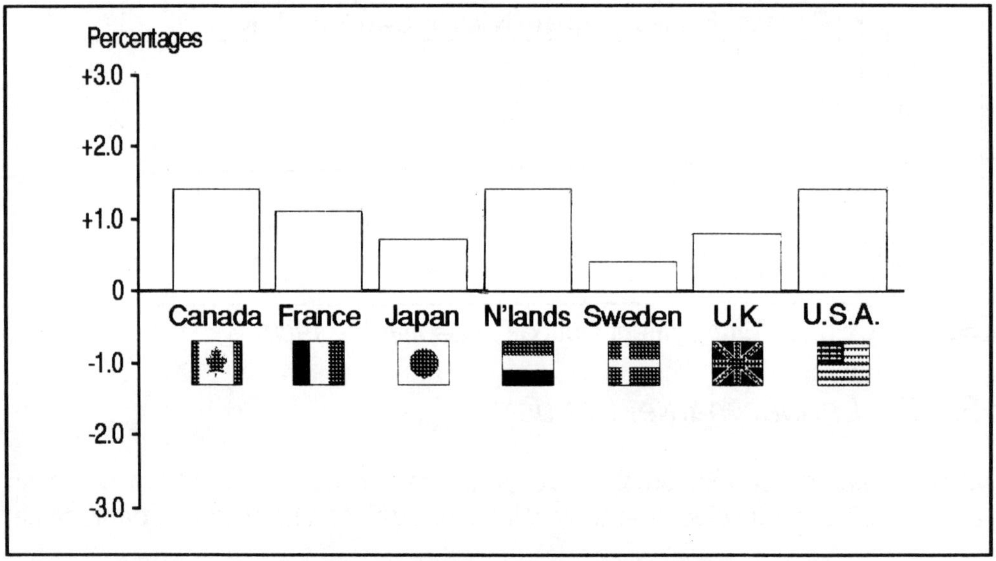

Source: OECD, 'Employment Outlook',   September 1988

- **Compositional changes in self employment:** the share of self employment has declined in all countries except the UK. The decline, however, reflects a substantial contraction in the agricultural labour force. Once allowance is made for this factor, there is, in fact, an increase in self employment, especially in professional and retail services which are noted for their poor training provision.

- **Significant structural unemployment:** in all the member states, the underlying trend in the rate of unemployment has been up, once allowance is made for cyclical fluctuations. There has been some improvement since 1987, but the problem of long-term unemployment persists, reflecting poor vocational preparation on the part of those out of work.

- **Continuation of trends:** the above four labour market trends are likely to continue, at least until 1995. This is emphasised by all the available long-term qualitative forecasts.

Figure 9.3   Age group 55-64: Labour force projections, 1990-2000

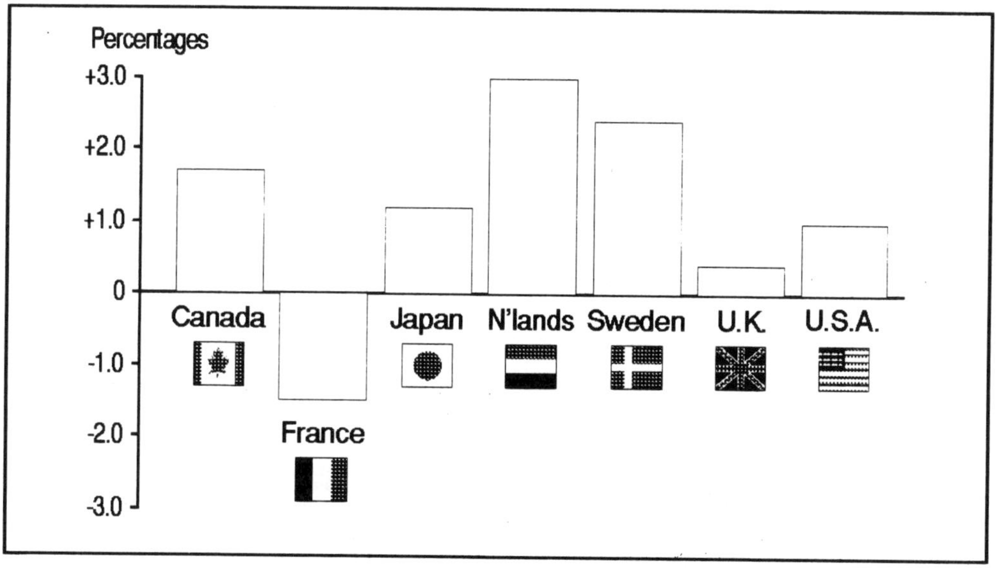

Source: OECD, 'Employment Outlook', September 1988

129

9.1.3   Implications of the identified trends

The implications of past and prospective trends identified in the previous two sub-sections are distinctly onerous, to say the least. On the face of it, it is clear that:

- Newcomers to the labour market as well as a large segment of the established workforce will have either inadequate basic education (e.g. older workers) or skills obsolescence (married women) or both.

- New jobs are emerging and will continue to emerge in areas where the provision for vocational training or re-training remains (and will continue to remain) inadequate.

  As a result, the existing skills or training 'gap' is likely to be perpetuated into the future. Of late, individual member states — notably Denmark, France, the UK and West Germany — have shown awareness of this problem and initiated a number of measures. Welcome though they are, their initiatives are unlikely to bridge the identified gaps in the foreseeable future.

  This is because alongside demographic and labour market trends other durable forces are at work. Their central thrust is towards continuously increasing the know-how and skills content of work in many industries, on a scale that poses formidable challenges for the system of education and training in individual member states. Even in relatively prosperous countries such as France, Italy and the UK, the present achievements of the system fall well short of requirements. This is because the requirements themselves are increasing rapidly at a rate which has surpassed the ability of the education and training systems to respond. In order to understand the nature of these emerging training and skills gaps, it is now essential to examine the impact of technology and industrial restructuring since the late 1960s.

9.1.4   Technology and industrial restructuring

Underlying the economic growth pattern in the Community, has been a fundamental shift in the way capital and labour — the two main factors of production — are being utilised. Figure 9.4 summarises this shift in a clockwise fashion, starting with the north-east quadrant. In the period 1968-75 economic

Figure 9.4   A cycle of innovation and economic growth

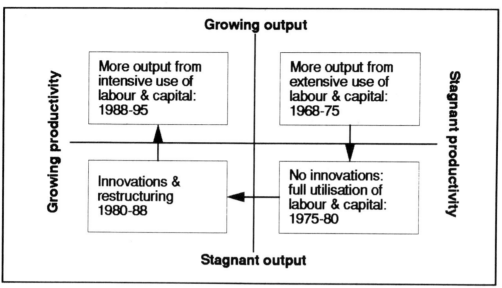

Source: CREATE Research Programme

growth came mainly from more extensive use of capital and labour — that is, from bringing into use hitherto under-utilised economic resources. This occurred at a time when the rate of labour productivity growth had slowed down markedly [3].

The period was punctuated by the 'oil crisis' of 1973 and the ensuing economic recession. In the period 1975-80, both economic growth and productivity growth stagnated (south-west quadrant). This recession was so severe that:

- The overall rate of growth of demand in the economies of member states slowed down, thereby slowing the overall rate of economic growth.

- There was a major deceleration in the new rate of investment in innovations, leading to a marked slow down in productivity growth.

Then came the second 'oil crisis' in 1979, ushering in an even more serious economic recession. The severe competitive pressures released by it sparked off the application of new technologies—particularly informational and materials (south-west quadrant). Under their combined impact European economies entered a new (and the latest) phase in the model (north-west quadrant). Under it, the dominant thrust is now towards:

• achieving more intensive use of capital and labour for business survival

• achieving economic growth mainly through growth in labour productivity.

Member states such as Denmark, France, Italy, Netherlands, the UK and West Germany are definitely in this fourth stage. The position of other member states is a matter of conjecture. But the fundamental point here relates to the shift from extensive to intensive use of capital and labour that is occurring across the Community in response to growing competitive pressures. This shift has far-reaching implications for the scale and content of training, as we shall see in Chapter 13.

9.2   Country focus

So far, this chapter has highlighted trends that are applicable at the level of the Community as well as most of the individual member states. In this section, we initiate a more disaggregated approach which draws out the main themes from separate studies relating to Denmark, Ireland and West Germany, derived from a separate CEDEFOP project [see reference 1]. This approach focuses on recent and prospective trends in individual economies, as well as discussing similarities across economies.

9.2.1   Denmark

The Danish study examined the macroeconomic outlook to the year 2000 and its implications for training [4]. The study considered four possible scenarios that could prevail individually, jointly or sequentially in Denmark between now and the year 2000. They are:

• **Turbo-Denmark:** involving trade and commercial liberalisation; high economic growth; increased competition; weakening of structures influencing industrial democracy and wage bargaining.

- **Environment-Denmark:** involving 'Green' viewpoints on economy and society; a self-contained economy and moderate economic growth.

- **Consensus-Denmark:** involving close co-operation between Government, social partners or other special interest groups; strengthening of co-operation with the European Community; and moderate economic growth.

- **Subculture-Denmark:** involving a breakdown of shared attitudes and values; weakening of special interest groups; more emphasis on the work ethic; and low economic growth.

Having considered the detailed features of each scenario, the report concludes that none of the scenarios are likely to prevail on a mutually exclusive basis: a *composite* scenario has greater likelihood. In it, the following outcomes are likely:

- Women's participation in the workforce will increase for most (but not all) age groups to the levels of their male analogues, as prevailed in 1982.

- As a result of the higher female participation rate, the overall labour force will increase at an annual rate of 0.95 per cent in the rest of the 1980s; average at 0.56 per cent in the period 1990-4; and 0.19 per cent in the period 1995-2000.

- Part-time work will increase at an annual rate of 0.6 per cent over the whole period in production, construction and private services sectors and by 1.5 per cent annually in the public sector.

- Hours of work will decline.

- Self-employment in agriculture will decline.

- Unemployment or early retirement will particularly impact on unskilled workers with the result that the employed labour force will, over time, have fewer people without any training.

- New entrants to the labour market will have a strong pro-training and pro-retraining outlook.

- The number of supervisory and management staff will increase, that of skilled and unskilled workers will decrease.

Industrial concentration will continue. The organisational rigidity that will result from it will be partially offset by the more flexible arrangement of working time. However the net effect on training could be adverse.

Against these developments, the Danish economy will have three phases: Phase One: 1985-90, Turbo-Denmark; Phase Two: 1991-5, Turbo and Consensus Denmark; and Phase Three: 1996-2000, Structural Change. Many macroeconomic developments that are likely to occur over the three phases have been identified. The principal ones are:

- Unemployment will rise until 1990 and begin to fall thereafter, but only slowly.

- The fall will be inspired by an increase in public expenditure overtly aimed at job creation.

- The modest decline in employment is but a reflection of the persistence of the structural weakness of the Danish economy throughout this decade.

- This heightens the importance of training and retraining as amongst the principal measures of revitalising the country's economic base.

Two principal conclusions emerge from these developments. First, changes in the structure of the workforce will move in favour of those with a higher training propensity. Thus, demand for training and retraining will increase. Second, this increase will be underpinned by a simple economic imperative: unless training provision is increased, the economic base will remain weak, notwithstanding the growth in public spending that would be overtly designed to create new jobs.

9.2.2   Ireland

Covering the period 1986-92, the Irish study had a shorter time horizon. But that does not detract from its important conclusions [5]. Its projections rely heavily on estimates emerging from the Government's latest three-year economic plan and the 1986 population census. The study's main findings can be summarised as follows:

- The population will decline slightly—from 3.53 million in 1986 to 3.50 million in 1992 through falling birth rate and emigration (mainly to EC countries).

- As a result, the age structure of the population will change: the average age will rise from 27 in 1986 to 30 by 1992.

- Unless there are marked changes in female participation rate, the labour force will remain static at 1.3 million; but if the rate is higher, the labour force could increase by 5,500 per annum.

- If the labour force remains static, unemployment may stabilise at about 18 per cent; but if the Government is able to implement its declared job creation plans, the rate could come down significantly.

- Long-term unemployment will continue to be the major labour market problem.

- Although the average age of the population will rise from 27 in 1986 to 30 in 1992, this will still be below the European norm. Up to 1992, there will be a continuing level of young persons entering the labour market in contrast to declining numbers in many European countries. The main question is whether the economy can provide enough jobs for them.

These findings have significant implications for vocational training. They are as follows:

- The ageing population will save government resources in certain child-related areas, making them available for training and job creation.

- As the population ages, an increasing proportion of potential applicants for training programmes will come from the age group 'over 25', with the result that the focus of vocational training will move from initial training to continuous retraining.

- The regeneration of industry, as envisaged in the economic plan, will require a major input from the vocational training system, to provide for high-skill training, relevant for financial, tourist and hi-tech manufacturing-based industries.

- Overall, government resources for vocational training programmes in Ireland will increasingly need to be targeted towards:
  - Young persons who leave school without adequate qualifications. These persons find it relatively more difficult to obtain employment.
  - Long-term unemployed persons whose skills are out of date. The proportion of such unemployed persons has grown in recent years.
  - Ensuring an adequate supply of highly qualified and skilled labour for the needs of the economy. This will be especially important in the run up to the single market.
  - Assisting enterprises and workers to cope with occupational and technological change.
  - Providing skills required for the start-up and growth of new enterprises.

From sectoral studies and other research carried out by the Training and Employment Authority, several major educational and training issues can be stated. They are likely to be important in the sectoral, corporate and occupational context.

At sectoral level, there will be a need to identify, prioritise and provide for re-training and updating skill needs. Some sectors, especially those with a high number of small indigenous firms, will face more problems than others.

At company level, Irish firms will need to analyse and plan their human resource needs much more strategically than ever before. There will be a need for the workplace to become the focal point for the planning and implementation of continuing training and education programmes. This will require that companies are able to form strategic training plans and articulate them. Generally, within the workplace there will be a move towards a higher skill level amongst employees.

At occupational level, people will have to utilise their skills in an increasingly multi-technology environment. Initiative, adaptability and team-work abilities will become increasingly important. Because of the move at a European level towards the mutual recognition of academic and vocational training qualifications across countries, there will be a need to examine and modify courses in Ireland if necessary. To promote a wider European dimension for education and training programmes, there will be a need to encourage more young worker exchange programmes between Ireland and other European countries.

From the above analysis, three principal conclusions emerge. First, high unemployment, ageing population, higher female activity rates and weak industrial structure will call for more training and retraining. Second, training is increasingly viewed as one of the main instruments of countering a number of potentially adverse developments in the economy. Third, there is a paramount need for Irish firms to remain competitive because Ireland exports half its industrial output. In the run-up to 1992, the skills of its workforce will need to be at least comparable to other European countries to ensure competitiveness.

9.2.3   West Germany

The German study was based on two independently derived scenarios: one looking at vocational training systems to 1995; and one examining the qualifications structure required for the world of work to the year 2000 [6]. Each of these is considered separately below.

A.   Scenario of vocational training

In the past decade, the system of vocational training has undergone a fundamental change owing to four factors:

- larger cohorts of young people

- a slowing down in the rate of economic growth

- increasing risk of unemployment

- changed education behaviour; resulting in more pupils holding higher school-leaving qualifications.

  Of late, this list has been augmented by:

- greater awareness of vulnerability to changing economic environment

- the increasing role of women in society

- new information technology

- shorter working hours and greater working time flexibility.

Against the background of these developments, two scenarios were constructed: Scenario A assumed an average annual economic growth of 3 per cent to 1995; Scenario B assumed 1 per cent. The critical difference between the two scenarios shows up in unemployment. Under Scenario A, unemployment declines markedly; under B it persists at its 1985 level. Beyond that, both scenarios generate certain similar changes, but at different degrees of intensity. They include:

- relative decline in manufacturing and construction employment and relative increase in service employment

- relative decline in industrial occupations and relative increase in technical, administrative and office occupations

- a step increase in investment in information technology: three-fold in Scenario A; two-fold in Scenario B

- an increased interest in training and employment by women, leading to part-time work and career occupations

- a 35 per cent reduction in the number of school leavers between 1985 and 1995 due to demographic changes. In schools, the first cycle of secondary education will continue to decline. Those holding the 'Arbitur' (qualifying for university entrance) will increase substantially in numbers, because of growing competition in the labour market in response to continuing unemployment.

The prevalence of these enduring factors means that imbalances between demand and supply of training places will be largely conditioned by the state of the economy. Under the optimistic Scenario A, supply will exceed demand because more economic resources will be available for training provision. Under Scenario B, demand will exceed supply, partly because of the more limited availability of resources partly because of the accumulated back-log and partly because of the heightened importance of training for individual workers on account of the fewer job opportunities. Under either scenario, three other tendencies are likely to prevail:

- craft training will decline because in-company vocational training will be directed at job-specific skills that can generate a return on investment in training

- the spread of information technology will raise skill requirements in many training occupations

- the attainment level of school-leaving certificate will become an important criteria for access to in-company training. This is because employers will be increasingly looking for those who are 'trainable'. As a result, problem groups—such as trainee drop-outs, young people from remedial schools, and young people without school-leaving certificates—are likely to be further disadvantaged.

These tendencies suggest that a decisive factor for occupational success will be individual commitment to continuing training. Also, the demands placed on trainers will increase substantially for three reasons: the trainees will be older; they will have a higher standard of school education; and the required training will be intensive and compact, using new media and teaching methods.

B. Scenario of qualifications structure of manpower requirements

The second part of the study was based on the *premise* that there is a link between work occupations and educational qualifications. Thus, if future labour force requirements can be defined in terms of occupations, then their qualifications implications can be worked out in advance. In this context, four categories of qualifications are used:

- no vocational training certificate (Level 1)

- in-company semi-skilled training, apprenticeship or equivalent school certificate (Level 2)

- master craftsman's or technician's certificate (Level 3)

- a degree from higher education college or university (Level 4).

These qualification levels were cross-linked with job details obtained from the latest (1982) Census. For the period 1976-82, the results showed that:

- Employers' recruitment behaviour has changed to the effect that they are demanding ever higher qualifications.

- In part, this is due to the changes in the content of work, requiring higher level skills.

- In part, it is also due to an over-supply of qualified workers; with the result that many workers were over-qualified for the jobs they hold. The over-supply was, in turn, partly due to increased educational provision and partly due to scarcity of jobs.

As for the period to the year 2000, various alternative projections yield the same message: namely, the qualification level required of the working population will continue to rise. Within this overall assessment, three messages are noteworthy:

- The absolute and relative number of unskilled jobs—those with Level 1 qualifications — will decline, causing unemployment amongst the less qualified members of the workforce.

- The number of workers with vocational qualifications will either remain stable or increase markedly (Levels 2 and 3), as will the number of workers with degree level qualifications will increase (Level 4).

- The demand for qualifications will rise steadily — a process that will be intensified by the continued surplus of skilled workers competing for fewer jobs. Technological development will result in a higher demand for hybrid qualifications, in industrial as well as service occupations. In particular, the importance of social skills (ability to co-operate and communicate, for example) will increase.

- Although in-company training will remain the largest source of training, its attractiveness vis-a-vis other sectors (e.g. universities) will decline.

- The 1990s will be a decade of continuing education and training. This is partly because of new technological developments and partly because the qualified people passing through the dual system will demand greater education and training provision in response to rising aspirations and relative scarcity of job opportunities.

Thus, two principal conclusions emanate from the German study. First, under a favourable economic scenario, the demand for and supply of vocational training could be more realistically handled. Whatever the economic outlook, however, the demand will increase owing to a number of enduring factors. Second, the educational qualifications required of the workforce will increase over the rest of this century. The precise and dominant cause of this increase is hard to discern. It could be partly due to the changing content of work, requiring higher level skills and partly due to rising aspirations.

9.3 Summary

This chapter has attempted to highlight various demographic, social, labour market and technological trends. It has also considered their education and training implications.

  This has been done first at the level of the Community and then at the level of three member states: Denmark, Ireland and West Germany. The breadth and depth of the approach adopted here has been dictated by the availability of the comparable data. The main points emerging from the chapter are as follows:

- The identified trends are common across many member states, though their intensity varies between them.

- The demographic, social, labour market and technological trends considered here have one over-riding common feature: they all suggest that the Community's workforce will require extensive training or retraining.

- This broad conclusion applies even if there was no single market. This is because the economies of individual member states have undergone major structural and technological changes in the last decade and will continue to do so in this decade as well.

- If anything, the single market will intensify these trends and, as a result, call for an even greater effort in developing new work skills.

- Focused analysis of three economies — as disparate as Denmark, Ireland and West Germany — corroborate the broad conclusions.

10

CASE STUDY 1: FRANCE

10.1   Background

This and the next two chapters present separate case studies on three member states. They were carried out as a part of a CEDEFOP project on future training needs. The project aimed to identify factors that influenced the scale and content of training. This was done through a series of interviews with researchers and policy makers in a number of institutions in the countries concerned.

The interviews used a discussion guide which is given in Appendix A. Their object was to collect and analyse information within a common framework. This, of course, necessarily meant that some information was slightly out of date because there is usually a long time-lag in the availability of internationally comparable information. Be that as it may, the data and observations emerging from the interviews are useful because they serve to highlight the challenges posed by the single market for education and training systems in member states.

At the outset, it is as well to emphasise that the case studies do not provide an account of education and training systems. This has been done in two recent reports [1,2]. Rather, their main aim is to identify the nature of the forces that will impinge on these systems, on the one hand, and the kind of responses that is expected of the systems, on the other. Once the three case studies have been considered in Chapters 10, 11 and 12, we move on to draw out their salient messages in the Community context in Chapter 13.

The information presented in this chapter is based on interviews held with national experts based at the following organisations in Paris:

- Delegation a la Formation Professionnelle

- Delegation a l'insertion des Jeunes en Difficulte

- Centre d'Etudes et de Recherches sur les Qualifications

- Bureau d'Information et de Previsions Economiques

Within the European Community, France is one of the countries which has a lot of published material in the areas of employment, education and training [see, for example, 3;4;5;6;7;8;9;10]. This chapter does not repeat this material: instead it attempts to provide either fresh perspectives on the available material or offer new insights that build on it. Either way, its aim is to go beyond this material and draw out the salient messages.

Table 10.1   France: Key labour market trends: 1965-86

(Absolute numbers in thousands; shares in percentages)

	1965	1975	1980	1986
A. Total labour force	20,616	22,353	23,369	24,009
Percentage shares of:				
a. Civilian employment	96	93	92	87
b. Armed forces	2	3	2	2
c. Unemployed	2	4	6	11
B. Total civilian employment				
Percentage shares by status:				
a. Employees	75	82	83	84
b. Self-employed	25	18	17	16
Percentage shares by sex:				
a. Male	65	62	60	58
b. Female	35	38	40	42
Percentage shares by industry:				
a. Agriculture	17	10	9	7
b. Industry	39	39	36	31
c. Services	44	51	55	62

Source: 'Labour force statistics' (OECD, 1988 edition)

This modest attempt at obtaining a fresh slant has been mounted against the background of key labour market trends evident since 1965, as covered in Table 10.1. They show that:

- There has been a notable upward trend in the rate of unemployment, despite the cyclical economic recovery since 1982. The implication is that unemployment has been structural in nature, due to the mismatch between the available jobs and the skills of those out of work.

- The share of self-employed workers in total civilian employment has declined, largely due to a relative decline in the share of agriculture in national output. Indeed, as we shall see in the next section, the decline in the share of the self-employed masks a very significant compositional change.

- The share of female employees has increased, to a large extent due to the rising participation of married women in the employed labour force.

- There has been a contraction in the shares of agriculture and industry in the employed workforce. In other words, the structure of employment has changed markedly in favour of service activities.

It is, therefore, clear that the structure of employment has changed. Indeed, the change looks even more pronounced when occupational changes in the workforce are considered. The latest available data are given in Table 10.2. They show that there has been a marked shift in favour of two sets of occupations: those requiring higher level formal qualifications (e.g. health and 'intellectual' occupations); and those classified as 'intermediary' professions (e.g. draughtspeople, technicians, clerical and service workers). In contrast, the biggest contraction has been recorded by craftsworkers and operatives. The precise compositional changes are a matter of definition: after all, occupational boundaries can never be defined clearly. But the substantive point is that the occupation structure is becoming more knowledge and skills intensive, and it is also becoming more oriented towards service activities.

It is against the background of these two developments that our interviews with national experts attempt to identify the nature of the factors influencing the scale and content of training in France, both now and in the foreseeable future.

Table 10.2 Labour force structure by industries, professions and occupations: 1975-81

Industrial groups Occupations	Marketable service		Non - marketable service		Whole labour force	
	1975	1981	1975	1981	1975	1981
Primary Farmer	0.7	04	1.4	1.3	10.2	8.6
Secondary						
Engineer	1.6	2.1	1.7	1.7	1.5	1.7
Technician	2.9	2.9	3.0	2.6	4.2	4.2
Skilled worker	13.4	12.7	6.2	6.2	22.2	22.4
Non-skilled worker	6.0	5.5	3.3	3.5	15.6	13.6
Sub-total	23.9	23.2	14.2	14.0	43.5	41.9
Tertiary						
Top executive	8.0	9.9	15.0	16.6	6.0	7.5
Middle executive	18.3	21.2	25.0	24.2	11.6	12.9
Qualified employee	32.7	30.8	17.0	18.0	17.4	18.2
Non-qualified employee	16.2	14.4	27.0	25.8	11.3	10.9
Sub-total	75.2	76.4	84.0	84.7	46.3	49.5

Source: 'Bureau d'Informations et de previsions economiques' (BIPE, Paris)

10.2   Factors influencing the scale of training

Before identifying the factors, it is worth making an important caveat. The labour market and occupational changes identified in the last section have been substantially influenced by the world-wide recessions of 1973-4 and 1979-81—both of which hastened the pace of industrial restructuring that had been evident since the late 1960s. However, as we look at the evolution of education and training policies in the last five years, as described in the first eight bibliographical references for this chapter, one point stands out above all others: this evolution has also been substantially influenced by a highly pro-active stance on the part of successive governments. Under this stance, education and training have been specifically singled out as areas of major social investment and meriting high priority in national economic and social objectives. Thus, policy formulation has not only recognised current national needs but also anticipated their future evolution, in the light of potential developments in the economy to the year 2000.

Such a pro-active stance rendered many of the questions in our interview guide (given in Appendix A) irrelevant. Thus, if the rest of this chapter seems to deviate from the format laid down in the guide, that is only because of the over-arching influence of the policy stance.

10.2.1   Policy and supply factors

In order to understand the reasoning behind the pro-active policy stance, it is necessary to examine the occupational forecasts of the economy to the year 2000, as given in Table 10.3. There are two main features: numerical growth in the period 1982-2000 in various occupations; and the educational background of employees within each occupation in those two years. These occupational and educational forecasts over the rest of this century have been derived on the basis of the most plausible macro-economic scenario of the economy. The forecasts indicate that:

- Certain occupational groups will increase numerically. They include the civil service, teaching, managerial and others engaged in services and personnel functions. On the other hand, occupations involving farming and manual work will contract.

- The educational background of every occupational group will change in favour of higher educational qualifications, irrespective of whether the group is likely to contract or expand numerically over the rest of this century.

- Although the number of self-employed will not change significantly overall, there will be a compositional shift in favour of those engaged in various professions requiring higher educational qualifications.

These three changes therefore indicate that over the rest of this century there will have to be a major shift in the emphasis of educational policy, if the education system is to meet the needs of the economy. Specifically, it means that 38 per cent of the workforce will need the first four levels of qualifications in the year 2000, compared to 22 per cent in 1982. Although necessarily approximate, these percentages provide a clear indication of the scale of increase that is needed in the output of the national education and training system.

Already, there are indications that the system is responding. Three examples support this view.

First, a new baccalaureate-level stream has been created, offering more vocationally oriented qualifications that lead to 'professional maturity'. Quite simply, the underlying idea is to increase the staying-on rate at school for those in the age group 15-19, and at the same time prepare them for the world of work through vocational education. At present, the staying-on rate for this age group is around 50 per cent. It is hoped to increase this rate to 80 per cent by the early 1990s. Vocational preparation apart, the expectation is that the basic education for this age group will be significantly improved so that it can form the basis of life-time learning which is imperative if France is to prosper in the single market with its increasing orientation towards service activities.

The second example relates to enterprise-based training and its national recognition. Companies are encouraged to produce their own in-house training packages which are given national recognition through the system of homologation as operated by Delegation a la Formation Professionnelle. The system encourages trainees to learn by granting economy-wide acceptance to their achievements.

The third example relates to the concept of open learning. This is gaining widespread acceptance in France. It has two-fold objectives: to encourage the love of learning, irrespective of the subject areas covered; and to promote self learning. In the last year alone, about 120 million FF have been paid out in the form of state subsidies to organisations engaged in the preparation of open learning material.

Table 10.3   Occupational structure by levels of aggregate educational
            categories: 1982-2000

Categories	Year	Total number (thousands)	Percentage distribution by level of education *				
			I+II	III	IV	V	VI
Farmers and	1982	1,739	0	1	4	13	82
agricultural workers	2000	1,127	4	4	12	27	53
Self-employed	1982	2,115	9	4	12	21	54
	2000	2,192	16	4	13	30	37
Civil service	1982	3,160	5	15	14	19	47
	2000	3,644	7	21	20	26	26
Teaching	1982	1,108	38	26	26	3	7
	2000	1,424	46	38	12	2	2
Senior and middle	1982	3,156	13	9	23	22	33
Company management	2000	5,233	24	17	28	18	13
Manual workers	1982	6,737	0	0	3	26	71
	2000	6,268	0	0	9	43	48
Service employees and	1982	3,452	1	2	13	27	57
Personnel	2000	4,735	0	2	21	38	38
Total	1982	21,467	5	6	11	22	56
	2000	24,623	11	10	17	30	32

* Level VI = Initial cycle of secondary education (1st, 2nd, 3rd years) and
            one-year pre-vocational schemes
  V = Final year of short vocational courses and short cycle courses
  IV = Final year of full secondary education but not post-baccalaureat
       education
  III = Diploma at BAC + 2 level (eg. DUT, BTS, DEUG)
  I+ II = Graduate or post-graduate diploma or diploma from 'grande ecole'

Source: 'Haut comite d'education economie (BIPE, 1987, Paris)

These three examples highlight three separate thrusts of current policy on education and training:

- to improve basic education so as to create a viable and lasting base for life-time learning

- to encourage the love of learning

- to offer due recognition for educational achievements in the labour market.

Although laudable in its objectives, the policy is not entirely straightforward. Indeed, a number of problems have emerged, as can be appreciated by looking at a few examples. First, raising the staying-on rate to 80 per cent has created acute shortages of teachers, particularly those engaged in the preparation for professional maturity. Second, the homologation system is also resource constrained in the face of an exponential growth in the number of company-based courses. Furthermore, many employers are slow to recognise the homologated training because of historical prejudice against anything that operates outside the state system. Finally, most of the open learning material is company specific. As such, it is very expensive, because it is not subject to economies of scale through large-scale nationwide use, as is the case in the UK, for example, with material produced by the Open University.

Be that as it may, there is little doubt that the scale of training—both now and in the future—is and will be driven by stated policy goals. It is now time to turn to some of the pertinent demand and social issues which are increasingly underpinning the policy.

10.2.3   Demand and social factors

According to the national experts interviewed, there are two critical factors influencing the demand for training. They are:

- **The single market:** the French manufacturing industry already has a strong global orientation. The single market will merely reinforce it. But the same cannot be said about services. Most of the growth in services employment in the past two decades has occurred as a result of organic growth in domestic demand and externalisation of functions that previously were performed in-house but are now increasingly sub-contracted [12,13]. The completion of the internal market in Europe after 1992 will rapidly promote the cross-border trade in producer services: financial, business, telecommunications, transport and wholesaling. As we saw in Part A, such services require a high degree of customisation and are therefore know-how or skills intensive. Success in the single market will, therefore, require new resources for the development, deployment and management of the necessary skills. It is worth emphasising that without extra resources for training the single market will be noted only for its hardship. This is because those services-dominated economies who do not develop the requisite skills will be severely disadvantaged.

- *Productivity improvement:* as the base of the economy comes to be predominated by service activities, economic growth will be difficult to achieve without improvement in labour productivity in the service industries. Such an improvement will require large scale continuing investment in new technologies and work restructuring. Either way, the skills of employees will need to be upgraded independently of the three policy-driven thrusts mentioned above.

Indeed, both these demand factors cannot be readily isolated from three social factors which are now also calling for a step-increase in education and training provision.

The first of these relates to the rising participation of women (particularly married) in the workforce (Table 10.1). Most of them are involved in service activities, as can be seen from Table 10.4 which is the main contributor to the feminisation rate within the fast growing intermediary professions. It is well known that all these professions are becoming skills intensive [13,15,16]. Married women entering these professions after a prolonged absence during the child-rearing years are obviously disadvantaged because of the risk of skills obsolescence due to technological changes. They are also disadvantaged in terms of pay. As the last two columns in Table 10.4 show, women's average wage in all intermediary occupations is considerably below their male counterparts. However, in order to improve their relative pay, there needs to be a substantial improvement in labour productivity. This can only occur through work restructuring, leading to the performance of multiple functions under one job. But without extensive retraining, work restructuring is unlikely to succeed.

The second social factor relates to those who are long-term unemployed (LTU). In France, a significant proportion of the LTU are youths and young adults [17,19]. Their principal characteristic is their relatively low academic attainment.

Table 10.4   Intermediary professions

Categories	Employees (thousands)	% of total	% of women in category	Wage indicator (Average = 100) Man	Woman
Foremen-supervisors	550	14.4	6	128	101
Technicians	656	17.2	9	125	108
Admin and commercial intermediary occupations of the firms	923	24.2	39	131	111
Intermediary professions of the civil service	277	7.2	47	126	102
Intermediary professions of health and social work	590	15.4	74	112	104
Primary school teachers and equivalent	759	20.0	63	119	110
Clergy	59	1.5	44	125	107
Total	3,814	100	40	125	107

Source: 'Haut comite d'education economie' (BIPE, 1987, Paris)

On leaving school, they have gone from one tenuous job to another before drifting into LTU status. As the structure of the economy becomes more services oriented, their labour market disadvantage is compounded. As a result of demographic changes, it is vital that the LTU are reintegrated into the labour market. There are at present a number of special measures targeted at the LTU [for details see reference 20]. But only sustained economic growth (and, by extension, improvement in labour productivity in services) can ease the plight of the LTU. On this argument, better training and utilisation of labour resources in service industries ultimately lie at the heart of the solution to the problem of the long term unemployed.

The final social factor relates to rising social aspirations. The proactive stance of the national education and training system is, to a certain extent, rooted in the rising educational aspirations of the population. As skills and know-how have emerged as vital resources in what is, after all, a highly open economy, society at large has come to place a growing value on education and training.

10.3 Factors influencing the content of training

Just as the factors influencing the scale of training have been largely over-shadowed by a proactive policy stance, much the same applies to factors influencing the content of training.

10.3.1 Education system: Targets and evaluation

On the face it, the national education and training policy attempts to achieve seemingly divergent objectives. But on closer inspection, the policy aims to achieve variety and complementarity in different areas. For example, the substantive thrust of the policy is to encourage a broad-based and general curriculum that precludes early subject specialisation in secondary schools. As we saw in the last section, subject generalism is viewed as providing a broad basis on which to base competency development in future. Yet when it comes to the system of professional maturity, some specialisation becomes inevitable. This is justified on the grounds that professional maturity is essentially targeted at preparation for the world of work rather than for further education.

Such differing emphasis is not a feature of inconsistency but a matter of satisfying the needs and aspirations of diverse groups of students. But in the final analysis, the content of training is fundamentally influenced by one or more of the following imperatives:

- Vocational preparation for those who do not wish to pursue post-school formal education. For example, 'professional maturity' prepares school leavers explicitly for the world of work.

- Basic high quality general education for those who wish to pursue further education. It is seen as vital for achieving three objectives: development of skills for effectiveness at work; development of a knowledge-base that enhances the overall competency levels; and development of attitudes that are favourably disposed to continuous learning and team work. Ultimately, the objective is to promote the development of competency which goes well beyond the notion of multiple or specialist skills, and centres on the issues of personal effectiveness at the work place.

- Opportunities for those who wish to have a change in career or occupation. This is already happening, for example, under the scheme called 'Ingenieurs et Cadres Superieurs'. It encourages technicians to become engineers through regular attendance at a well-defined conversion course. About 2,000 candidates are now covered by the course, half of whom are unemployed and the other half come from industry. Such conversion courses are being planned for other subject areas as well.

These three imperatives are underpinned by a centralised system of vocational training. The details are described in a document from Delegation a la Formation Professionelle [18]. Centralisation, however, does not detract from the fact that there are regional councils, trades union and employer bodies who are involved over a large area of policy implementation. There are periodic evaluations of programmes, mainly carried out by those directly involved in their implementation.

One of the most distinctive features of the education and training system is the role of social partners. The manufacturers' associations and labour unions play a vital role by conducting collective negotiations which culminate in:

- inter-professional agreements which guide the general training system

- industry-specific agreements on the goals of training. In 1987, there were more than 20 such agreements.

Management and unions collectively manage more that six billion FF for the purpose of providing vocational training.

In collaboration with central government, they contribute to the definition and adaptation of vocational training law. They also participate in drawing up training policy both at national and regional level. They participate in regional committees for vocational training, social advancement and employment.

Within companies, too, the unions have the facility to comment on company training plans. Finally, management and unions also participate in the administrative boards and advanced training councils of training organisations that are managed jointly. In these bodies, they contribute to the definition of training programmes, their objectives, and also to the awarding of certificates and diplomas in joint consultative committees (e.g. AFPA).

Overall, the corporate commitment to training is ensured by the legislative stipulation that companies with a minimum of ten employees must allocate at least 1.2 per cent of their wages bill to in-service training. In 1987, about 2.3 per cent was allocated for this purpose. This investment is targeted principally at training for effective use of new technologies and/or productivity improvement. Over and above the legal requirements, companies can also enter into agreements with the Government to obtain financial assistance from the National Employment Fund for in-service training.

10.3.2 Structural factors

The all-pervasive emphasis on training and retraining is but an overt recognition of the deep-seated changes occurring in the economy and society. It recognises that technological and economic changes have a two stage effect, as was discussed in Sub-section 8.2.4 (and Figure 8.1).

The first effect is felt at the direct point of impact where the changes are actually occurring. This is the point of maximum impact where new occupations are created and the established ones are weakened. For example, the rapid diffusion of new information technology has created many new occupations in those industries producing the associated hardware and software [19,20]. In this context, the state system of secondary and higher education is being geared increasingly towards meeting new occupational needs.

The second effect is felt elsewhere in the economy as a part of a knock-on or multiplier effect. For example, as the pace of work restructuring has accelerated, the intermediary occupations have become important because of the rising skills content of their work. As a result, training plays a pivotal role, partly because of its flexibility in catering for emerging skills requirements, be that due to technology or work restructuring; partly because of the significant involvement of social partners; partly because of the over-riding emphasis on local needs and circumstances; and partly because the system is innovative enough to experiment with new concepts such as open learning, computer-based training and national homologation of company-based training [18].

10.4   Summary

This chapter has attempted to identify the nature of factors that have influenced the scale and content of training in France in the past and those that will do so in the future. In the process, it has also looked at the role of the single market. The main points emerging from the chapter are as follows:

- There have been significant structural changes in the French labour market under the combined impact of the two world-wide recessions in 1973-4 and 1979-81. The nature of the economy has become more services-oriented, requiring higher levels of educational qualifications and skills. These changes will continue over the rest of this century, especially with the creation of the single market.

- It is against the background of prospective educational and skills needs that successive Governments in the last decade have adopted a highly proactive stance towards education and training. For example, ambitious targets have been set in the area of professional maturity in the system of secondary education; a system of homologation of company-based training has been established; and the concept of open learning is being promoted over a wide segment of society. The basic thrust of these actions is directed at achieving three objectives: an improvement in basic (secondary) education; promotion of love of learning in order to encourage life-time learning; and national recognition for company-based training.

- These three objectives overshadow many other factors influencing the scale and content of training. On the demand side, these include the creation of the single market and the need to promote productivity growth in services as a way of achieving higher economic growth. On the social side, they include the need to assist disadvantaged groups such as women returning to work after child-rearing, and the long-term unemployed. On the institutional side, they include the need to assist those who wish to change their career or occupation.

- Overall, although the policy actions are significant, prospective changes in the French economy will require additional stimulus to education and training efforts.

11

CASE STUDY 2: ITALY

11.1   Background

The information presented in this chapter is based on interviews with experts at two national research centres:

- Centro Studi Investmenti Sociali (CENSUS) — Rome

- Fondazione Agnelli — Turin

   The interviews were carried out against the background of key labour market trends evident over the past two decades, as outlined in Table 11.1. They show that since the mid-1960s:

- the size of the labour force has expanded by nearly 20 per cent;

- the underlying trend in employment is rising, irrespective of the cyclical improvement associated with economic recovery since 1982. The implication is that unemployment is becoming structural in nature in the sense that unemployed workers do not have the skills required by the changing structure of the economy;

- the share of self-employed in civilian employment has been declining, largely reflecting the contraction in employment in the agricultural sector. If anything, the number of self-employed workers in non-agricultural activity has been increasing;

- the share of women in total civilian employment has been increasing;

- the shares of agricultural and production industries in total civilian employment have been contracting. In other words, the economy is becoming more oriented towards services activities.

Table 11.1   Italy: Key labour market trends, 1965-86

(Absolute numbers in thousands; shares in percentages)

	1965	1978	1980	1986
A. Total labour force	20,836	21,233	22,553	23,851
Percentage shares of:				
a. Civilian employment	92	92	90	86
b. Armed Forces	2	2	2	3
c. Unemployed	6	6	8	11
B. Total civilian employment				
Percentage shares by status:				
a. Employees	63	71	71	70
b. Self-employed	37	29	29	30
Percentage shares by sex:				
a. Male	72	71	68	66
b. Female	28	29	32	34
Percentage shares by industry:				
a. Agriculture	25	17	14	11
b. Industry	36	39	38	33
c. Services	38	44	48	56

Source: 'Labour force statistics' (OECD, 1988 edition)

Alongside these labour market changes, some deep-seated educational developments are also discernible, as shown by Table 11.2. Two noteworthy points emerge from the table. First, the education level of the workforce has been increasing since 1977: there has been a substantial increase in the proportion of the labour force with secondary school and university degree qualifications. Secondly, unemployment has impacted disproportionately on those with none or minimum (elementary school) qualifications.

Overall, the identified labour market and educational trends are but the visible end of a number of major changes taking place in the Italian economy. The changes in question and their training implications are covered in the next section.

Table 11.2   Labour force by educational level: 1977-85

(percentages)

	School			University degree	Total
	Elementary	Middle	Secondary		
Labour force					
1977	55.9	26.1	13.7	4.3	100.0
1980	48.5	30.1	16.5	4.9	100.0
1985	37.0	35.6	21.4	6.0	100.0
Persons in employment					
1977	57.5	25.5	12.7	4.3	100.0
1980	50.2	29.4	15.5	4.9	100.0
1985	38.8	34.6	20.3	6.3	100.0
Persons in search of employment					
1977	35.5	34.1	26.4	4.0	100.0
1980	27.8	39.0	29.5	3.7	100.0
1985	21.9	44.1	30.7	3.2	100.0

Source: 'ISTAT, Labour force survey' (1987, Rome)

11.2 Factors influencing the scale of training

According to national experts, there is little doubt that the need for training has been increasing in this decade and will continue to do so in the next. Currently, there are a number of factors that are elevating the role of training. These need to be taken into account when assessing the country's training needs over the rest of this century. Although different in nature, the factors have one common feature: they call for a step-increase in:

- the number of students with senior secondary school and university degree qualifications; and

- the scale of enterprise-based training.

Although the factors cannot be readily quantified, the national experts felt that they were having a fundamental influence on the structure of work directly, and on the training needs indirectly. In sum, they were changing the content and form of work on a scale that gave rise to major education and training implications, both now and in the foreseeable future. The factors in question are discussed under the appropriate headings in the rest of this section.

11.2.1 Demand factors

There are three factors that are promoting a step-increase in the demand for training provision. They are:

- **Demographic changes:** key demographic changes have been given in Chapter 6. In the period 1975-85, the proportion of the Italian population in employment has increased by 6.3 per cent. Of this, according to the Eurostat statistics, 7.4 per cent of the increase was due to population increase and -1.1 per cent decrease was due to the contraction in employment opportunities. Most of the increase, in turn, has been due to the rising longevity rate: for example, the share of the age group 45-64 has increased from 22 per cent in 1975 to 24 per cent in 1985. By 1995, this figure will rise to 26 per cent [1]. This overall ageing will be accompanied by an increase in the share of female workers, as pointed out in the previous section. It also transpires that a significant proportion of these female workers will be married and returning to the labour market after having children. Thus the key growth component of the labour force will be older workers and those who have been away from the labour market. In the face of technological and industrial changes (see below), the emerging work groups will not have the skills required by the economy in the next decade.

- **Industrial, technological and occupational changes:** in Section 11.1, the trend towards service-based activities was noted. This is likely to continue into the next decade, albeit at a lower rate [2]. However, alongside the changing industrial structure, two tendencies have become evident and are likely to continue into the next decade. First, the new information and materials technologies will continue to be applied. As well as automating various processes, these will result in the redesigning of work such that individual workers will be increasingly performing multiple functions under one job, both in the production and services industries. This observation applies equally to vehicle manufacturing at one extreme and retail trades at the other. As a result, the skills content of intermediate and higher level occupations is increasing, and will continue to do so in the next decade. Yet these occupations are predominantly filled by those who either have junior secondary school qualifications (in the case of intermediate occupations which are mainly filled by mature adults) or graduates (in higher level occupations) who have had minimal on-the-job formal training. Accordingly, across the whole band of occupations covering intermediate and higher level skills, there is a 'training gap'. The rising qualifications content of the labour force, as shown in Table 11.2, is only a manifestation of the more elaborate training requirement across a large number of occupations that are growing in either qualitative or quantitative terms.

- **Single European market:** the prospect of an internal market in Europe will create new business opportunities, especially in customised products and services, as companies attempt to cater for the specific needs of different segments of customers in the expanded market. Under customisation, the role of know-how will increase because it is only through rapid adoption of the new know-how that companies can promote product differentiation. As a result, new demands will be made on the competences and skills of the work force, especially in light and heavy engineering industries and in business and financial services industries. These are, after all, the area where the Italian economy has a strong relative advantage at present.

11.2.2 Social factors

Demand factors have increasingly required growth in training provision because of the impact of on-going structural changes on the skills content of work. The same structural changes are generating new social pressures on training needs. These pressures are manifesting themselves through three developments:

- **Rising participation rate of women:** most of the increase in the number of women workers this decade is accounted for by married females returning to the labour market after child-rearing [3]. Such returners have one of two characteristics: low level of schooling in their formative years or exposure to skills obsolescence during their absence from the labour market. Most of the returners are engaged in less skilled tasks in retail distribution, banking, insurance, business services, tourism and recreational services. But under the combined impact of technology and new competitive pressures, work is being redesigned in these industries to the extent that returners are now requiring extensive retraining for which there is no formal provision at present in either the private or the public sector.

- **Rising social aspirations:** there is growing awareness in Italy about the role of education and training in achieving business success in the competitive 1990s. In this context, there is a strong consensus among most sociologists that family pressures on and encouragement to the younger generation are more intense than ever before. The importance of learning is now an essential part of social conditioning.

- **Growing problem of long-term unemployment:** in the last decade, this problem has worsened: the rate of long-term unemployment has persistently increased to the point that some 58 per cent of those out of work in 1987 had been seeking work for more than 12 months [4]. They are beginning to share the same characteristics as returners who have become increasingly disadvantaged in the face of rapid structural change. They are being assisted through a number of programmes such as Labour Mobility Fund, 'Fondo di Rotazionne', and early retirement. Although welcome, these programmes are extremely modest in relation to the size of the problem [5]. However, in the face of impending demographic contraction in the 1990s, there is an urgent need to consider more ambitious programmes, if the Italian economy is to sustain its economic growth.

All the social partners are aware of the fundamental changes taking place in the structure of the economy and the labour market. Indeed, employers and trade unions have been involved in the conception and administration of vocational training at the regional level. But their role in this context has, so far, been rather modest — more consultative than participative. The power and influence of central government is all too pervasive now and will continue to remain so in future. Among the employer and trade union groups, there is a strong body of opinion that over the next decade, the importance of enterprise-based training will increase. As a result, there is an urgent need to define and develop the interface between the state education system and the enterprise-based system. This observation applies particularly to engineering and vehicle production industries where the role of enterprise-based training is becoming crucial.

11.2.3 Supply factors

The demand factors outlined above have already given rise to skills shortages. In the meantime, the education system has seen a rapid expansion as expressed by the number of schools, classes and the number of students (see Table 11.3). Alongside this expansion have come two developments.

First, there has been a rapid growth in the vocational training provision from regional authorities, working in collaboration with private companies. The popularity of local provision is growing because of the involvement of private companies. However, there is a serious risk that spontaneous growth in local provision may become unstructured. Furthermore, it also carries the risk of displacing the national system.

Second, the growth in private and public provision of education is long over-due in relation to the speed of structural changes in the Italian economy. However, this growth is occurring in response to needs that are felt currently rather than in anticipation of the labour market developments in future. The relative lack of proactivity in this context is due to the fact that no detailed analysis of future skill needs of the economy is available.

As a result, three tendencies are evident. First, in many services industries, (especially financial and tourism), jobs have become deskilled by new technologies. Yet many qualified people continue to hold these jobs. To a certain extent, this is also due to the adverse impact of the 1979-81 recession on the labour market. Against the background of rising unemployment,

Table 11.3:   Synopsis of the evolution of the school system

School year	Schools	Classes	Total students
Junior secondary school			
1952-53	3,374	32,044	963,926
1962-63	8,563	53,927	1,595,111
1972-73	9,437	110,557	2,421,799
1982-83	10,064	133,141	2,849,898
1983-84	10,050	132,038	2,815,922
1984-85	10,039	131,192	2,797,766
1985-86	10,033	129,980	2,764,535
Senior secondary school			
1952-53	2,533	19,449	460,003
1962-63	4,490	36,269	929,033
1982-83	7,516	105,576	2,470,036
1983-84	7,546	106,015	2,508,800
1984-85	7,552	108,890	2,546,772
1985-86	7,564	112,876	2,607,749

Source: CENSIS processings of Italian education ministry data

employers have preferred to recruit more qualified candidates, irrespective of the needs of the job. At the higher end of the occupational spectrum, technology has promoted job loading such that individual workers are expected to perform multiple functions under one job. Yet the same individuals have not had the appropriate training. Consequently, across the occupational spectrum there are pockets of over-qualified and under-qualified workers existing simultaneously, indicating mis-allocation of valuable human resources. There is considerable scope for the restructuring of work in order to achieve a better match between qualifications and work. In this context, a significant start has been made in the engineering and vehicle manufacturing industries. Under the competitive pressures released by the single market, this process will undoubtedly hasten.

Secondly, in many manufacturing industries, employers increasingly recruit those with senior secondary school qualifications in preference to graduates. The underlying objective is to avoid the unnecessary recruitment of over-qualified individuals. However, such qualification holders then do not receive the 'add-on' training in the enterprises that is necessary to upgrade their skills in preparation for structural changes. This is largely because these changes are not anticipated and planned for.

Finally, there is growing mobility between occupations. Skills shortages compounded by relative lack of in-house training have increasingly enabled workers to move up the occupational ladder. The phenomenon applies mainly to intermediate level occupations—such as multi-skilled craftworkers and clerical employees—where occupational demarcations are weakening. It owes more to the relative tightness of the labour markets for these occupations and less to organic growth in their skills base.

11.2.4   Policy factors

As far as vocational training is concerned, there are two key policy issues worthy of mention:

- **Funding:** this is far from adequate as can be seen in Table 11.4. Even discounting the fact that the youth training measures incorporate an element of unemployment subsidy, the programme investment is viewed as small in relation to the emerging size of the skills gap, according to the national experts.

- **Over-supply of teachers:** as a result of the demographic contraction, there will be a significant contraction in the number of school leavers, as shown in Table 11.5.

The implication is that there could be a consequent surplus of some 800,000 teachers. It has been proposed that the present complement should be retained with a corresponding improvement in the teacher-pupil ratio. But there remains the significant task of retraining teachers in order to secure the targeted improvement in the quality of teaching. Additionally, the trainers in the regional programmes need to be retrained, too. In either case, there is no clear vehicle for upgrading the skills of teachers and trainers. Accordingly, the most critical

Table 11.4　Investment in training programmes: 1985-87

		1985 billion lira	1987 billion lira	per cent of GDP in 1987
a.	**Labour market training for adults of which:**	459	139	0.01
	Labour Mobility Fund	164	67	
	Fondo di Rotazionne	272	-	
	Other	23	72	
b.	**Youth measures of which:**	2,452	2,823	0.35
	Employment training contracts	800	1,000	
	Vocational training run by regions	857	870	
	Training funded by European Social Fund	795	953	

Source: 'Employment Outlook' (OECD, Paris, 1988)

problem for public policy is one of acquainting teachers and trainers with the skills changes in different occupations and ensuring that they have the competences to promote the development of the requisite skills among the trainees. The root cause of the problem is a lack of reliable information on the nature and scale of current and future skills gaps. This hinders planning in the state sector. But that is not all: it also hinders the development of greater complementarity between the state education system and the enterprise-based training system, which will become increasingly vital after 1992.

Table 11.5   Demographic impact on school leaver population

	Change in the number of leavers in the period 1985-2000
Primary School	- 485,668
Junior Secondary School	- 813,924
Senior Secondary School : if present trends continue : if there is levelling off in future : if there is compulsory education up to 16 years of age	- 654,040 - 724,329 - 295,478

Source: 'Italy Today—Social Picture and Trends' (CENSIS, Rome, 1986)

11.3 Factors influencing the content of training

In our discussions with the national experts, it emerged that the factors influencing the scale of training also had a major impact on the content of training. Thus the analysis of the previous section equally applies here. However, some additional ideas and insights also emerged from discussions with the national experts. These are reported in this section under appropriate headings.

11.3.1 Structural factors: Target and evaluation issues

A notable development in this decade has been the growing importance of regions in the organisation and delivery of training. The predominance of manufacturing industries in the northern half and of service activities in the southern half of the country is duly reflected in the regionally-provided training. In both cases, training provision is targeted at developing basic technical competences and a defined set of 'add-on' skills that permit the performance of multiple functions under one job. For example, engineering workers with one basic area of specialisation now also receive training in the allied mechanical, hydraulic, electrical and electronic trades.

To a certain extent, such multi-skills training is also a reflection of the application of new information and materials technologies which are creating possibilities for work redesign that permit the performance of multiple functions under one job. Indeed, this form of restructuring has far more impact on skills requirements in relation to the emergence of new occupations in, for example, the area of information technology. The education and training systems are beginning to fathom this fact. But its translation into effective training solutions has yet to become apparent. As always, there are exceptions. For example, the Fiat Car Company already has elaborate training programmes that are firmly based on current and future skills needs. But in an economy with a high incidence of self-employed and small firms, multi-skilled training still remains a highly localised and large company phenomenon.

Indeed, over the next decade, the critical training problems will arise not so much in relation to new occupations but to existing long-established occupations which are undergoing dramatic changes in their functional and skills contents.

This much is clear from results of the 1981 Census of Population [see reference 2]. This observation applies equally to many of the traditional occupations in manufacturing and services alike.

This development raises two issues. First, it implies that the knowledge or know-how component of work over a large segment of the workforce is increasing. In other words, an increasing proportion of people in employment can be classified as knowledge workers. The single market will, if anything, reinforce this trend because of its heavy emphasis on product customisation. Thus, this decade will witness an increasing proportion of knowledge workers who will need the type of training that can promote three objectives: skills development for effectiveness in their current jobs; professional development in preparation for the next job; and attitude development for facilitating the job rotation and teamwork that is vital for the effective performance of multi-functional jobs. In future, the content of vocational training will need to have all these three elements. Also, the training in question will have to come from multiple sources because it would be impossible for one source to meet all three imperatives.

The second issue relating to the expanding skills content of work concerns long-term unemployed (LTU) people. As knowledge emerges as a prime resource in future, this group will be even more disadvantaged. This is because its reintegration into the labour market will mean having exposure to all three elements referred to in the previous paragraph. According to the national experts, so far no *ex post* evaluations have been done on the effectiveness of the various training measures. Furthermore, in their view, the measures currently attempt to equip the LTU workers with no more than the most basic skills. As a result, unless new initiatives are forthcoming, LTU will remain a permanent feature of the Italian economic landscape.

11.3.2   Education and training system

The trend towards multi-skilling is most evident in the vocational training provided by the regions and individual enterprises. This is manifested by a more structured approach with varying emphasis on the three elements identified under the previous sub-heading. An analogue of this development is the inclusion of general education subjects in training programmes. These include numeracy, linguistic fluency and basic science subjects. The underlying objective is to widen the knowledge base of trainees and thereby facilitate the subsequent teaching of more specialised techniques, procedures or ideas.

That said, it would be a gross exaggeration to say that the teaching of general subjects constitutes an important element of vocational training: it does not. If anything, until recently even the senior secondary schools appeared to focus on narrow specialisms as far as technical teaching was concerned. This was done in the mistaken belief that the depth rather than breadth of the knowledge base mattered most. There is a gradual move away from this tendency. Again, its pace is held back by a lack of clear strategy on the upgrading of the competences of trainers and teachers. But there is no doubt that generalism is featuring in education and training courses under the sheer weight of structural changes. It has another useful spin-off: it is promoting the recognition of vocational training—irrespective of its source—on a national basis. Many companies now provide training that has national recognition. As a result, a clear trend has been established towards the weakening of occupational boundaries and greater inter-occupational mobility across significant segments of manufacturing and service industries. As a result, and over time, Italy will witness greater mobility within its own labour market first, before experiencing Community-wide mobility.

11.4 Summary

This chapter has attempted to identify the nature of factors that have influenced the scale and content of training in Italy in the recent past, and those that are likely to do so in the future. It has also looked at the role of the single market. The main points emerging from the chapter are as follows:

- There are a number of demand and social factors that are promoting the importance of training and retraining. The demographic contraction and the single market will reinforce the ascendancy of these factors in the 1990s.

- On the supply-side, public policy is responding but its achievements so far fall short of requirements. Not only is the current funding level inadequate in relation to emerging needs, but there is also less coherence in public policy in three areas: training of trainers and teachers; advance planning in anticipation of the emerging skills needs; and the interface between the state-run vocational education and the enterprise-based training.

- In future, the main influence on training will be the increasing need for multiple-skills due to the restructuring of work, thereby elevating the role of know-how as the prime resource in the creation of customised products or services.

- The proportion of knowledge workers will rise. This trend will require a more comprehensive approach to training, with multiple strands, with each strand directed towards the development of specific types of competences. The approach will require an improved interface between state-provided training and enterprise-provided training. It will also require better evaluative mechanisms.

- In both these contexts, the current education and training systems fall well short of requirements. To make matters worse, they hardly meet the minimum needs of today's long-term unemployed people, let alone the multi-skilled workers of tomorrow. Indeed, disadvantaged groups will be even more disadvantaged in future, unless new measures are introduced to assist them.

12

CASE STUDY 3: UNITED KINGDOM

12.1 Introduction

The information presented in this chapter was derived from interviews held with the following organisations in the UK:

- Training Agency

- Banking, Insurance and Finance Union

- Business and Technician Education Council

- Construction Industry Training Board

- National Council for Vocational Qualifications

- Union of Shop, Distributive And Allied Workers

The interviews relied on the question set given in Appendix A. They were conducted against the background of four critical longer term trends in the UK labour market as shown in Table 12.1:

- a firm upward underlying trend in the rate of unemployment which has begun to ease noticeably since 1987

- a firm upward underlying trend in the share of self-employment

- a rising share of female workers, particularly married women holding part-time jobs

- a substantial shift in the structure of employment from manufacturing to services.

Table 12.1   United Kingdom: Key labour market trends, 1965-86

(Absolute numbers in thousands; shares in percentages)

	1965	1978	1980	1986
A. Total labour force	25,632	26,357	26,840	27,771
Percentage shares of:				
a. Civilian employment	97	94	93	87
b. Armed Forces	2	1	1	1
c. Unemployed	1	5	6	12
B. Total civilian employment				
Percentage shares by status:				
a. Employees	93	92	92	89
b. Self-employed	7	8	8	11
Percentage shares by sex:				
a. Male	65	60	60	57
b. Female	35	40	40	43
Percentage shares by industry:				
a. Agriculture	4	3	3	2
b. Industry	46	39	38	31
c. Services	50	58	59	67

Source: 'Labour force statistics' (OECD, 1988 edition)

These structural changes constitute only one aspect of change in the labour market. The other, equally significant, relates to the occupational background of civilian employment, as given in Table 12.2.

Table 12.2 Occupational change: 1971-90

Occupation	1971 level	1995 level	Change (% p.a.) 87-95
Corporate managers and administrators	1347	2086	1.66
Manager/proprietors: services & agric.	1197	1448	1.10
Science and engineering professionals	374	774	2.43
Health professionals	98	177	2.72
Educational professionals	738	1148	1.49
Other professionals	287	647	2.23
Science & eng. associated professionals	580	806	1.72
Health associated professionals	416	719	2.48
Other associated professionals	427	906	2.48
Clerical occupations	3285	3454	0.75
Secretarial occupations	989	1211	0.67
Skilled engineering trades	1442	1101	0.23
Skilled construction trades	581	678	1.85
Other skilled trades	2599	2110	0.49
Protective service occupations	280	354	0.77
Personal service occupations	1162	1602	1.26
Sales occupations	1618	2106	0.24
Drivers and mobile machine operators	1236	859	-0.41
Other operatives	2411	1628	-0.37
Other occupations in agriculture	297	190	-1.50
Other occupations (exc. agriculture)	2792	2376	-0.15
All occupations	24165	26379	0.84

Source: 'Review of the economy and employment, 1988/9 Volume 1' (Institute of employment research, 1989)

175

It shows that the occupational structure is becoming electric light bulb-shaped in that:

- the higher level services-oriented white collar occupations are expanding creating a growth in the number of knowledge workers performing know-how intensive jobs

- the lower level manufacturing-oriented blue collar occupations are contracting.

In sum, these changes are indicative of the growing tertiarisation of the economy. Under it, new jobs have been created in marketed services partly due to the externalisation of services previously performed in-house (e.g. catering, contract cleaning and business services); and partly due to organic growth [1]. A majority of these new jobs are part-time and held by married women [2]. According to the latest forecasts, these trends will continue into the 1990s [3].

12.2 Factors influencing the scale of training

In order to understand the nature of the forces that influence the scale of training now and over the next decade, one has to examine the longer term changes in the country's industrial structure. Since the early 1960s, the relative competitiveness of manufacturing industry had started to decline for a number of reasons. The first 'oil shock' of 1973 ushered in a severe recession under which domestic productive capacity could not withstand the new competitive pressures. As a result, some 500,000 jobs were shed. In the ensuing economic recovery, which lasted over the period 1975-8, a number of macro economic and labour market measures were introduced to halt the decline in manufacturing employment. However, before they could take full effect, the second 'oil shock' occurred in 1979, once again exposing the relative weakness of the country's manufacturing base. By 1981, over a million jobs (15 per cent) were shed, making the UK one of the countries most severely affected by the world-wide recession of 1979-81.

With the worst of the recession over, and with a free-market Conservative Government in power, the central thrust of labour market policy began to change—from influencing the demand for jobs towards improving the quality of labour supply. The underlying idea was that in the 1980s skills would become the cutting edge of business competition and only a qualitative improvement would reverse the problem of manufacturing competitiveness in the longer-term. In 1981, the National Training Initiative (NTI) was launched against this background and also in the belief that there was a strong training gap which had to be filled over the rest of the decade.

Implicit in the NTI is the so-called market failure argument. It posits that employers should provide their own training solutions as far as possible. After all, so the argument runs, having a better trained workforce is in the employer's own economic interests. However, there may be circumstances in which the free functioning of the market will not necessarily generate training for certain disadvantaged groups of individuals, such as unqualified school leavers or the long-term unemployed. In such cases, the state will accept responsibility for training them. This argument is not explicitly stated in the NTI but its essential thrust is easy to discern in the now all too frequent Governmental exhortations to companies to provide greater in-house training provision.

The logic of this position is clear. Dictated by technology, deregulation, gathering competition and product diversification, the pace of change in the UK economy is so rapid that individual employers are best placed to identify the repertoire of skills they need and to supply them by in-house training as far as possible. The national institutions of education and training can provide only the basic elements. In a dynamic environment, these need to be topped up by skills that are specific to individual employers' products, work processes, technology, markets and customers. Furthermore, the process of topping-up should be structured and systematic in order that the resulting competences should have national recognition.

Thus the central thrust of policy on education and training is clear. It is to:

- improve the quality of basic (primary and secondary school) education which is seen fundamentally as the responsibility of the state

- encourage employers to provide their own training needs as far as possible and in the light of their own business, market and technological circumstances

- promote national recognition of the competences developed through enterprise-based training

- have special state provision of training for those who are unlikely to be helped by employer-based training.

Over time, there have been a series of publicly-funded training measures in order to implement the NTI. Conspicuous among them have been:

- Youth Training Scheme (YTS)

- Technical and Vocational Education Initiative (TVEI)

- Adult Training for Employed, Self Employed and Unemployed People

- Employment Training for the Long-Term Unemployed (ET).

The details of these and other training programmes are given elsewhere [4]. They need not concern us here. The substantive point is that as in France, so in the UK: the factors influencing scale and content of training are over-shadowed by macro-economic imperatives which have substantially conditioned the policy response. Some factors have indeed influenced policy; others have, in fact, been influenced by it. In the final analysis, it is difficult to be explicit about these factors and virtually impossible to evaluate their relative importance. It is with this caveat in mind that we present below the information from the interviews with the national experts. The presentational format corresponds with the question set given in Appendix A.

12.2.1   Demand factors

The demographic trends are outlined in detail by *Eurostat*[10] and summarised in Chapters 6 and 13. They point to three critical developments over the rest of this century:

- the number of school leavers will contract by about a third in the period 1985-95

- the population structure will age

- women will comprise the largest component of growth in the civilian labour force to 1995.

Over the same period, the skills and knowledge component of work is likely to increase, as we saw in Table 12.2. The UK economy is already now in the midst of a severe shortage of staff in know-how based occupations. The shortages are likely to worsen partly owing to the continuing trend towards tertiarisation, and partly owing to the single market which, as we saw in the previous two chapters, will promote greater customisation of products and services that are skills-intensive in nature.

It is therefore clear that demand-side forces will promote skills-intensity at a time when supply-side forces will promote the emergence of worker groups who have not had adequate training in the past (older workers); or those exposed to skills obsolescence during enforced absence from the labour market (married women). The emerging mismatches are likely to worsen for three reasons relating to the development of the necessary know-how that the economy will increasingly demand over time.

The first of these concern the system of education. Among the Western industrialised countries, the UK has the lowest proportion of the 15-19 age group staying on in post-compulsory education, a fact we shall consider in Chapter 16. Its participation rate in higher education involving those in the age group 20-24 is correspondingly low. The details are given in a recent OECD report [6]. This low participation rate combined with the demography-led decline in the number of students in the two younger age groups will deprive the economy in the sense that there will be fewer workers with the potential to become knowledge workers around the turn of the century.

Second, the basic knowledge-base of the economy will not be wide enough to promote the necessary topping-up of skills that is needed within individual enterprises if they are to compete successfully in the 1990s. This is because to convert an educated worker into a knowledge worker a number of skills have to be added to basic formal qualifications [7]. This problem has been recognised by the Department of Education and Science [8]. A revised curriculum is being introduced for pupils of compulsory school age under the Education Reform Act 1988. Its object is to enable pupils to acquire the basic theoretical as well as practical skills. That way, some pupils will receive significant vocational preparation at school. Others can acquire a broad base on which to develop 'add-on' skills after a period of further studies [9].

Finally, currently there are no major programmes—either in the public or private sector—specifically addressing the needs of the two groups: women returning to work after child-bearing, and knowledge workers (but see below). The problem of returners is a significant one: they are neither vocationally nor experientially prepared for the growth occupations. As for knowledge workers, the numerical and knowledge-based problems have already been cited above. Beyond that, they require significant training towards the formation of attitudes that are favourable to life-time learning and team-work as we saw in the two previous chapters. Unless they undergo a continuous process of self-enlightenment and successful social interaction with their peers, the knowledge-base will not necessarily be augmented at the desired rate. More worrying still, there do not appear to be any training efforts directed at the economic effects of the single market. Doubtless, this will change as we approach 1992.

12.2.2 Supply factors

The Government's main vocational training programme for the long-term unemployed, i.e. those people registered unemployed for more than six months, is Employment Training. ET provides up to 12 months' directed and practical training based on a personal assessment of the individual's needs. The programme acknowledges the problems and needs of disadvantaged groups in three respects.

First, the use of personal assessment is of particular benefit to disadvantaged groups as it means that special training needs (e.g. basic literacy/numeracy, provision for people with disabilities) are identified and addressed within the trainee's overall training package.

Second, to enable the identified special needs to be met, organisations delivering ET have access to supplementary grants of up to £20 per week per person, in addition to the basic training fee, to help meet the cost of special training. Disadvantaged trainees can also make use of an 'extended introduction' option which provides them with a more gradual entry into the training regime.

Third, there are modifications to the normal six month unemployment eligibility condition to ease entry to the programme for certain disadvantaged groups; e.g. people requiring help with English as a second language, ex-offenders, people returning to the labour market following family commitments, and lone parents. Lone parents may also receive help towards the cost of childcare.

So much for ET. We now turn to other supply related issues, covered in the question set in Appendix A. As far as the supply of teachers and trainers is concerned, there are significant shortages of teachers in science and maths subjects. These are being remedied. But the more significant problem relates to trainers. As the focus of training is shifting to companies, there is no corresponding increase in the number and quality of in-house trainers. The notions of 'knowledge workers' and 'add-on' skills have yet to permeate the corporate community, especially at a time when the influence of trade unions has progressively diminished through gradual exclusion from participation in various public bodies.

12.2.3 Social factors

There is little doubt that social expectations are giving rise to an increasing demand for higher levels of education and training among parents and young people in general. The rise in the numbers of school leavers gaining accepted school leaving qualifications, and in the numbers of girls gaining such qualifications in the last 20 years, is testimony to this. There has also been a steady increase in the UK in the numbers gaining higher degrees, and also in the proportion of women gaining higher degrees. However, there are local variations in the staying-on rates and the rates of pupils proceeding to further and higher education. Also, the differences between socio-economic groups remain pervasive.

Looking at training, since 1983 well over 2 million young people have been trained through YTS, over 1 million of them since the scheme became a two-year programme in 1986. In September 1988, there were about 435,500 young people in training on YTS and the latest figures show that 74 per cent of young people leaving YTS go into jobs or take up further education or training. There is now a commitment to offer every young person leaving full-time education who cannot find a job a YTS place. However, the scheme needs to build on its success to ensure that, in future, there is more emphasis on qualifications and employers taking on a fuller share of the costs of the scheme.

As far as women are concerned, since the 1960s their economic activity rate has risen steadily and is predicted to rise over this decade. A high female activity rate in the UK goes hand in hand with very high comparative levels of part-time employment and a large tertiary sector. This increasing activity rate does not necessarily result from changing social values (although it may contribute). The causes are diverse and relate more to changes in the occupational structure, particularly the development of service sector work in the UK.

Activity rates are already high, especially in the South East of the country, and employers are increasingly competing for women returners. A number of employers are introducing recruitment and retention schemes. A further issue concerns adequate deployment of the skills that women have. Women still cluster in the lower level occupations and employers are often still reluctant to provide a full range of training and career opportunities to women, especially those working part-time. Occupational segregation by gender continues to create labour market rigidities and to reduce the pool of talent from which employers can recruit and promote employees.

12.2.4 Policy factors

Skills shortages in the UK are currently monitored in an annual Skills Survey of Manufacturing Industry, jointly sponsored by the Training Agency (TA) and the Confederation of British Industries, the main employers' body. There have been five surveys to date. The survey asks employers about the occupations in shortage, what action they are taking to overcome those shortages and what they anticipate in the future.

An employers' skills and manpower practices study, extending the coverage to all main industry sectors, is currently being developed through a survey by the TA. This in-depth survey aims to look at the issues behind employers' manpower and skills needs, their perceptions of skill shortages, the problems they experience and how they deal with them.

Other organisations outside Government also conduct surveys of their members which include questions on skill shortages.

As far as overall training strategy is concerned, this was first set out in the National Training Initiative. It has been restated in the recently published White Paper 'Employment in the 1990s'. The strategy for higher level training was set out in 'Higher Education: Meeting the Challenge'. The key objectives are:

- To set up a National Training Task Force to assist the Secretary of State for Employment to develop new local training arrangements and to promote greater investment by employers in the skills of the workforce.

- To invite local employer-led groups to establish a national network of Training and Enterprise Councils (TECs) to plan and deliver training and promote the development of small businesses at the local level.

- To launch the Business Growth Through Training programme to help companies develop a training strategy to meet their business objectives.

- To begin consultations with statutory Industrial Training Boards and employers' representatives to draw up a timetable to ensure they become independent non-statutory bodies.

The principles underlying these objectives are:

- That training advice for small firms must be seen to contribute to business success and economic growth.

- That employers and individuals must accept a greater share of responsibility for training, although government has a role in setting a framework for funding the training of unemployed people.

- That there must be nationally recognised standards of competence, administered through the establishment of the National Council for Vocational Qualifications.

- That delivery of training and enterprise must be developed in local areas bringing together public and private investment.

- That arrangements for training must be flexible to meet the needs of individuals and local communities.

12.3　Factors influencing the content of training

12.3.1　Structural factors

In the UK, standards for government funded training are set out nationally but local variations are very significant. The TA has a regional and local network with 57 local area offices. Area offices are able to adjust national standards to meet local needs such as the skills mix of the local industrial and occupational structure.

The new system of TECs (Training and Enterprise Councils) will take the local accountability of national training schemes even further. TECs will be even more 'local' in their coverage — one hundred TECs are envisaged — and at least two-thirds of TEC members will be employed at top management level drawn from the private sector. No trade union representation is envisaged. The TECs will tailor national programmes to suit area needs and to achieve agreed performance outcomes.

Turning now to the new technologies, the TA monitors and funds research on relevant aspects of the impact of new technologies and new materials on future labour markets. Information is provided for regions and areas on such developments via a publication called the *National Labour Market and Skills Assessment*, which is issued annually to inform planning for training. Policy branches are kept informed of developments. Through the special programme within ET and through other means outlined above, training is provided in emerging skill areas.

In addition, the TA has a dissemination role in terms of the training implications of technological change through national and local level. The TA works closely with the Department of Trade and Industry (DTI) in this area. However, employers are obviously best placed to provide relevant training in new technologies. In particular, suppliers of equipment and materials are an important source of such training. Increasingly employers in the UK are becoming aware that investing in new technology will not provide competitive advantage unless it is accompanied by other changes in working practices which importantly include training.

The training provided in small firms is currently of particular concern to the UK Government. The DTI's Enterprise Initiative provides help to small and medium size enterprises in the form of assisted consultancy for the development of key management skills and the Employment Department provides counselling and training for small firms. The fact that advice on training is to become a more important element in future is reflected in the move of the small firms counselling service to the TA. As noted above, a new initiative, called Business Growth Through Training, started in 1989, aims to target information and help with training issues more specifically in small and medium size enterprises.

As far as unemployed people are concerned, ET is a major new initiative to train them in the skills they need for work. The initiative started in September 1988. By March 1989, 150,000 people were in training on the programme. People who want to join the programme are referred first to a Training Agent who provides assessment, counselling and guidance and agrees an individual action plan. The aim is to equip unemployed people, especially those out of work for six months or more, with relevant skills. People with disabilities, returners to the labour market, people whose first language is not English and ex-offenders can enter the programme without having been registered unemployed for six months. It offers training at all levels.

12.3.2 Evaluation factors

Each of the Government-sponsored programmes is periodically evaluated. The evaluations are not usually published, but the results are always used to refine the programmes concerned. The more intractable problem, however, relates to company-based training. An overwhelming majority of companies do not evaluate their in-house programmes. Worse still, many treat training as a stand-alone phenomenon with no clear interface with business plans or objectives. At a time when companies are expected to undertake greater responsibility for training and development, these practices are a major cause for concern.

In 1986, there were about 300 bodies awarding vocational qualifications, a situation which gave rise to confusion, overlap and unnecessary restriction on entry to some occupations. The National Council for Vocational Qualifications (NCVQ) was set up by the Government in April 1985 to design and implement a new national framework of vocational qualifications, setting standards of occupational competence and ensuring that vocational qualifications are based upon them. Initially this task has been carried out within a four-level framework incorporating qualifications up to Higher National awards and their equivalents, although the NCVQ is investigating how professional awards could be fitted into an enlarged framework.

One problem with the exercise has been that standards of occupational competence have been seen in rather narrow vocational and job specific terms; issues of knowledge and understanding as elements of competence have been overlooked. The NCVQ is currently considering introducing a component which covers these issues, as well.

12.4   Summary

This chapter has attempted to identify the nature of factors that have influenced the scale and content of training in the UK in the recent past and those that are likely to do so in the future. The main points emerging from it are as follows:

- The employment structure of the UK economy is being dominated by service industries. Under it, the occupational structure has been changing in favour of white collar jobs at the expense of manufacturing-based blue collar jobs, leading to a significant growth in intermediate and higher level occupations. There has also been a pronounced increase in self employment and female employment, involving part-time work. All these trends are also expected to continue into the next decade.

- Collectively, they have elevated the importance of training. But more fundamentally training has become the focal point of labour market policy as a part of a major switch in government policy — from demand-side job-creation to supply-side improvements in the quality of skills of the workforce.

- Under the new policy stance, more responsibility for vocational training is being put on employers, through the creation of Training and Enterprise Councils. The role of the state is viewed as intervening in those areas where the private provision of training may not materialise. As far as compulsory education is concerned, the role of the state is viewed as promoting improvement in basic education and higher staying-on rates in the post-compulsory sector. In all these respects, the enabling mechanisms have gradually been put into place only since 1983. As a result, it is difficult to assess the impact.

- The policy initiatives have been many and varied. On the one hand, they show awareness of various critical factors influencing the scale and content of training. On the other hand, they have a clear entity of their own under the free-market philosophy.

13

NEW CHALLENGES TO EDUCATION AND TRAINING POLICIES

13.1 An overview

The previous four chapters have highlighted the nature and, in some cases, the magnitude of forces that are currently impinging on education and training systems in the member states. Two over-riding messages emerge from them. First, a training gap has emerged in the Community under the combined weight of demographic, social, economic and technological developments. Second, this gap will, if anything, persist and widen over time. The rationale underlying the analysis so far had made some allowance for the single market, but not much because the underlying assessment has been based substantially on the structural changes that have occurred since the early 1970s.

This chapter now turns its attention to the single market and it analyses the challenges arising from it. It has two objectives: to identify and describe those challenges; and to provide a backcloth against which various critical actions can be devised in Part D. Such a backcloth is essential if, in response to the fresh round of structural changes, individual member states are to devise appropriate responses in a way that serves to minimise the potential social and economic hardships that are likely to arise in the immediate aftermath of the single market.

The completion of the single market will, if anything, intensify pressures on education and training systems because of its emphasis on customisation of products and services. In the age of growing customisation, a training gap could have severe adverse consequences because it would fail to augment the know-how and skills base which is so vital for generating new products and services, as we saw in Chapters 3 and 4. At the level of individual firms or regions, it can be the main source of business uncompetitiveness directly, and unemployment indirectly. At the level of the Community, it can be the main source of unbalanced economic development directly and relative international decline indirectly. In sum, the gap could be an expensive luxury for individual firms in the 1990s, just when competitive pressures will almost certainly intensify, because medium-term macro economic gains from the single market are likely to be rather modest whilst major industrial restructuring is in progress. For the Community, the gap could well nullify attempts to create a new industrial dynamism which can enhance its economic strength *vis-a-vis* Japan and the USA. Clearly, major new challenges have to be faced if the single market is to live up to its promise.

The nature and scale of such challenges clearly depend upon the extent to which the quality and quantity of existing education and training systems will fall short of the emerging requirements of the single market. The size of the prospective shortfall is difficult to quantify at this stage because it requires a more detailed evaluation of the skills needs of each member state for the rest of this century. This has yet to be attempted by any organisation or individual. However, a modest attempt in the previous six chapters has shown that demand for vocational education and training will grow across a large area of the Community. When projected growth is examined against the background of existing education and training policies (as described in references 1, 2, 3 and 4), two points emerge as noteworthy:

- *Improvement:* there is a need for a step-increase in the quality of basic school education, both in terms of promoting a higher participation rate and developing a more secure base for life-time learning.

- *Public-private sector collaboration:* there is a need for developing greater collaboration between national systems of education and training on the one hand, and the system of company-based training on the other. In countries such as Denmark, the Netherlands, the UK and West Germany, this is already happening. But even these impressive examples fall well short of the requirements dictated by the developments identified in the previous four chapters. Unless significant moves are made across the whole Community the economic effects of the single market will be noticed only through declining competitiveness and rising unemployment.

Seeking and securing greater complementarity between macro and micro systems is the biggest challenge generated by the single market, in terms of education and training. This is because the issue here is not just one of establishing formal institutional links between them, but it is also one of creating an overall framework that is at once:

- *comprehensive,* in terms of coverage of all the necessary strands of education and training

- *responsive,* in terms of constant adaptability to on-going structural changes and their disproportionate impact on various worker groups, industries and regions

- *motivative,* in terms of encouraging individuals to engage in the process of life-time learning that is vital in the management of industrial restructuring

- *integrative,* in terms of bringing together all providers of education and training in a way that clearly identifies their roles on the one hand and establishes a complementarity on the other.

The construction of this framework is a difficult task, fraught with numerous problems, some of which are objective in nature and others normative. There are numerous issues that need to be debated, discussed, researched and evaluated. It is difficult to list them all here, but as a way of initiating the debate, it is possible to start with five sets of issues which are deemed vital in the construction of the framework. At the very least, they serve to identify the nature of the forces that need to be accommodated because they are currently putting strains on existing systems of education and training in the member states.

These sets are summarised in Figure 13.1 over the page where the outer ring identifies each set and emphasises the links between all of them. The inner ring lists the issues which need to be tackled if the Community is to have an education and training framework that meets the four imperatives, as spelt out above. Each of the sets is considered separately in the rest of this chapter, starting with structural changes and then moving clock-wise.

Figure 13.1   Challenges to education and training policies

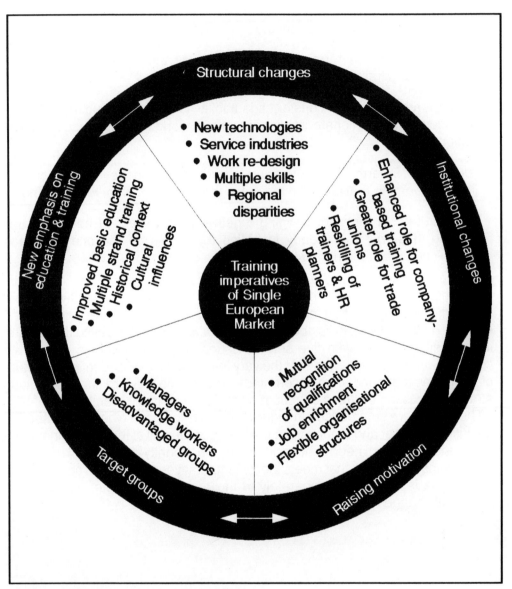

Source: CREATE Research Programme

13.2 Structural changes

There are five factors here which present challenges:

- **New technologies:** the challenges emanating from new technologies are three-fold. First, they are automating a number of tasks previously performed by semi-skilled employees, whose skills are no longer suited to the emerging needs of the economies of the member states. As a result, they drift from one job to another before becoming long-term unemployed. Thus the initial challenge here is how to devise special re-training programmes for those whose jobs have been displaced. Until 1987, there was a major gap in this area [5]. Although, new initiatives have been mounted in countries such as France, Spain and Greece, the gap remains. The second challenge comes from the new high-tech service industries based on the new technologies [6]. They promote the need for skills which the conventional education system does not provide either in sufficient quality or quantity. As a result, their growth has resulted in a massive over-heating of the labour market. Finally, through its integrative capability, technology is also causing the redesign of work in user industries on a scale that far outstrips the capabilities of these industries to retrain their employees, as we saw in Figure 8.1. As technological diffusion occurs, these three challenges will intensify. So far, education systems in the member states have responded by providing technology-based training. This is only a small part of the solution. The fundamental need is to provide multiple-skills training among the user industries.

- **Emergence of service industries:** this is a well-documented phenomenon [7, 8]. Yet the education and training systems have yet to adapt themselves to it.

- **Work redesign:** this phenomenon, too, is well-documented [9]. Across the Community firms are resorting to job loading, leading to multiple functions under one job. Yet the education and training systems continue to operate as if functional specialisation is the predominant form of work for most employees.

- **Multiple skills:** the rationale for this is all too obvious yet employers continue to rely on the slow and tedious process of learning-by-doing. This applies just as much in advanced economies like the Netherlands and West Germany as to the lesser developed economies like Greece, Portugal and Spain.

- *Regional disparities:* owing to structural differences between the economic regions in each of the member states, new jobs and skills development have occurred unevenly. This unevenness will intensify with the onset of the single market, unless the education and training systems make special provision for disadvantaged regions.

In sum, structural changes in all the member states have been significant since the Community-wide recession of 1979-81. The single market will provide a fresh impetus to this process [6]. Yet the existing education and training policies have barely begun to cope with the last round of changes [9].

13.3 Institutional changes

In this context, the challenges derive from three sources:

- *Need for enhanced role for company-based training:* in the age of product customisation, companies have a paramount role to play. Yet, with the exception of Denmark, France and West Germany, companies in most of the member states have yet to discharge this role effectively. A recent UK study covering fast-growing and prosperous service industries found that 65 per cent of employers did not even have well defined training departments [10]. The story is equally dismal in the contracting manufacturing industries in most of the member states [9]. This poses a formidable concern: how can companies develop new skills to promote customisation if they lack basic in-house training infrastructure? Beyond that, how can we also achieve the essential complementarity between the public system and the company system, if the latter is only conspicuous by its absence? The perceived inadequacies in company-based provisions are a major worry for most of the member states at present.

- *Greater role for trade unions:* another significant short-coming of company-based and public sector-based training is the exclusion of trade unions from the whole process of skills formation. As social partners, they deserve to have a participatory role. More pragmatically, however, their involvement is needed if only to promote the concept of life-time learning among employees. At present, unions have some involvement in West Germany, and, to a lesser extent, Denmark, France and Italy. But even then, their role appears to be consultative rather than participative.

- **Re-skilling of trainers and HR planners:** those responsible for developing and managing the growing corps of skilled and know-how intensive employees need new competences that go far beyond the simplistic functions of personnel or training work. The individuals concerned, too, need to be trained and developed. Currently, neither company-based nor public sector-based education and training systems appear to have made significant provision for such individuals, with the notable exceptions of Denmark and West Germany.

In sum, these institutional changes are vital if the education and training systems are to command credibility and effectiveness.

13.4 Raising motivation

Above all, the concept of life-time learning needs to commend itself to employees themselves. Before that happens, however, they need to be convinced about the associated monetary and psychological gains. Three preconditions are vital in this context:

- **Mutual recognition of qualifications:** the idea of a 'training passport' and other means of mutual recognition are a step in the right direction. They need to be implemented soon if a new momentum is to be generated. In the past, far too much time elapsed before agreement was reached at the Community level, as we saw in Chapter 8.

- **Job enrichment:** as know-how becomes a prime resource, two challenges will arise: how to develop it and how to deploy it? In collaboration with trade unions, companies need to devise job enrichment programmes that improve the intrinsic features of work through greater variety and responsibility. But such programmes have clear training implications which extend beyond on-the-job, learning-by-doing training. There needs to be widespread and explicit recognition that job enrichment requires multiple skills which, in turn, can only be developed through extensive training.

- **Flexible organisational structures:** the challenge for education and training systems — both nationally and within companies — is how to provide training that is conducive to the formation of appropriate attitudes and culture at the work place. As the importance of know-how increases against the background of customisation, companies will increasingly have to devise flexible organisational structures that promote greater autonomy, discretion and self-expression on the part of employees. On their part, employees will need to have an attitude and ethos that promotes teamwork and a sense of corporate loyalty. After all, employees are known to have greater loyalty to their 'craft' or profession than to their employers. No member state appears to have paid due attention to providing training that is focused on personal development which encourages the necessary behavioural changes. Nor, for that matter, does there appear to be any recognition of the importance of attitude and culture training. We return to this point in detail in Chapter 16.

13.5   Target groups

Currently, both company-based and public sector-based education and training systems do not appear to pay adequate attention to the needs of three specific groups of workers in the Community:

- *Managers:* in a rapidly changing business environment, managers need multiple-competences to manage the change successfully. Currently, much of the management development occurs informally on the job. A formal approach is needed that attempts to develop competency in three broad areas: technical, human and conceptual. Technical competency can be taught in conventional ways, and then practised under supervision; human skills have to be learnt rather than taught, preferably with help from some sort of mentor; and conceptual skills have to be developed by constant practice, stimulated by reading, observation and argument. The main point is that there is an undoubted need for a multi-strand approach because, compared to the USA and Japan, management development has had a lower profile in the Community. This is a gap that needs to be closed [11].

- *Knowledge-workers:* the concept of knowledge-workers is not novel. Since about the middle of the last decade, the restructuring of work under the impact of technology and global competition has increased the number of knowledge-workers, who possess three attributes: higher educational qualifications, intellectual skills and greater discretion at the work place. Yet the Community's education and training systems neither recognise the concept nor cater for its needs. In contrast, Japanese company-based training is entirely structured around it. Unless there are major initiatives within individual member states in this area, the pace of product and service customisation will be slow because it depends directly on the rate of human resource development of knowledge-workers.

- *Disadvantaged groups:* currently three groups of workers are disproportionately under-represented in programmes of vocational training in the member states: women returning to work after having a family; long-term unemployed workers; and disabled people [5]. Recently there has been a number of new initiatives in countries like Denmark, France, Italy and the UK. But these fall short of the requirements, if the Community is to face impending demographic changes effectively. By 1995, the Community's overall labour force will be contracting annually by about 250,000, and by nearly a million in the early part of the next century [12, 13]. This argues strongly for a large-scale retraining programme for groups who have been forced to remain hitherto at the fringes of the labour market.

In sum, the challenges here relate to providing a clear focus on various employee groups whose needs have remained unmet, and yet who are expected to play a critical role, at least over the rest of this century.

13.6   New emphasis on education and training

The challenges discussed so far come from outside the system of education and training. Yet there are others which derive from within it. It is all very well to show what needs to be done if the single market is to generate the expected economic gains. Equally, it would seem unrealistic not to recognise the inherent problems in the system itself. These are three which merit attention:

- *Improved basic education:* the problem here is two-fold; namely, how to raise pupil participation rates and how to improve the quality of instruction. Countries like France, Greece, Italy, Portugal and Spain have a high drop-out rate with the result that their systems have the propensity to turn out successive generations of under-qualified employees. For example, under the present trends an overwhelming majority of Portuguese workers in the first two decades of the next century will have no more than seven years of basic schooling. In countries like Belgium, Ireland, Netherlands and the UK the perception prevails that even with higher retention rate in schools, the quality of instruction is at variance with the emerging needs of their economies. Indeed, across the Community the most deep-seated problem is the seemingly low quality of publicly provided secondary school education. This is partly a matter of inadequate financial resources, especially in the southern member states. But more fundamentally, it is also a reflection of the quality of teaching resources. The problem thus lies at the heart of the system. Unless it is tackled on a substantial scale, post-school skills formation will necessarily be sub-standard.

- *Complementarity:* this does not require further elaboration, other than a basic observation that the education system needs to recognise its role in the overall human resource development. The challenges are two-fold: how to identify the role of the education and training system in this context and how to establish bridges with the system of company-based training. Currently, neither of the challenges are being understood in most of the member states.

- *Historical and cultural influences:* there is little doubt that individual member states will need to have greater complementarity between the state systems and company-based systems. Progress, however, will be slow and at times difficult because of historical and cultural influences. This is perhaps best exemplified by the differences in the approach to management education in the member states. Systems in Belgium and the UK rely on the concept of action-learning, based on the view that managers learn best when finding real solutions to real problems in the company of friendly peers who can use each other as a 'set' of consultants. West Germany relies on the model of apprenticeship; and France, quite distinctively, on the notion of scientific rational analysis. These differences make it even more difficult to 'import' a set of tried and tested solutions to the emerging challenges. Indeed, each member state has to devise its own solution. But there is little doubt that historical and cultural influences are very real and could well impair the ability of education and training systems to rise to the needs of the single market.

In sum, the challenges from within the systems are just as formidable as those from without. They will not only require increased financial resources but considerable ingenuity in promoting excellence in teaching within the long-established constraints of history and culture.

13.7 Summary

The previous four chapters have identified the nature of forces that are serving to create a training gap in the Community before the effects of the single market are taken into account. This chapter has now identified the challenges posed by the single market. The challenges in question are:

- *Structural,* because they require flexibility in the education and training systems in order to cope with various enduring changes.

- *Institutional,* because they require upgrading of the separate roles of company-based training, trade unions, trainers and HR planners.

- *Motivational,* because they require the systems to orientate the motivations of employees towards life-time learning.

- *Sectional,* because they require greater selectivity in the systems towards certain sections of workers.

- *Historical and cultural,* because the systems are a product of their past history and culture and are not susceptible to new ideas and initiatives.

  The challenges in turn require a new framework that is:

- *Comprehensive,* in terms of coverage of all the necessary strands of education and training.

- *Responsive,* in terms of its adaptability to the disproportionate impact of on-going structural changes on various worker groups, industries and regions.

- *Motivative,* in terms of encouraging individuals to engage in the process of life-time learning that is vital in the management of industrial restructuring.

- *Integrative,* in terms of producing the essential synergy between all providers of education and training.

PART D

1992 and Beyond

Parts A, B and C have described the 1992 programme and assessed the business, labour market, education and training challenges arising out of it. This final Part now draws together the salient points emerging from the assessment. In the process, it develops two critical themes that have arisen from our analysis: namely, the economic gains from the 1992 programme are likely to take the form of a zero sum game but it ought to be possible to enhance the scale of gains so that winners just don't win because the losers lose.

This Part starts with a detailed explanation of why the 1992 programme could well be a zero sum game (Chapter 14). It then goes on to identify the micro levels actions that will enhance the scale of gains (Chapter 15). It argues that such actions will involve major changes in company-based education and training systems, given the ascendancy of know-how as the prime resource. Among other things, such actions will also involve greater complementarity between education and training systems, in both private and public sectors (Chapter 16). Having outlined the essential changes, it goes on to consider macro level actions, especially those associated with the Social Dimension of the 1992 programme (Chapter 17). The final chapter brings together the identified actions. Against the background of various favourable developments, it argues that these actions can underpin a new vision for the integrated Europe.

14

A ZERO SUM GAME

14.1   Winner takes all

First and foremost, the 1992 programme is about the elimination of various administrative, technical and financial 'distortions' so that products, services and financial markets can operate more effectively, thereby ensuring a more efficient allocation of resources. The fact that such distortions have prevailed some forty years after the formation of the Community is not a surprise: some, like technical standards, are embedded in national cultures; others, like financial controls, are part of an essential economic armoury for running a modern industrial state.

In sum, their removal is bound to initiate major structural changes. More significantly, they will occur under Adam Smith's 'invisible hand' of the market. In that sense, they will be different because similar upheavals in the past have occurred, at least in part, under the benign hand or the invisible boot of the state. Either way rapid and major changes are inevitable.

However, it is essential to put these changes into perspective. As we saw in Chapters 3 and 5, the overall employment impact of the programme is expected to be modest. In the macro-economic context, the projected impact does not resemble anything that, in any sense, can be called a step-change.

After all, in the first instance, the size of the impact depends on the cost reductions generated by the programme. The European Commission's estimate puts the potential cost reduction at about 2.5 per cent of the value of the trade affected, of which 1.5 per cent is attributed to the abolition of customs formalities and the balance to other sources [1]. This figure, however, errs on the high side because it is unlikely that all trade formalities will be eliminated completely in the foreseeable future. According to a recent study, a more realistic figure for cost reduction would seem to lie between 1 per cent and 1.5 per cent [2]. A gain of this order is far from significant.

Looking at other dimensions of gains, as shown in Table 14.1, much the same observation applies. The fact that estimates have a 30 per cent error margin does not detract from this observation. Concentrating on employment, the projected gain of 1.8 million jobs in the medium term to 1998 is small, being equivalent to around 1 per cent of the Community's total workforce. Even the highest estimate of 5.7 million envisages changes in macro-economic policy over and above the single market programme. At a time when unemployment is expected to remain in double figures in many member states, a 5 per cent boost in jobs will be welcomed. But even this higher figure invites two caveats.

First, other comparable countries such as Australia, Canada and the USA have individually achieved some 25 per cent growth in employment in the 1980s through a conventional mix of monetary and fiscal policies [3]. Against their recent achievements, the Community's potential job boost looks rather modest. Much the same observation applies to the projected performance of other macro-economic indicators in Table 14.1. Their implied order is well within the reach of country-specific conventional macro-economic policies relating to changes in taxes, interest rates and exchange rates.

Table 14.1   Medium term macroeconomic consequences of the single market

Economic policy stance	GDP (%)	Consumer prices (%)	External balance (as % of GDP)	Employment (millions)
a. Without accompanying measures	+4.5	-6.1	+1.0	+1.8
b. With accompanying measures on:				
• government budget	+7.5	-4.3	-0.5	+5.7
• external trade	+6.5	-4.5	0.0	+4.4
• price reductions	+7.0	-4.5	-0.2	+5.0

Source: The Economics of 1992 (European Commission, 1988)

This leads to the second caveat. Small though they may look, the macro-economic effects present only an aggregate picture: they are merely the tip of the iceberg of fundamental restructuring, as we saw in Chapter 5. Its equation of the net gain has two large offsetting items on the other side. In other words, there will be major winners and major losers. It is just that their summation results in a small net gain. Once allowance is made for the error margins in the estimates, the gains could well be not significantly different from zero, at least in the next five years. This cautions against reading too much into the estimates of gains: *they conceal a lot more than they reveal.*

From this analysis, it would appear that the 1992 programme is essentially about industrial restructuring, to be achieved under the freer operation of market forces leading to greater competition. In plain terms, it is about the survival of the fittest. That restructuring will occur is not in doubt: that it will be major is equally certain. Against a background of modest gains, such restructuring will produce winners but mainly at the expense of losers, such that the overall gain is not different from zero. As we saw in Chapter 5, in the first year of the single market programme, employment will decline by 0.4 per cent, which is equivalent to some half a million job losses, with the UK bearing the brunt of them at 157,000. Almost certainly, this is the 'best case' scenario because it does not appear to have discounted the acceleration in pace of structural changes since the publication of the White Paper on the Single Market in 1985. This acceleration will either bring forward the timing of job losses or increase their scale: in all probability it will do both, the more so because it is already happening under the fierce operation of market forces that have their own momentum and logic. For the next five years or so, this momentum will accelerate. Under it, the outcome will be simple and deterministic: the winner will take all. The 'invisible hand' of the market will ensure that. This assessment raises various social issues which are covered in Chapter 17. Before then, though, it is essential to highlight certain salient features of the gathering momentum in order to underline the proposition that, for the first five years or so, the single market will be a zero sum game.

14.2 End of the dinosaur age

The Single European Act was passed in 1986 and ratified by the member states in 1987. Since then, progress towards the creation of the single market has been far slower than public perceptions would seem to indicate.

This much is evident from details of the implementation programme. The single market is expected to be created through 279 specific measures identified in the European Commission's 1985 White Paper. By January 1990, 152 of them had been adopted by the Council of Ministers, the EC's main executive forum for national politicians. Member states are usually allowed 18 months to implement these measures by rewriting national laws or changing administrative rules. On this reckoning, therefore, some 90 measures should have been implemented by now in all the 12 member states. But only 14 of them have been implemented. Furthermore, the implementation process is rather uneven. For example, 55 measures have been implemented by only eight member states. So far, Italy has implemented the lowest number—about 35. Unless the pace hastens exponentially, it is unlikely that the enabling measures will be implemented by the target date of 31 December 1992.

Yet, when one looks at the pace of corporate mergers and takeovers, it is easy to be deceived into believing that the programme is, if anything, ahead of schedule. This is starkly evidenced by the huge upheaval that has occurred in the last six months in the French insurance and air travel industries even before the European Commission has had the chance to decide on the eventual shape of the relevant directives.

Why? Because the spirit of 1992 has taken on a significance that far exceeds the detail of the programme. Perceptions and not the programme contents are influencing the preparatory pace. This is despite the high probability that, in many areas, the implementation phase will indeed be drawn out beyond 1992 as national governments pay heed to various vested interests. Yet fundamental changes have been initiated by companies. Stakes have been raised. Corporate rationalism has taken on a new meaning which has yet to be understood widely: how else can one explain the hyper-activity on the part of, for example, France's Compagnie Financiere de Suez? It has just pieced together a giant conglomerate in the heart of Europe at a record speed, involving business areas in which it has no management expertise; and all this at a time when conglomerates in the USA are being 'unbundled' by corporate predators in order to unlock the trapped dynamism.

For a while at least, perceptions have superseded fundamentals. In this context, previous experience is rather illuminating [4]. The United States became a single market in the true sense of the term around the turn of this century. One consequence was a series of corporate mergers, peaking around 1902, that consolidated 15 per cent of all manufacturing sector plants into several market-leading firms. Some 35 years later, a study examined the long-term consequences of this historic merger wave, involving some 159 firms, and found the following:

- 33 per cent were early failures

- 6 per cent were later failures

- 11 per cent could be characterised as 'limping'

- 7 per cent were successes after rejuvenation

- 36 per cent were 'clear' successes

- 6 per cent were 'outstanding' successes

Fewer than half of the successes survive today in recognisable form. Accordingly the message is clear: about 1 in 2 mergers were successful over a 30 year period. Over a 90 year period, even the winners went through further significant changes.

From the foregoing analysis it is clear that major restructuring is occurring and will continue to occur within the Community. Furthermore, it has its own momentum which appears to be divorced from the reality of the 1992 programme's implementation pace. Finally, restructuring will cause major rationalisation of capacity, partly through changing corporate ownership and partly through the freer operation of market forces that will ensure the survival of the fittest. If there are winners—and doubtless there will be some—they will be at the expense of others because in the medium term to the late 1990s, the single market will be a zero sum game.

However, that is not to say that there would be no gains after the turn of this century: quite the reverse. Out of the restructuring process—warts and all—the Community stands a good chance of curing itself of the so-called Eurosclerosis and repositioning itself on a new and higher growth trajectory. Indeed, the restructuring will usher in a new age in which industrial dinosaurs will find it hard to survive. But that is not all. Like America and Japan, Europe is rich in natural, physical and human resources. It is equally rich in cultural diversity, social traditions and political heritage. Hitherto, these advantages have not been fully utilised because of political developments that served to compartmentalise its nation states. Indeed, what Europe has lacked is a mechanism to 'orchestrate' resources in a way that produces a collective outcome greater than the sum total of outcomes currently prevailing at the level of individual states.

The 1992 programme is the principle orchestrator in this context. It is about producing an economic, social and political entity that is greater than the sum of its parts. But this historic mission should not detract from two critical imperatives:

- *Social considerations in the short term:* the immediate challenge for the Community is to minimise the adverse social consequences of restructuring, at a time when overall economic gains will be at best modest and at worst negligible.

- *New dynamism in the longer term:* as we approach the next millennium, the challenge for the Community is to ensure that a new phoenix does rise from the ashes of restructuring, such that the Community does reap handsome rewards out of the most critical initiative in its history.

Both issues require action over a wide area of social and economic policy. Specifically, they should aim to achieve three objectives: an orderly transition in the short term; a revitalised economic base in the longer term; and a more equitable distribution of economic gains, leading to higher living standards for *all* citizens of the Community. These are laudable aims which can easily degenerate into rhetoric, unless they are backed by numerous actions. The rest of this part of the book will concentrate on those actions deemed to be critical. Given that the restructuring process is first and foremost a micro level phenomenon, the next chapter starts with the essential actions at the level of individual firms. It paves the way for a more detailed look at the education and training issues which are important in the development of the know-how that can revitalise the European economic base (Chapter 16). Chapter 17 then moves on to the essential actions at national and community level.

It is our contention that both sets of actions—individually and collectively—will go a long way towards meeting the two imperatives outlined above.

14.3 Summary

This chapter has attempted to explain why the single market will be a zero sum game in the sense that the industrial restructuring initiated by it will produce winners and losers, with no significant net gains for at least the first five years. The main points emerging from the chapter are as follows:

- The medium-term macro-economic gains arising from the single market are likely to be extremely modest. They could just as easily be delivered by changes in conventional macro-economic policies, as evidenced by the recent performance of countries such as Australia, Canada and the United States.

- However, the modest overall gains are but the tip of the iceberg. They are the net result of two large sets of offsetting effects, arising from the process of industrial restructuring.

- Under it, major capacity rationalisation will occur due to the intensification of competition and changing corporate ownership, the latter through mergers and takeovers. The invisible hand of the market rather than the benign arm of the state will determine the pace and scale of industrial upheaval.

- Out of this process, there is no guarantee that the new streamlined capacity will automatically generate greater economic gains in the longer term, if the comparable American experience is any guide.

- Clearly, some further actions will be needed at the level of individual companies, governments and the European Commission.

- Such micro and macro level actions need to impinge on two critical issues that merit attention: in the short-term, how can the adverse social impact of the zero sum game be minimised; in the longer term, how can European industry be revitalised in a way that generates social and economic gains for all the Community's citizens? These two issues are covered in the next three chapters.

15

PRECONDITIONS FOR SUCCESS: A MICRO APPROACH

15.1   Know-how: The prime resource

As we saw in Figure 3.2 in Chapter 3, the new economic forces released by the single market will promote intra-Community trade in customised products and services, given the diversity in the cultural, social and economic background of its 320 million 'domestic' consumers. Against the background of fresh competition and industrial restructuring, that figure also explained why successful companies will be those who put a premium on sound industrial relations, skills development and technological progressivity. In other words, they are the ones who will be developing and valuing all their resources — human, physical and technological.

Accordingly, the development and management of know-how will become important in its own right as customisation grows apace. But that is not all. For its pace, too, will need to accelerate as products and services come to have a progressively shorter shelf life. This is amply corroborated by the example of motor vehicles. In the 1970s, an average car had a model life of about eight years. In the 1980s, this was reduced to three years. In the process, the R&D component of total cost over the life cycle of a car has risen markedly — anywhere from 10 per cent to 30 per cent, depending upon the model. This trend has been evident across a whole array of products and services. The single market will merely accentuate it. In any event, there is no doubt that know-how will become a vital competitive weapon in the new environment characterised jointly by the release of fresh market forces and customer targeting.

However, for individual companies, having the requisite know-how will be one thing, but developing and managing it will be quite another. Indeed, the notion of know-how as a competitive weapon raises a range of issues in the whole area of human resource management. Chapter 8 identified the skills gap and suggested certain solutions. But this new notion of know-how as a competitive weapon is more wide ranging: it certainly extends beyond the bridging of the gap. Not only is it about acquiring the necessary work skills, it is also about developing and motivating employees in a way that helps to achieve a competitive edge in one or more of the following: R&D, design, production, delivery and after-sales service.

In fact, it is about converting human ingenuity — both innate and acquired — into a capital resource which can legitimately be included in a company's asset base. After all, in the age of customisation, flexibility and adaptability on the supply side are essential ingredients of success because the market environment is rendered highly uncertain by changing consumer psychology. In such a situation, the only factor of production that can be truly flexible and adaptable is know-how.

As a result, a radical rethink is called for in employers' perceptions of labour. In conventional accounting terms, employees are looked upon as 'costs'. As such, they appear in the profit and loss account. In the evolving environment, as know-how is in the ascendant, this convention will have to be replaced by one which treats employees as 'assets' in the balance sheet [1].

Indeed, notwithstanding technological advances, many companies will find their payroll costs rising as a proportion of total sales. This could be for many reasons, of which the main one will be the rising know-how content of products and services. In other words, some of the value added by employees will rise and with it will rise payroll costs, as the ascendancy of know-how to the prime factor of production changes corporate costs' structures.

After all, in the age of customisation, know-how intensity is not the same as labour intensity: one is about brain power, the other about muscle power; one is a senior partner of the new technology, the other rendered obsolete by it; one requires years of education, training and work experience, the other only normal physical and emotional maturity.

In short, customisation is about redefinition of work and labour input. But this redefinition is not a matter of semantics, or of fancy new buzzwords. Essentially, it is about initiating a number of strategic changes in order to fulfil a set of pre-conditions that are vital for business success in the single market - success for individual companies during the restructuring process in the medium-term; and for the Community as a whole in the longer-term.

15.2 Preconditions for success: Caveats and overview

This section attempts to identify and outline those preconditions. However, before considering them, it is essential to make two general observations.

First, our discussion of the identified pre-conditions is necessarily general, and deliberately so. After all, the object is not to provide a blueprint for action; rather it is to make companies aware of the critical areas in which actions will be needed. The precise scope, timing and strength of possible actions will, as always, depend upon the circumstances of individual companies in aspects such as business plans, product-mix, technology in use and occupational-mix.

Second, the generality of the discussion does not detract from the importance of the identified areas. Indeed where further details are essential, as in the case of know-how development, they are given in Chapter 16. The fact remains that if employers across the Community initiated actions in areas where there is none at present or accelerated those that are in progress currently, then the single market will begin to live up to its promise.

In particular, these actions have the potential to soothe the socially adverse impact of the transitional phase by bringing about a notable improvement in the competitiveness of companies that survive the restructuring process. More optimistically, perhaps, they can alter the balance within the restructuring process: less through corporate mergers and take-overs and more through the improved efficiency of the existing firms. As we saw in Chapter 5, mergers and take-overs tend to achieve higher productivity by obtaining the same level of output with reduced labour inputs. In contrast, improved labour productivity in the existing firms tends to achieve improved labour productivity by obtaining a higher level of output with the same level of inputs. In other words, the first option involves unemployment; the second does not, or at least less so.

In the longer term, the identified actions have the potential for revitalising the Community's economies and improving their relative position in global markets. After all, under the present 'Uruguay' Round of trade liberalisation under the auspices of the General Agreement on Tariffs and Trade (GATT), world trade is set for a major boost. As in the Community, so in the world at large, a major part of this growth will be in customised services. Various strategic actions in the preparatory phase of the 1992 programme could prove highly proactive. Nearer home, at the very least, they can serve to ensure that the process of generating new industrial dynamism in the Community is at once faster, wider and deeper.

The actions in question are summarised in Figure 15.1, which shows the nature of responses needed as companies switch from standardised products, largely targeted at their home market, to customised products, targeted at diverse customer groups in the economies of other member states. Between them they comprise two distinct sets of actions: structural and human resource management, as discussed in the next two sections respectively.

Figure 15.1   Preconditions for success in the single market

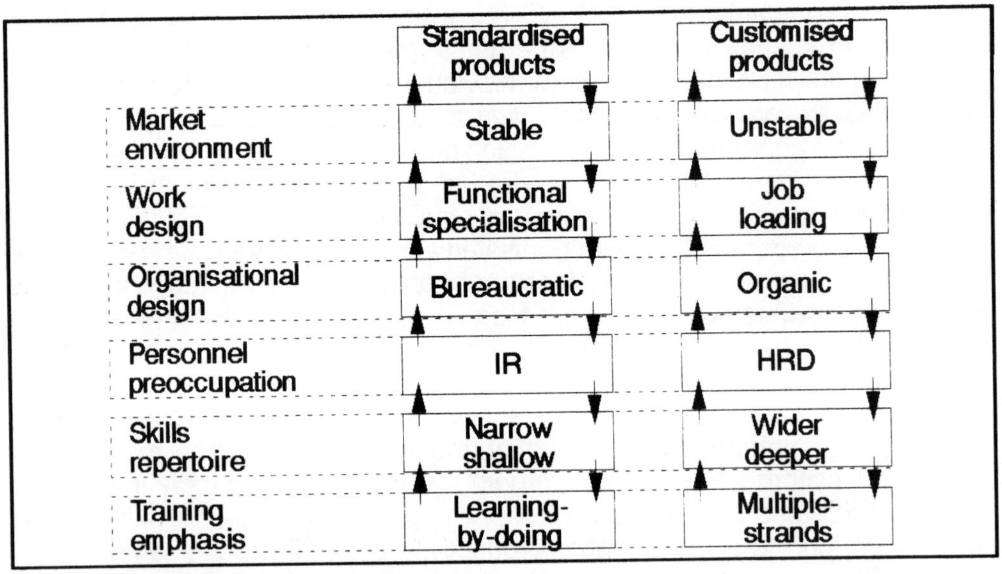

	Standardised products	Customised products
Market environment	Stable	Unstable
Work design	Functional specialisation	Job loading
Organisational design	Bureaucratic	Organic
Personnel preoccupation	IR	HRD
Skills repertoire	Narrow shallow	Wider deeper
Training emphasis	Learning-by-doing	Multiple-strands

Source: CREATE Research Programme

15.3   Structural imperatives

There are two distinct imperatives here: one affecting the content of work performed by employees involved in the conception, design, production, distribution and after-sales service of customised products and services; and the other affecting the organisational setting in which work is performed. Between them, the two imperatives aim to improve labour productivity on the one hand; and employee satisfaction on the other.

15.3.1 Work redesign

As we saw in Part C, work redesign has been in progress in various member states in the last decade. It has resulted in two forms of job loading - horizontal and vertical.

More prevalent in the service industries, horizontal loading has brought together disparate functions under one job. This is well exemplified by the banking industry where clerical work, involving some 75 per cent of employees, has been subject to this form of redesign (see Figure 15.2).

More prevalent in manufacturing industries, vertical loading has brought together certain sequentially related functions under one job. This is well exemplified by the engineering industry where craft work, involving between 40 and 60 per cent of employees, has been subject to this form of redesign (Figure 15.3).

Although evolving work patterns conform to the needs of customisation, the pace of redesign across the Community has been slow and piecemeal, on the whole. New information technology has played a crucial role in this context because of its potential for integrating various functions in the three conventional

Figure 15.2   Horizontal loading of clerical work in banks

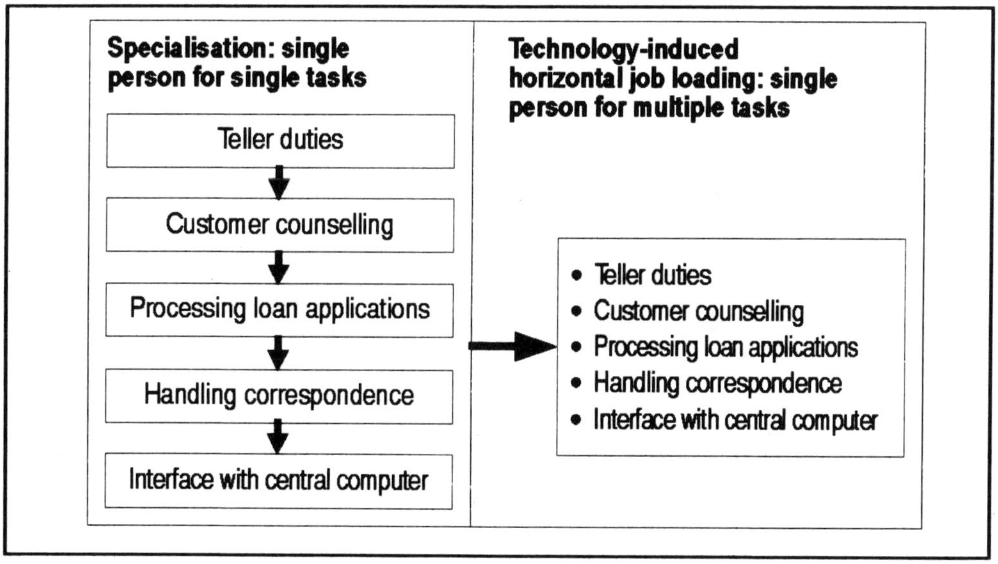

Source: CREATE Research Programme

211

spheres of activity: production, distribution and (office-based) co-ordination. But the introduction of technology has not been used as an opportunity to mount major redesign initiatives. As a result, technology has yet to deliver high productivity, except in a handful of industries such as vehicles manufacturing, printing, air travel and banking.

Doubtless, there are problems in redesign: not least because of the need to eliminate long established functional demarcations. But the Japanese and the Scandinavians have shown that with enlightened management initiatives resistance to redesign can be overcome. Stripped of the rhetoric, the whole point about creating industrial dynamism is, in the final analysis, about creating a flexible and adaptable workforce. That is why these countries have been so successful in world markets. In the case of Sweden, for example, the achievements are all the more remarkable: its highly adaptable workforce is one of the principal factors compensating for a small domestic market.

Within the single market, as customisation of products and services continues apace, individual employees will require considerable flexibility in order to adapt constantly to changing consumer needs. This, in turn, will require well worked out initiatives on work redesign and job rotation from their employers.

Figure 15.3   Vertical job loading of craft work in engineering

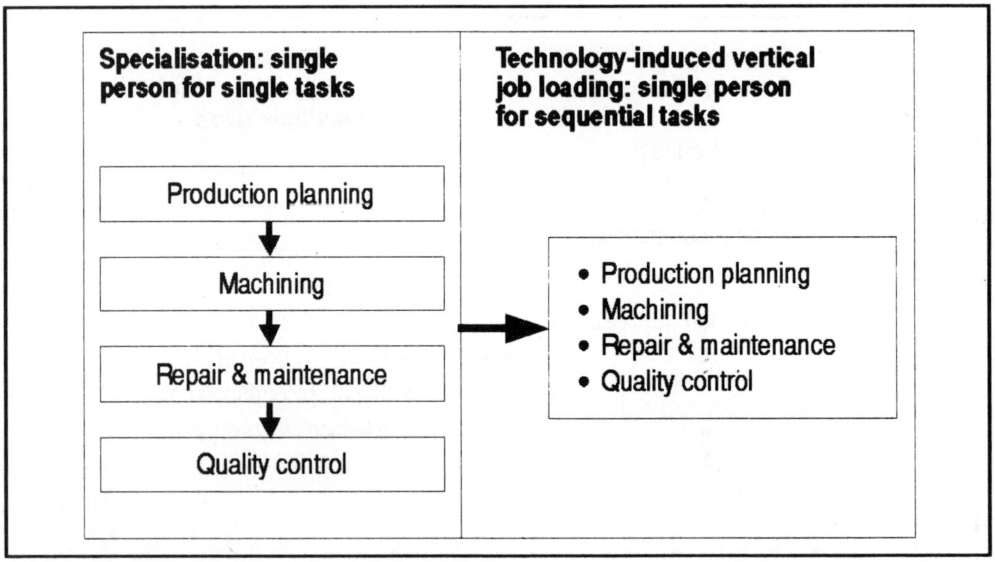

Specialisation: single person for single tasks

- Production planning
- Machining
- Repair & maintenance
- Quality control

Technology-induced vertical job loading: single person for sequential tasks

- Production planning
- Machining
- Repair & maintenance
- Quality control

Source: CREATE Research Programme

15.3.2   Organisation design

As the skills and know-how content of work rises, the issue of organisation design will once again come to the fore. This is because the conventional bureaucratic model, based on command and control, has been found to be singularly ill-suited to motivating, developing and managing employees who rely more on brain than muscle power.

Across the Community there have been considerable changes in the 1980s in organisation design, aimed at achieving decentralisation of work as well as decision making.   However, many of them have inadvertently ended up generating tribal structures amounting to fragmented bureaucracies (see the north-east quadrant in Figure 15.4). Yet their aims had been to generate either matrix structures or dynamic networks, with fewer managerial layers and more devolved responsibilities (as shown in the lower half of the figure). Fresh efforts are needed to redesign the structures in order that individual employees enjoy greater discretion, work variety, and job rotation. Without them, it will be difficult to ensure worker motivation and on the job skills and know-how development.

Figure 15.4   New organisational forms: 1950-2020

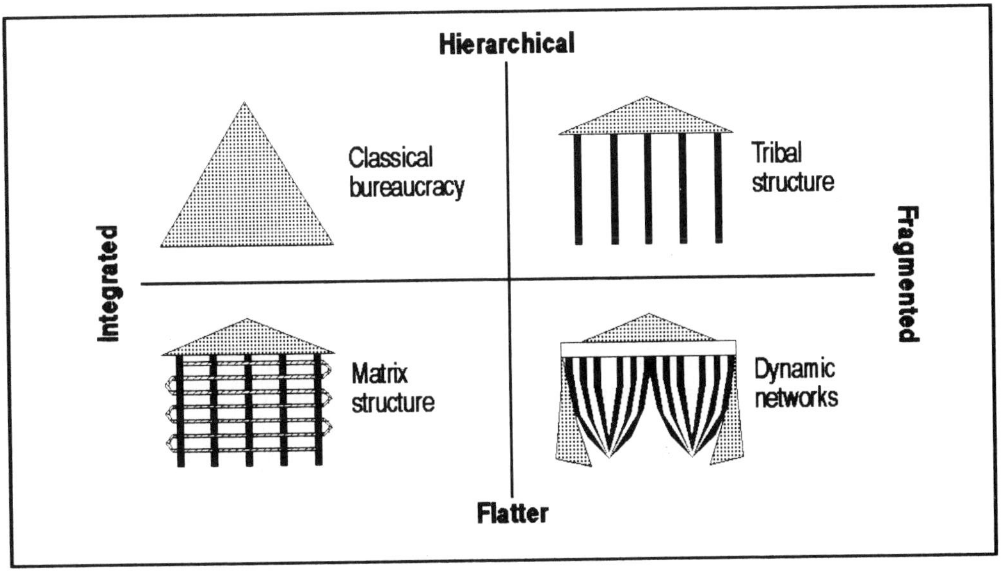

Source: CREATE Research Programme

213

15.4   Human resource management imperatives

Here there are three distinct imperatives: one relating to the content of the personnel function, one to the repertoire of work skills and one to training emphasis. Among them, they aim to improve the deployment of skills and know-how on the one hand and their development on the other.

15.4.1   Personnel function

Hitherto, throughout the Community, the personnel function has been dominated by industrial relations (IR) issues, typically involving pay and terms and conditions of work. As a result, personnel professionals have not been able to play a significant role in the development and deployment of essential skills and know-how. Although the importance of these conventional issues cannot be denied, it is as well to realise that as we move towards an economy increasingly based on brain power, the IR function will need redefinition.

More immediately, however, personnel professionals need to widen their portfolios to include three areas which will require significant actions in the 1990s.

The first of these involves recruitment and retention of women returners. As we saw in Chapters 7 and 8, there is a strong case for devising returner schemes which facilitate an orderly return to work for women with children. Essentially, such schemes require initiatives in three specific areas: retraining aimed at confidence building; retraining aimed at countering skills obsolescence owing to absence from the labour market; and changing work patterns to suit the family circumstances of returners [2]. As yet, such schemes are novel in most of the member states, but especially in Belgium, Greece, Italy, Portugal and Spain. Yet they are important because as women's rate of participation in higher education has increased, they have become increasingly capable of entering occupations that are know-how intensive. There still remains the substantial task of attracting women into these occupations which will comprise the main growth areas in the 1990s (see Chapter 8).

The second area of concern relates to the prevailing inefficiencies in the deployment of existing skills and know-how. As was shown in Part C, there is some evidence of educational 'overkill' in the recruitment practices of many employers in member states such as Italy, the UK and West Germany. As a result, there is considerable misallocation of valuable resources, as shown in Figure 15.5:

- At the left-hand extreme, there are many over-qualified employees in the sense that they have qualifications far in excess of the needs of the jobs they hold. This has come about as a result of two factors: the availability of educationally qualified candidates within the ranks of the unemployed; and the well known practice under which many employers use qualifications to over-compensate for any disadvantages that they associate with certain groups such as women returners, disabled people and ethnic minorities. As a result, these groups tend to get recruited into jobs for which they are seemingly over-qualified. The result is an over-supply of talent in the 'wrong' jobs.

- At the right-hand extreme, there are many under-qualified employees in the sense that they have not received training that is commensurate with the rising skills and know-how content of work, resulting from new technology, growing competition and work restructuring. The implied training gap (or deficit) is particularly notable amongst the intermediate occupations (e.g. technicians, supervisors and senior clericals), where there is excess demand for talent.

Thus, a combination of myopic recruitment practices and neglect of training has brought about a paradoxical situation where surpluses and deficits in talents co-exist within the same organisation. Unquestionably, there is ample scope for reducing these imbalances, especially since the skills gap is set to widen in the 1990s, as we saw in Chapter 7. Accordingly, personnel professionals need to reappraise their organisation's recruitment criteria as well as address training issues.

The final area of concern for personnel professionals relates to the development of international expertise for certain categories of employees. Two factors are promoting a pan-European orientation of the Community's companies: corporate mergers and takeovers; and the proposed statute of the European Company. These two factors are only the outward manifestation of a long-established trend towards serving the European, as distinct from the domestic, market. In the single market, this trend is bound to accelerate especially in various service industries such as banking, insurance, air travel, telecommunications and wholesale distribution. In the management of

Figure 15.5   Qualification mismatches in different occupations

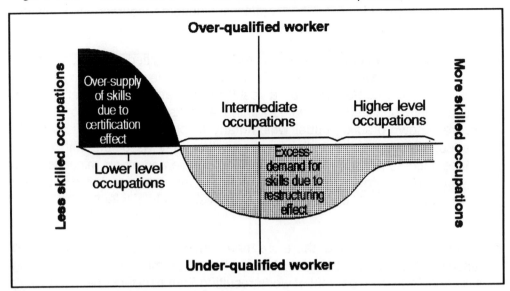

Source: CREATE Research Programme

transnational operations, the role of 'international experience' will become even more crucial: the more so because of the scale and rate of industrial restructuring that started in 1987 and will continue well into this decade.

Many companies in both manufacturing and services already have schemes that are significantly designed to develop such experience, largely through international transfers of employees. However, such schemes tend to concentrate on operational rather than strategic areas (see Figure 15.6 overleaf). They are also orientated towards the performance of specialist tasks (left-hand side of the figure). Either way, they have lacked a strategic focus. For most of this decade, industrial restructuring rather than organic growth will be the dominant corporate preoccupation. This means that companies are more likely to be concerned about the initiation and management of change through transnational strategic alliances leading to joint production, marketing, distribution and resourcing strategies. Accordingly, the focus of international experience will need to be re-examined.

Figure 15.6   International transfers

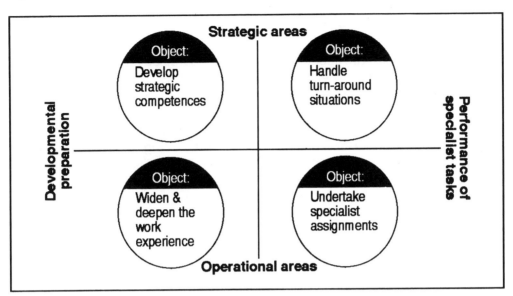

Source: CREATE Research Programme

15.4.2   Repertoire of work skills and training emphasis

The last two preconditions in Figure 15.1 are considered together here because they are evaluated in greater detail in the next chapter which is concerned with changes in the whole system of education and training. For now, there are two separate points worthy of note, one relating to the repertoire and one to training emphasis.

Taking them in turn, there needs to be a sea-change in the existing repertoire of skills, interpreted here loosely to cover know-how as well. It needs to becomes at once wider and deeper, in terms of three elements:

- the number of distinctly different skills targeted at different functions within a job

- the intensity of the use of these skills

- the know-how base which can comprise skills as well as wider knowledge about the business in terms of, for example, its products, markets, technology, customers and working methods - in other words, any cognitive elements that serve to enhance the value added.

The three elements are essential because standardised products and services tend to require function-specific and procedural skills, whereas customisation requires a number of additional skills such as entrepreneurial, diagnostic, decision-making and intellectual ones [3].

Turning to the training emphasis, the main imperative here is to move away from the over-reliance on on the job learning-by-doing and towards a more comprehensive approach with multiple strands. If skills and know-how are important, then the process leading to their development is just as important. In this context much needs to be done, both by companies and governments of the member states, as we shall see in the next chapter.

15.5   Summary

The chapter has had two objectives. First, to develop the argument that know-how, loosely defined to include work skills and other cognitive attributes, will become a prime resource as customisation grows apace in the single market. Second, to identify and outline various pre-conditions that have to be met if companies are to develop, deploy and manage their valuable human resources in a way that ensures business success in the single market. The main points emerging from the chapter are as follows:

- Growth in intra-Community trade in the single market will be largely confined to customised products and services that are intensive in know-how. As a result, development, deployment and management of know-how will be a crucial success factor because they convert human ingenuity—both innate and acquired—into a capital resource.

- The notion of know-how as a competitive weapon and a capital asset raises a range of issues in the area of human resource management. Furthermore, it requires an attitudinal change. In the age of customisation, know-how intensity of work is not the same as labour intensity: one is about brain-power, the other about muscle power; one is technology's senior partner, the other is being rendered obsolete by it; one takes years of education and training, the other mainly physical, mental and emotional maturity.

- Accordingly, the pre-conditions of business success in the new environment focus on five critical human resource issues. They call for changes in:
  - work design
  - organisation design
  - the personnel function
  - the repertoire of work skills
  - the emphasis on training.

- In each case, it is a matter of moving away from the practice consistent with standardised products and services to those consistent with customisation.

16

KNOW-HOW DEVELOPMENT: TOWARDS A NEW PARTNERSHIP

16.1   An overview

The previous chapter has identified various preconditions that have to prevail at the level of individual companies if they are to survive the new competitive forces released by the single market. However, when it comes to education and training issues the required actions extend beyond the scope of the corporate sector, given that governments in all the member states have dominant responsibilities in this area. It is therefore difficult to talk about company actions in isolation.
  Accordingly, the object of this chapter is three-fold:

- to identify some base-line actions that need to be taken at the level of individual governments, *irrespective* of historical and cultural differences in their education and training systems

- to show how the essential complementarity can be established between the education and training systems run by states and those run by companies

- to highlight the essential thrust of the training effort needed at the level of individual companies.

16.2 Government-level actions

There are three areas in which immediate action is needed if individual member states are to contribute towards the process of know-how development and thereby help to generate the gains from the single market. They are closely linked to the key challenges identified in Chapter 13. The areas in question are:

- *Raising the participation rate in post-compulsory education:* as Figure 16.1 shows, with the exception of Belgium and the Netherlands all member states have considerable potential for raising the participation rate of teenagers (15-19 age group) in post-compulsory education. Much the same observation applies to young adults (20-24 age group). In the age of growing customisation of products and services, continuous (life-time) learning is essential on the part of employees. But if the concept of continuous learning is to become viable then the Community needs a significant improvement in the participation rate of both these age groups. A higher participation rate will provide a wider base for the subsequent development of add-on skills at the work place.

- *Changing priorities in secondary education systems:* a wider base is a necessary but not sufficient condition for the development of add-on skills. For that, there needs to be a reversal or, at least, a significant change in the priority order in the education systems. As Figure 16.2 shows, the current classroom curriculum in most of the member states is built around the conventional triad with the following descending order of emphasis: development of theoretical knowledge; development of practical know-how; and development of attitudes and skills. As a result of the structural challenges outlined in Chapter 13, the conventional triad has become increasingly irrelevant, almost to the point of being unstable. This rank order serves to help those pupils who wish to further their education because of its predominant emphasis on theoretical knowledge. As a side-effect, it provides inadequate vocational preparation for those who aspire to go straight into the world of work. In other words, the conventional system suits pupils with more academic aspirations. When considering reform, there are two options shown respectively by the second and third triads in Figure 16.2. The first of these options involves retaining the rank order of the three elements as in the first triad, while shifting the balance towards the development of practical know-how, attitudes and skills. Under this option, the system of secondary education can continue to prepare youngsters for further education, whilst providing vocational preparation for those who wish to enter the labour market on completion of compulsory education. The second option involves reversing the rank order from the first triad so that compulsory education puts maximum emphasis on vocational preparation. Thus the second and third triads in Figure 16.2 involve a step-improvement in the quality of basic education in the sense of providing a broad-based education for those students wishing to pursue higher level education; and vocational preparation for those wishing to enter the labour market after compulsory education. Either way, basic education should be tailored to complement rather than substitute curriculum for the continuous learning that has to occur during working life.

- *Creating complementarity:* raising the participation rate and changing the priority in the curriculum by themselves will not be enough. There is an urgent need to create greater complementarity between the education and training systems run by the individual governments on the one hand, and company-based training systems on the other. This complementarity is essential in achieving life-time learning because it relies on the former to provide the essential *base* and the latter to provide the *add-on* skills. The complementarity is developed further in the next sub-section, which examines the actions needed at company level.

Figure 16.1   Proportion of youths in education, 1986

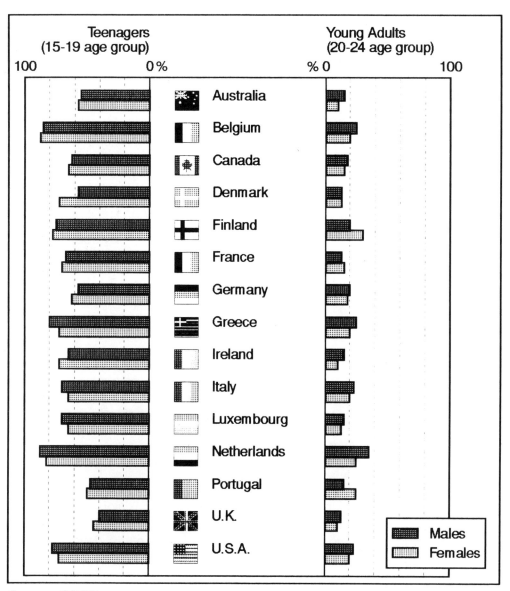

Source: OECD

Figure 16.2   Changing priorities in education system

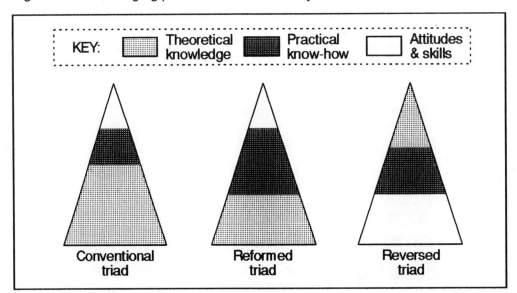

Source: CREATE Research Programme

16.3   Company-level actions: A case study approach

Whereas it is possible to pin-point the areas of action at governmental level, it is more difficult to do so at company level because of major inter-company differences in products, market environment, technology, culture and working methods. Thus in order to convey a stronger feel for company level actions, it is necessary to be more specific and look at the circumstances of a particular industry in a way that enables one to provide some fresh insights and general lessons. In this context, we focus on the situation in the banking industry in five member states: France, Ireland, Italy, the Netherlands and the UK. The choice of this industry has been influenced by two considerations: the know-content of its services is rising rapidly and the 1992 programme will accelerate this trend. We first examine the present arrangement in training in this industry and then go on to indicate the changes needed in it. In the final section we draw out the key messages from the case study as well as provide the usual summary.

16.3.1   Remedial approach

Three recent publications from the European Commission outline the principal features of the education and training systems prevailing in all member states [1, 2 and 3]. Between them, they prompt two key generalisations:

- *Diversity:* there is enormous variability in the nature, scale and institutional framework of education and training systems between the member states. For example, at one extreme there is Portugal with no more than seven years of compulsory education. At the other extreme there is West Germany, where the comparable period is eleven years for all pupils, and some 14 years for nearly 50 per cent of the pupils who traditionally stay on to take Abitur or Hochschulreife — the university entrance examinations. Much the same observation applies to vocational training. It is relatively underdeveloped in Greece, at one end but notably advanced in Denmark at the other.

- *Similarity:* in a large majority of the member states, two tendencies predominate. First, the secondary school system is not organised around the pupil as a worker but around the pupil as a product. In other words, systems tend not to be responsive to the needs of the economy. Second, vocational training is mainly viewed as having a *remedial* role: rectifying the skills deficiencies caused by the education system or rapid economic change to which individuals may find it difficult to adapt owing to inadequate personal development.

Diversity and similarity apart, the primary objective of the education and training systems in the chosen countries, then, is to produce as many 'faultless products' as possible. How does this concept interact with the world of banking?

Figure 16.3 conceptualises the interaction between the education and training systems in question. As a generalisation, it is fair to state that until recently most of their banking employees went through three layers, as defined overleaf:

- **Foundation layer:** new entrants to the industry were expected to have some basic qualifications in formal or vocational education. For example, in the UK until 1987 this had been expressed in terms of passes in five subjects at 'Ordinary' level of the school leaving examination. In France, it had been based on a certificate of completion of college studies, leading to either Lycees or Lycees Professionnels. The nature and content of entry qualifications, however, is a matter of detail. The substantive point is that the basic school leaving qualifications formed the foundation of the follow-up human resource development within banks.

- **Inductive layer:** this layer incorporated the basic elaborate in-house training that is usually provided in the first year, as part of inducting the new entrant into a new work environment. It had two principal characteristics, both of which were aimed at developing some basic competencies. The first of these was its highly formal and didactic (class room) nature that imparted elementary information on a bank's organisational structure, philosophy, customers, products and markets. The underlying objective was to familiarise newcomers with all the important aspects of the bank. The second characteristic was the emphasis on the learning of basic techniques of doing the relevant job, with due emphasis on developing technical and procedural skills.

- **Developmental layer:** after induction training began the substantive task of the development of skills (the top layer in Figure 16.3). This layer had three critical features. First, it had some formal off the job training provided by outside institutions (public sector colleges, for example) or industry-specific Chartered Institutes, which are professional bodies who award certificates on successful completion of a course of formal instructions. The thrust of formal training was directed at enhancing the knowledge base. Second, there was also on the job informal training which was ill-defined because it was based substantially on the notion of learning-by-doing. It was ill-defined in the sense that individuals were encouraged to learn what they could while performing their jobs. In fact, a large part of the development layer comprised on the job informal training. In other words, after inductive training, acquisition of work skills was left mainly to individual motivation and innate learning abilities. Finally, and importantly, there was no:
    — distinction made between acquisition of skills for improving performance in the current job, and developmental preparation for the next job

Figure 16.3 Traditional remedial model

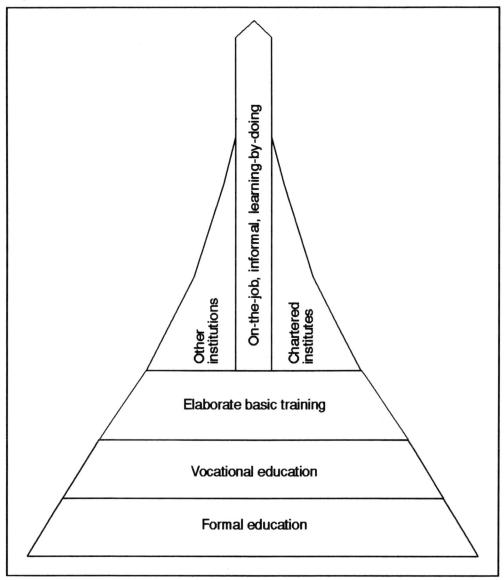

Source: CREATE Research Programme

— systematic and pre-defined balance between on the job and off the job training, and between formal and informal training
— distinction made between training for improved work skills and training for acquiring the requisite attitudes for teamwork.

This is a remedial model of training, in the sense that it viewed individual banking employees as having some basic deficiencies which prevented them from being effective at work. Training was thus primarily directed at overcoming these short-comings. This model is increasingly out of touch with the emerging reality because it is inconsistent with three developments: the growing need for job loading and consequent productivity improvement; the emergence of know-how as a prime resource in international competition; and the growing need for nurturing those attitudes that are conducive to teamwork. In fact the attitudinal issue is vital: like musicians, employees in a know-how business such as banking have to be nurtured and orchestrated in an organisational setting that has to encourage creativity, professional advancement, self-expression and autonomy, but within the confines of team-work and corporate objectives. Like musicians, such employees have a high propensity for individualism and discretion which may run counter to the business interests of a bank. The challenge here is to convert these traits into strengths through the development of a culture that is open, communicative and participative in a way that encourages employees to identify their interests with those of the bank, in the same way that musicians identify themselves with their orchestra, without sacrificing creativity and individuality in the process.

16.3.2   Developmental approach

The training model that is consistent with product customisation is given in Figure 16.4. In terms of orientation, it is different from the one in Figure 16.3 in two fundamental respects:

- **Base:** while retaining the foundation layer, it argues for a step-change in its quality, as a way of creating a strong base for skills development on a life-time basis. As we saw in Section 16.2, in all the member states the education and training systems tend to rely to varying degrees on the conventional triad of objectives that give acquisition of knowledge a precedence over know-how development and attitudes and skills formation.

Figure 16.4   Skills development model

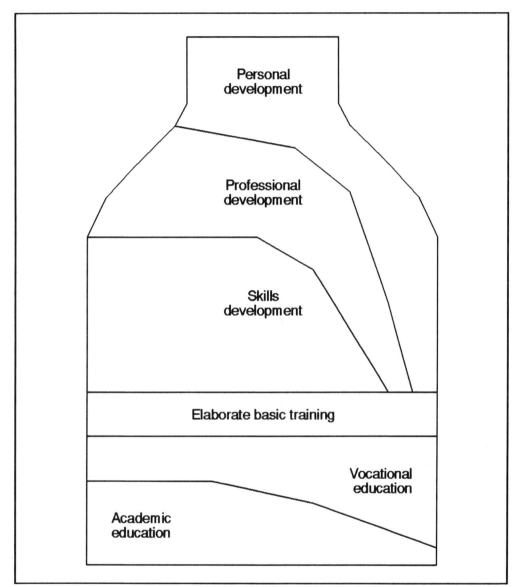

Source: CREATE Research Programme

The new model proposes a reversal in this triad as follows (see Figure 16.2):

Traditional Triad	**Revised Triad**
(in order of importance)	
1. Knowledge	1. Attitudes and skills
2. Know-how	2. Know-how
3. Attitudes and skills	3. Knowledge

The reversal is primarily based on the emerging reality that knowledge has to be acquired continuously throughout the individual's working life because of new technologies, new products and growing competition in a dynamic environment. This is only possible if the employees of today and tomorrow have the right attitude towards learning and a superior core of basic knowledge to form the basis of life-time learning. This approach argues that the object of the education system should be, first and foremost, self-discovery: i.e. the development of love of learning, and learning how to learn.

- *A focused developmental layer:* within this layer, there is a fundamental need to get away from the prevailing *ad hocary* and move towards a systematic approach based on triple strands:
  - the first of these involves the *development of skills* for improved effectiveness in the current job, to be achieved through formal on the job training as well as learning-by-doing.
  - the second strand involve *professional development* to widen the knowledge base, so as to enhance intellectual and problem-solving skills. This should result in greater effectiveness in the current job and also constitute developmental preparation for the next job.
  - the third strand involves *personal development* in order that correct attitude and corporate culture formation can take place. For employees in skilled and know-how occupations, this strand is vital if there is to be due recognition of mutuality of interest between them on the one hand, and their employers on the other.

There are two other noteworthy points about the revised model (Figure 16.4), both of which emphasise its pragmatism that is consistent with the emerging needs of post-industrial societies [4].

First, it puts the emphasis on every element of education and training systems: formal and informal; on the job and off-the-job; company-based and public

230

sector-based; and training for skills, professional development and personal development. In the final analysis, the balance in all these respects depends upon the occupational circumstances of employees, the extent and quality of in-house training provision, and the quality of nationally provided education and training.

Second, the model favours a far greater role for company-based training than that which prevails currently. This is because in a dynamic environment employers have a better awareness of the changes taking place in their products, markets, technology and working methods. National education and training systems are usually slow to respond to these changes. This is partly because it takes time for the changes to become widely known and partly because of the innate conservatism of the systems themselves. Indeed, the product customisation attendant on the single market, will favour 'niche' players whose market strength will be largely underpinned by the ownership of a body of know-how that is not generally available. If it is, then, by definition there will be no niche players. In fact, know-how will increasingly have to be developed in-house to create the niche. In this whole process, the national systems can perform only two functions:

- provide a sound base on which to build continuous training

- complement, where necessary, the corporate efforts in the three strands of development in the top half of Figure 16.4.

The foregoing analysis foresees a significant role for individual banks in the development of skills and competences of their employees.

To generalise, therefore, the economic forces that will be unleashed by the single market will require a sea-change in two respects. First, the national education systems in member states will have to discard the notion that schools produce 'products' and adopt a new notion that perceives them as producing tomorrow's workers. This will have to come through the changes in the traditional triad, as described above. Second, banks will have to take enterprise-based training far more seriously than they have up till now. They have not done so before because multi-strand quality training is expensive and its outputs are difficult to measure. As a result, training has always been treated as a 'soft' area of corporate financial budgets.

In order to change corporate attitudes in this context there is an urgent need to move towards an all-embracing framework of human resource development at the level of individual banks. Unless this happens, improvements in basic education — as is now being tried in Britain with the Education Reform Act 1988 — will fall short of securing the benefits of the single market. This is because such improvements can only form the basis of the requisite follow-up developments in skills, professionalism and personal attributes — as shown in Figure 16.4. In the age of rapid customisation, the improvements can never be adequate substitutes for them. At the same time, the follow-up developments require a coherent framework. So what is this new framework? Let us consider it first before drawing out the main lessons of this case study of the banking industry.

16.4 Human resource development: A systems approach

The emergence of know-how as a prime resource requires a shift in the focus of traditional manpower planning in banks away from numerical analysis to the planning and development of skills. This shift underlines four imperatives emerging from our analysis so far in this book:

- the single market will intensify competition

- know-how development is essentially a competitive response. It is important for creating new customised products and services as well as achieving improved labour productivity

- know-how development is expensive and therefore requires a framework which at once ensures its accountability and stipulates its essential thrust

- know-how development is essential for success in the single market.

These imperatives can be accommodated within what can be described as a systems approach to human resource (HR) planning and development; so-called, because it links training and development with a number of other critical considerations at the level of individual banks. The approach is summarised in Figure 16.5 and described in detail in a recent report from the London Human Resource Group [5]. It has four building blocks each with its own set of activities.

Figure 16.5   Model of HR planning and development

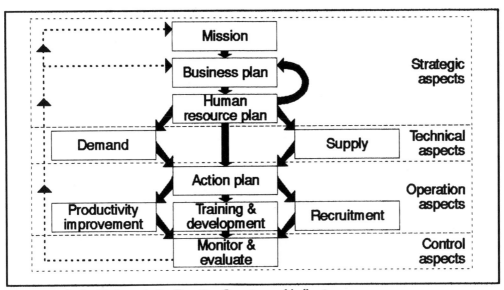

Source: Amin Rajan, Julie Fryatt, *Create or Abdicate:*
The City's human resource choice for the 90s

The first block covers strategic aspects of the HR plan by emphasising that there has to be a clear link between a bank's business plan and its HR plan. This linkage, in other words, sees the HR plan as a mechanism that enables the bank to achieve its corporate aims in a cost effective manner. In practice, this means having or developing those skills and know-how which are consistent with the successful implementation of the business plan, on the one hand, and the adoption of 'best practice' productivity methods on the other. The process of identifying an optimal inventory of skills and know-how consistent with these twin objectives has the merit of linking all aspects of the HR plan with pre-defined business imperatives. Be that as it may, the process is also *iterative* in that it envisages a revision of business plan if the HR plan anticipates major difficulties in the recruitment, development and deployment of the requisite skills and know-how.

The second block covers technical aspects. Once the optimal skills inventory is identified, it can be translated into a headcount figure broken down by different categories of skills, in order to estimate the overall demand for skills.

The corresponding figure for the supply of skills that are generated internally can be worked out by compiling a profile of career development of existing employers. The technical details of these approaches are more fully described elsewhere [5].

When demand and supply estimates are put together, three operational aspects — as listed in the third block — become clear: how much of the required know-how will be met through productivity improvement, how much through training and development, and how much through recruitment from the external labour market. When assessing the contribution of training and development, this approach needs to take into account the various layers identified in the skills development model in Figure 16.4. As such, the over-riding merit of the new approach is that training and development are firmly aligned to the needs of the business plan. That way, they come to occupy a central role in the successful implementation of the bank's business strategy. No longer can they be treated as the 'soft belly' of corporate budgets.

The final building block provides a mechanism for monitoring the extent to which the operational aspects measure up to the pre-defined objectives of business and HR plans.

The four blocks provide an elaborate systems approach with seven merits:

- they emphasise a two-way link between business objectives and HR plans

- they emphasise the importance of planning for skills and know-how rather than simply staff numbers

- they put the issue of 'best practices' and productivity improvement at the heart of HR planning and attempt to identify the enabling mechanisms

- they attempt to avoid educational 'overkill' in recruitment, by identifying essential skills and know-how consistent with business objectives

- they provide emphasis on the business and personal imperatives when it comes to training and development

- they eschew short-termism

- they help prioritisation, in terms of skills categorisation and work activities.

As outlined here, the systems approach has more relevance for HR planners in banks than the national institutions of education and training. That is not to say that the latter do not have a role to play, they do, as Figure 16.4 shows clearly. But as we have argued above, in the age of customisation the role of employers is crucial in the development of the requisite skills and know-how. After all, they are at the leading-edge of most of the critical technological and environmental changes in the free market economies of all the member states. The over-riding merit of the systems approach is the way it highlights the corporate role in the development of skills and know-how in the light of its own business plan. In the process, however, it also enables the corporate sector to generate objective signals for the education and training systems. At present, throughout the Community such signals are ill-defined at best and non-existent at worst.

16.5   Summary

This chapter has suggested a number of minimum actions that need to be taken by governments and companies in the field of education and training in order to ensure that the single market will serve to revitalise the economies of the member states. The main points emerging from it are as follows:

- Governments need to act in three areas. They need to:
  — raise the participation rate in post-compulsory education partly to counter the adverse impact of the projected demographic decline and partly to meet the growing know-how needs of their economies.
  — change the curricula in their secondary education systems in a way that helps those who wish to proceed to further education as well as help those who need vocational preparation.
  — create greater complementarity between their systems and those run by companies.

- Individual companies also need to act in a number of areas, as shown by the three general points arising from the results of the case study on the banking industry as covered in this chapter.

- First, companies need to move towards three-strand training that builds directly on the attainments reached in the state system of education and training.

- Second, the first of these strands should be directed at *skills* development; the second strand at *professional* development; and the third at *personal* development. Between them, the three strands should aim to ensure effectiveness of trainees in their current jobs and developmental preparation for the next.

- Third, the suggested approach to training and development could be expensive. Hence, it is essential to have a framework that integrates business and human resource planning. Under it, training and development should be firmly locked into business imperatives.

17

THE SOCIAL DIMENSION: A MACRO APPROACH

17.1 Aspirations-achievement gap

After the 1973-4 oil crisis, the economies of Europe and America began to lose their post-War growth momentum. The most visible manifestation of creeping stagnation was unemployment. However, since about 1983 there has been a sustained economic recovery in all the industrialised nations. Under it, unemployment has begun to decline sharply in the USA but only slowly in the Community (see Figure 17.1). However, such improvement as there has been in unemployment levels within member states — like Belgium, France and the UK — has been dominated by rapid growth in part-time employment so that on a full-time equivalent basis recorded progress looks even less impressive (see Figure 17.2).

Individual member states have attempted to tackle unemployment through various macro-economic and labour market measures. Whereas such measures can claim a certain degree of success, the fact remains that by January 1990 some 16 million (10 per cent) of the Community's workers were still without jobs — a rate well in excess of that of other economic regions (Figure 17.1). Worse still, a significant proportion of workers have had to resort to work status which they have accepted through necessity rather than choice, as shown by Figures 17.3 and 17.4 respectively giving the percentage of those on part-time work or short-term contracts who would rather have had a full-time job. It is clear that, what the economies of the member states achieved in the 1980s fell short of the aspirations of their workforce. The resulting gap emerged even before much needed industrial restructuring began in earnest. As we saw in Parts A and B, the single market will cause further unemployment in the short term, together with the social hardship that goes with it. Not surprisingly, therefore, the Community has been concerned about adding a significant Social Dimension to the 1992 programme — one that builds on the social traditions established by the Treaty of Rome — by adding elements that can help to ensure an orderly management of economic change.

Figure 17.1   Unemployment rates: 1968-88

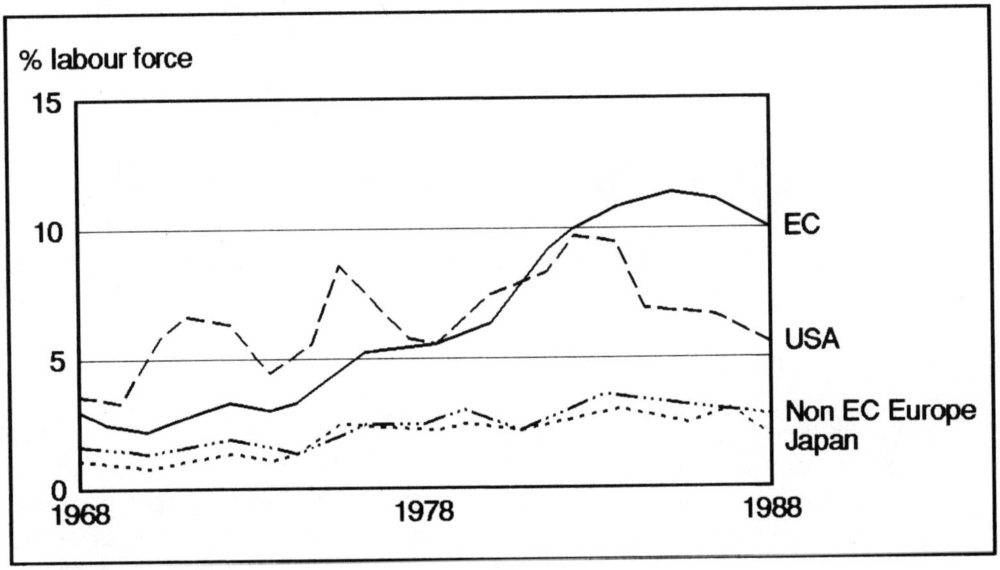

Source: EUROSTAT

This is the pragmatic interpretation of the European Commission's current efforts. There is, of course, a more idealistic interpretation. This posits that the creation of a single market is not an end in itself, but a means to an end: the regeneration of the European economies is needed for facilitating social progress for all their citizens. There is, however, no guarantee that market forces alone, so the argument runs, will ensure social gains except perhaps in the long run. Hence the need for a Social Dimension that can ensure that social progress occurs in parallel with economic progress.

The rest of this chapter has three objectives:

• to highlight elements of the Social Dimension

• to examine in detail the workings of certain elements that are already in operation

• to present the case for the Social Dimension as an instrument for ensuring the success of the single market.

Figure 17.2   Change in employment in the Community: 1979-88

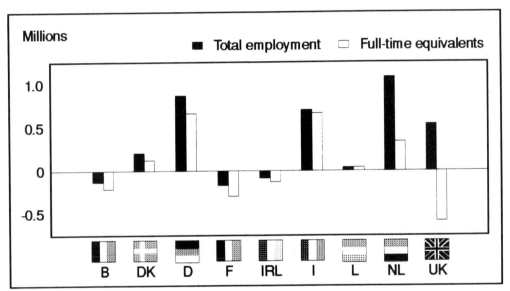

Source: EUROSTAT

Figure 17.3 Part-timers wanting a full-time job: 1987

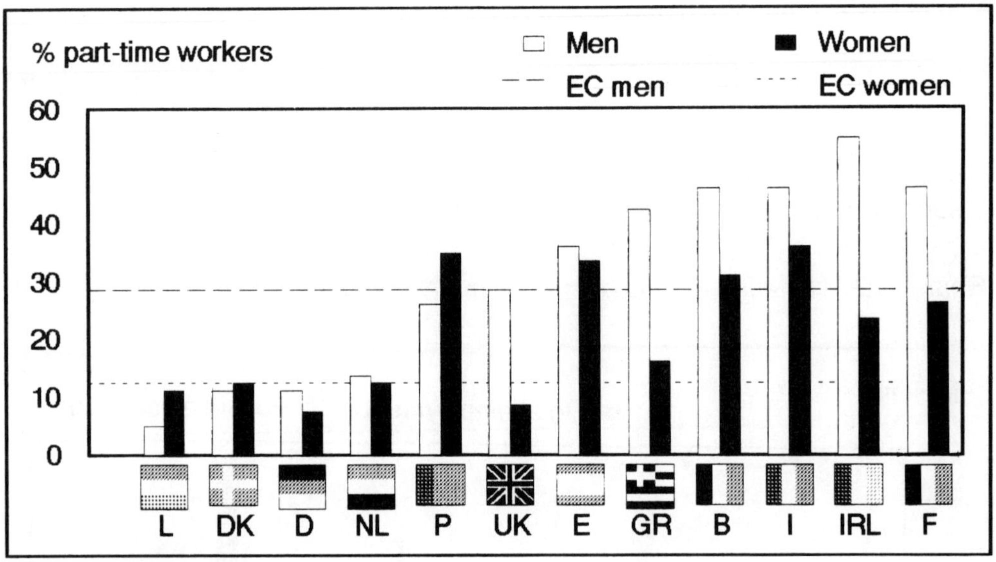

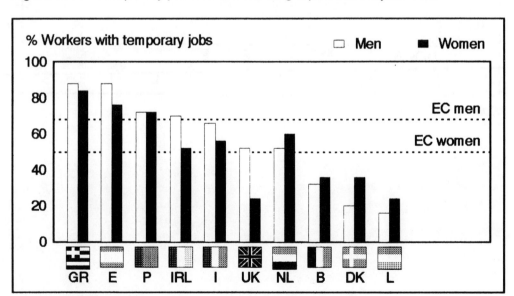

Source: EUROSTAT

Figure 17.4 Temporary job holders wanting a permanent job: 1987

Source: EUROSTAT

17.2 The Social Dimension: The principles

In an important sense, the Social Dimension is as old as the Treaty of Rome. Its recent sudden prominence has come about by the new provisions envisaged under the Single European Act 1987. Both those legal instruments encompass various elements, drawing the distinction between those that are binding and those that are not, as shown in Tables 17.1 and 17.2. This distinction apart, it is clear that the central thrust of the elements is directed at employment-related areas such as health and safety, freedom of movement, social security and training.

At the surface level, the individual elements are not contentious: after all, member states already have their own bodies of rules and regulations on most, if not all, those elements under prevailing laws on employment and social security. As such, those elements merely reinforce national laws.

17.2.1 The Social Charter

At the detailed level, however, the Single European Act 1987 envisages some radical changes which the member states like the UK and the Netherlands have found rather contentious. The proposed changes are best understood in the context of the so-called Community Charter of Fundamental Social Rights. Its details are already spelt out in two important recent documents [1,2]. Below are listed its main provisions. The Charter proposes 12 distinct rights:

- **Right to freedom of movement:** every citizen of the Community should have the right to freedom of movement throughout its territory, for family or occupational reasons without loss of rights under the social security and tax systems. Furthermore, wages and terms of conditions prevailing in the host countries should apply to all workers from other member states employed in the host country.

- **Right to fair remuneration:** decent wage rates should be established by law or collective agreements at national, regional, occupational, sectoral or company level.

- **Right to improvement of living and working conditions:** this applies particularly to the organisation and flexibility of working time, redundancies and paid leave. The right extends to all forms of employment and particularly to those on fixed term contract, seasonal work, part-time work, temporary work, weekend work, night work and shift work.

- *Right to social protection:* every adult, in or out of work, should have adequate social protection, providing a minimal accepted standard of living.

- *Right to freedom of association and collective bargaining:* every employer and every worker should have the right to belong freely to any professional or trade union organisation of his/her choice. This entails recognition of the right to belong to a trade union, freedom to negotiate through collective bargaining and the right to strike in the event of conflict of interests. Collective agreements may be established at the European level and, towards this end, the two sides of industry should develop a social dialogue.

- *Right to vocational training:* each worker should have access to training or retraining on a continuous basis so as to minimise the adverse social impact of industrial restructuring and technological change.

- *Right to equal treatment:* men and women should have equal treatment in matters of remuneration, access to employment, social security, education, vocational training and career development.

- *Right to information, consultation and participation of workers:* this applies particularly in areas such as technological change, industrial restructuring, corporate mergers and take-overs and other areas with direct implications for employment.

- *Right to health and safety protection at the workplace:* this involves ensuring satisfactory health and safety conditions and further improvements in them.

- *Rights for children and adolescents:* these involve setting minimum employment age at 16 years, offering equitable remuneration and complementary vocational training during working hours.

- *Right to decent standard of living for the elderly:* this involves ensuring that all citizens in retirement and early retirement have a reasonable income commensurate with a decent standard of living.

- **Right to integrate for the disabled:** the disabled should have the opportunity for the fullest possible integration into working life through vocational training, improved accessibility, appropriate means of transport and housing.

Table 17.1   *Main social provisions of the Treaty of Rome, 1957*

---

1 Binding provisions cover the following:

- In a general way, Article 100 allows the approximation of 'such provisions laid down by law, regulation or administrative action in member states as directly affect the establishment or functioning of the common market'.

- Freedom of movement for workers (Articles 48 and 49).

- Social security for migrant workers (Article 51).

- Freedom of establishment, ie. the right to take up and pursue activities as self-employed persons (Articles 52 to 58).

- Equal pay for male and female workers (Article 119).

- The European Social Fund (Articles 123 to 128).

2 Non-binding provisions cover the following:

- The standard of living and working conditions and the social field in general (Articles 117 and 118).

- Paid holiday schemes (Article 120).

- A common vocational training policy (Article 128).

- Moreover, the Treaty setting up the EEC includes a number of social provisions relating to the common agricultural policy (Title II) and the common transport policy (Title IV).

Source: Patrick Venturini, *1992: The European Social Dimension* (EC, 1989)

Table 17.2   The additional provisions introduced by the Single European
                  Act, 1987

---

1 New binding provisions concern the following:

- The approximation of national provisions relating to health, safety, environmental protection and consumer protection (Article 100a).

- The working environment, the health and safety of workers (Article 118a).

- The economic and social cohesion of the Community (Articles 130a to 130e).

2 A new provision of a non-binding nature concerns:

- A dialogue between management and labour which could lead to relations based on agreement (Article 118b).

Source: Patrick Venturini, *1992: The European Social Dimension*   (EC, 1989)

17.2.2   The Statute of the European Company

So much for the Social Charter. While many of its elements are non-controversial, it does have some that are. Those which have attracted most attention relate to the concept of worker participation and collective bargaining. The European Commission proposes to implement them through the so-called Statute of the European Company.

Under it, greater industrial democracy is to be achieved through an elaborate *quid pro quo* devised on the basis of the lesson learnt from two previous attempts: the Fifth Directive on the structure of limited liability companies; and the Vredeling Directive which catered for rights and procedures on information and consultation of workers. Both these Directives have been honoured more in the breach than in the observance. At any rate, the momentum behind them died out in the early 1980s against the background of a severe recession and rising

THE SOCIAL DIMENSION: A MACRO APPROACH

unemployment. Since then, a number of loopholes have been discovered, rendering the Directives almost useless.

Accordingly, in order to generate fresh momentum, the European Commission has come up with a carrot and stick approach through proposals on a new Statute of the European Company. Under it, trans-national firms can acquire the status of a Community company in order to avoid the current penal system of double taxation associated with their multinational operations. In return, these firms will have to accept greater worker participation. Two elements are noteworthy about the proposals:

- *Free choice:* each company will have the freedom to choose whether to register as a Community company or maintain the *status quo*.

- *Options:* as regards participation forms, companies have three choices: the German system under which workers are represented on the main board; the Franco-Italian system of a works council with employee representation and operating independently of the management board; or the Swedish system which lays down the rules for participation under a special agreement.

These, then, are the measures that have been proposed for the creation of what is called Social Europe or the European Social Area. Euphemistic though it may sound, the purpose behind it is at once bold and determined. Before developing the underlying rationale, it is helpful to have some idea about what the Social Dimension has achieved in practice so far.

17.3   The Social Dimension: The practice

This section focuses on two sets of programmes: one set established under the Treaty of Rome and the other under the Single European Act 1987. The first of these concerns the European Social Fund and the second concerns a multitude of educational and training programmes. Before looking at their specific features it is as well to realise that such programmes are difficult to evaluate, either in the national or Community context. This is because they have a strong social purpose which defies quantification of the type normally attempted in conventional cost-benefit analysis. In other words, their evaluation is largely a matter of individual value judgment. For this reason, this section merely provides the details of the programmes and leaves it up to the reader to decide their social worth. The section's secondary aim is to highlight the salient features of the specific programmes that have underpinned the development of the Social Dimension until now.

17.3.1 The European Social Fund

The Fund has now become the principal source of Community funding for vocational training and job creation. This funding is generally matched by national funds. Its budget has increased sharply: from 700 million ECU in 1977 to a planned target of 5,200 million ECU in 1993. Although subject to further reform in 1990, the essential thrust of the Fund will remain intact [3].

Figure 17.5 shows the distribution of funds by member states, after allowing for inter-country differences in the size of the labour force. Not surprisingly, the countries with the highest unemployment rates have been the main beneficiaries. Figure 17.6 shows the Fund's main target groups. It is clear that the overwhelming emphasis has been on the young and the long-term unemployed, indicating the Fund's primary role in the retraining of those who are adversely affected by the changing labour markets.

17.3.2 Educational and vocational training programmes

There are a number of programmes which extend beyond helping disadvantaged groups. These are listed in Appendix Tables B3-B7. Their main objective is two-fold: to enhance social contacts between the citizens of the member states; and to promote educational and vocational preparation consistent with the development of the know-how that individual member states will need as customisation of goods and services continues apace.

The foregoing description of the two sets of programmes shows the main thrust of the Social Dimension so far. It also serves to highlight the nature of the actions that the European Commission itself has been undertaking. At the very least, it serves to show that the Social Dimension extends well beyond the contentious issues relating to industrial democracy. Hence, a blanket rejection of its programmes carries a serious risk of throwing the baby out with the bath water.

Figure 17.5 Proportion of labour force assisted by social fund: 1988

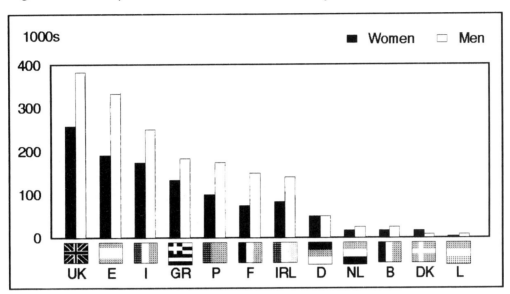

Source: Employment in Europe, 1989

Figure 17.6 Targeting of the social fund: 1988

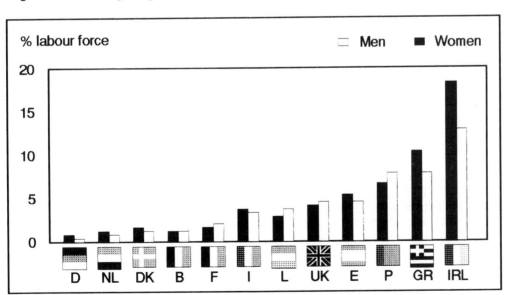

Source: Employment in Europe, 1989

17.4 Rationale for the Social Dimension

Until recently, the most vocal opposition to the Social Dimension came from the Union of Industrial and Employers' Confederations of Europe (UNICE), as well as from certain individual member states. UNICE now appears to feel that there is room for accommodation, although it reserves the right to oppose individual elements as and when the shape of the enabling legislation becomes clear. At the Strasbourg Summit in December 1989 all member states except the UK accepted the Social Dimension in principle. As and when the enabling legislation on individual elements appears, the UK can veto it since many of the contentious elements will require a unanimous vote in the Council of Ministers, as they relate to employment matters.

The clear majority now in favour of the Social Dimension is indicative of the role it is expected to play in the single market. As we have seen in Chapters 3, 4, 5 and 14, economic gains arising from the single market are unlikely to be substantial in this decade. If anything the single market will be first noticed through major industrial restructuring that will cause unemployment. Hence, the Social Dimension is viewed, first and foremost, as giving a human face to the single market. Furthermore, as we saw in Chapters 3 and 14, know-how will emerge as a prime resource. The Social Dimension is seen as an instrument of ensuring that the process of know-how development, deployment and management is at once fair and efficient. Unlike other factors of production, know-how is intangible and internalised by the individuals that possess it. It is, therefore, imperative that there is a proper social framework within which those individuals can thrive and create new wealth for the Community. Thus an important economic imperative lies beneath the traditional social considerations. This general argument, in turn, is underpinned by a number of considerations which are developed in the following sub-sections.

17.4.1 Equity versus efficiency

The Cecchini Report estimates that unemployment will rise by some 0.5 million in the first year of the completion of the single market, with nearly 30 per cent occurring in the UK. As we saw in Chapter 14, however, the programme of writing EC Directives into national laws may well extend beyond 1992. The process of industrial restructuring has already begun, though its substantive gains are unlikely to materialise in this decade. Furthermore, there is nothing inherent in the process of restructuring which pays special attention to the needs of specific groups of individuals or regions.

This is because the whole process is driven by market forces that have least regard for social considerations. The Social Dimension aims to provide a compensating mechanism. But more than that it has the potential to generate greater and quicker economic gains by providing a mechanism for speedy retraining, and rechannelling surplus labour into alternative uses. In sum, it aims both to provide a counterweight to market forces and to improve their allocative efficiency.

17.4.2 Market failure

This dual objective is all the more necessary when it is recognised that areas like health, safety and training generate significant externalities: the benefits arising from them can benefit the whole society in addition to those companies who are generating them.

History shows that where such spill-over effects exist, companies are unwilling to adopt a proactive stance, largely because they are left to bear the cost even though the benefits accrue to society. By this argument, in the circumstances of the single market, companies will have little incentive to promote a number of elements of the Social Dimension. This has been particularly borne out by employers' seemingly myopic attitudes to training in member states such as Italy, Portugal and the UK. Those 'good practice' employers providing quality training have ended up as unwitting recruitment pools for others who indulge in labour poaching. Unless all or many employers engage in good practices, the penalties for those who do are potentially high, with the result that progress in a number of essential areas may well be held back. Market forces alone will simply not generate the necessary actions. Recent evidence from the UK amply corroborates this view: for example, in 1986-7, seven out of ten of Britain's 26 million workers left school at the minimum leaving age. Seven out of ten had only a short initial training for their jobs. Seven out of ten had no training after that [4]. These figures are not additive: they merely serve to show the areas of market failure over different stages of an individual's life cycle, as far as training is concerned.

17.4.3   1992 equals zero

As we saw in Chapter 14, the process of rewriting national laws in the member states so as to incorporate the Commission's Directives has been slow. This has largely been caused by political lobbying on the part of various vested interests.

One such lobbying group which has yet to flex its muscles is the trade unions. They have adopted a supportive stance so far, believing that out of industrial restructuring will emerge tangible long-term economic gains, and also that in the transitional phase there will be a Social Dimension which will serve to minimise social upheavals. If this *quid pro quo* is not upheld then it is unlikely that the parliaments in Denmark, France, the Netherlands, and West Germany will be all that keen on implementing the Directives since they are subject to considerable influence by the trade unions in their countries.

Perhaps matters will not even go that far: the new socialist majority in the European Parliament after the 1989 election has already served notice that without the Social Dimension they are unlikely to enact the remaining measures of the 1992 programme.

Such fears are real rather than apparent. In all member states except the UK there is a strong groundswell of opinion in favour of the Social Dimension. Even in the UK it is arguable whether the opposition extends beyond governmental and CBI circles. Indeed, nine of those member states are already signatory to the separate European Social Charter drawn up by the Council of Europe. Many of them have also ratified a whole range of similar conventions produced by the International Labour Office. To them, having an explicit social dimension to economic progress is not new: on the contrary, the two are viewed as indivisible. The European Commission is, therefore, in the unenviable position of having to accommodate opposition from the UK on the one hand, and the collective social aspirations of all other member states on the other. Soon, it may have to decide on what aspects of the 1992 programme it can sacrifice if this impasse proves impossible to overcome. In all the other 11 member states there remains a strong feeling that the 1992 programme must have the Social Dimension: the invisible hand of the market may need to be countered by the visible boot of the Community in some areas and the long arm of Brussels in others. Otherwise, the burden of adjustment will be borne disproportionately by some worker groups and regions.

Whether the opposition from the UK Government will kill off the Social Charter is open to debate. In strict legislative terms, it can slow down the legislation process and thereby dilute many of the elements. On the other hand, the European Court of Justice is increasingly paying attention to both the letter and the spirit of the Community's laws. As a result, through the Court's rulings over time the charter may well come to have Community-wide applicability.

However, leaving aside the politics of it, it is clear that unless the proposed rights on training, retraining and industrial democracy are adopted, there is a serious risk that the process of industrial restructuring may be characterised by social discord in the short-term and negligible economic progress in the long-term.

17.5 Summary

This chapter has looked at the macro level changes that are deemed essential if the process of industrial structuring associated with the 1992 programme is to generate economic and social gains in the 1990s and thereafter. The main points arising from it are as follows:

- In an age when know-how will become a prime factor of production, actions taken by companies towards its development, deployment and management will not be enough. They will have to be complemented by other actions.

- The Social Dimension of the 1992 programme provides a coherent framework for such actions. But it goes even further. Building on the social provisions of the Treaty of Rome and the Single European Act 1987, the Social Dimension encompasses a number of measures in the area of employment that have four objectives: improvement of living and working conditions; continuous training and retraining; greater industrial democracy in the workplace; and special help for the old or the disabled.

- These objectives are to be pursued through the adoption of a new Charter of Fundamental Social Rights. It will add a human face to the process of industrial restructuring whilst complementing actions that need to be taken at the level of individual companies. Its object is to ensure that the invisible hand of the market is tempered by the visible arm of the Community, if and when necessary.

- It is essential that the Social Dimension is implemented. Otherwise, the freer operation of market forces may place a disproportionate burden on certain individual groups and regions. Also there is a risk that the whole 1992 programme may be jeopardised by certain vested interests. This is because in all the member states except the UK, the Social Dimension is viewed as a *sine qua non* of the orderly management of change and social progress in an integrated market.

18

A NEW VISION FOR THE KNOW-HOW CENTURY

18.1   The Second Industrial Revolution

There is now a general acceptance that many industrialised nations, including various member states of the European Community, are in the midst of the Second Industrial Revolution. As always, its starting date is a matter of debate but its origin can be readily traced to the scientific developments that have promoted computers as the new heartland technology: heartland in the sense that they now perform a vast range of diverse operations in manufacturing and services alike. That said, it is just as well to emphasise that technology is only the visible end of a dramatic transformation in the industrial structure as well as the working methods of these economies.   Under them, work skills and know-how have been emerging as a prime resource. If anything, this process is likely to accelerate with the creation of the single market, as was discussed in Chapter 3.

In an important sense, therefore, the Second Industrial Revolution is different from its precursor that first occurred in Britain in the eighteenth century and elsewhere in Europe some 60 years later. Both of them have been periods of discontinuity characterised by major scientific advances. But the First Industrial Revolution was essentially about converting physical raw materials into tangible products with the use of the newly discovered mechanical power; the second is about converting brain power into tangible services, some of which are sold directly to consumers (e.g. banking and insurance) and others to manufacturers as intermediate inputs (e.g. consultancy, marketing, software, engineering and research and development services). Thus, not only are more services demanded by consumers but they are also demanded by manufacturers whose products are becoming increasingly services-intensive.

Not surprisingly, therefore, the industrial base of the economies of member states is becoming increasingly dominated by services. This shift towards services has also been evident in the changing relationship between GDP and productivity. In an economy with a predominantly manufacturing base, growth in GDP tends to come substantially from growth in labour productivity, made possible by economies of scale associated with mass production or from improved use of labour and machinery. In a services dominated economy, on the other hand, such productivity gains are more difficult to generate because 'production' is in small batches and it is generated by brain power which, given its animate nature, cannot operate like machines. Hence, the emergence of the productivity gap, as discussed in Chapter 8.

As Figures 18.1 and 18.2 show, prior to 1984 productivity grew faster than GDP at a time when the Community's manufacturing industries were involved in a

Figure 18.1   GDP and productivity growth: 1979-84

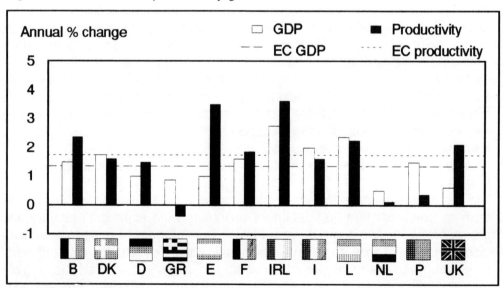

Source: EUROSTAT

large-scale labour shake-out. Since then, however, productivity has invariably increased more slowly than GDP because of the rapid growth in services. Indeed, this phenomenon is not recent: it has origins that can be traced back to the 1960s when the underlying growth in GDP first began to decelerate noticeably (see Chapter 2).

Figure 18.2   GDP and productivity growth: 1984-88

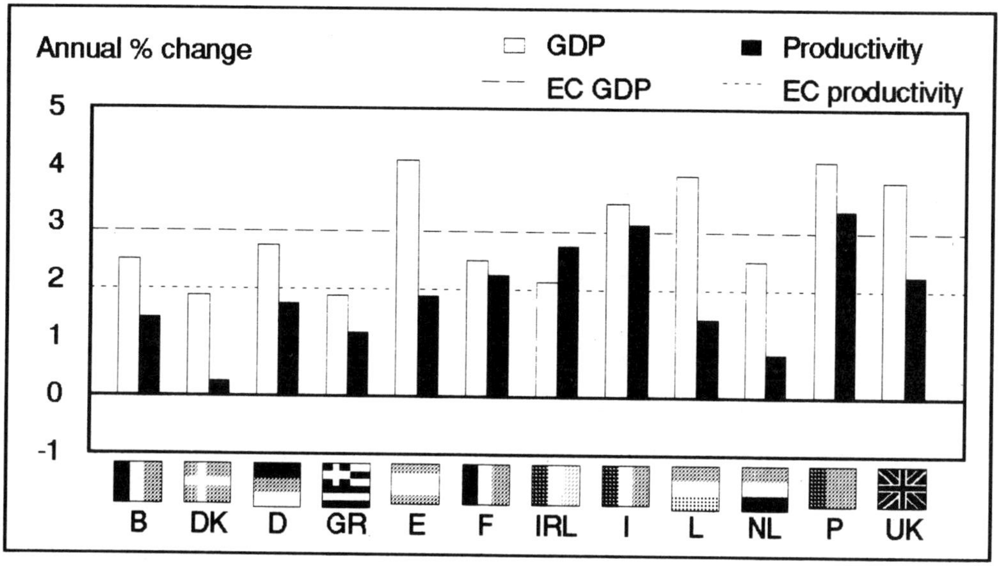

Source: EUROSTAT

18.2   New challenges and opportunities

The new forces released by the single market will accelerate the trend towards customised products and services. Given their high know-how content, it is most likely that the trend towards services will continue. Indeed, the next century could quite rightly be called the know-how century — one in which economic and social success will come to those who have the competitive edge in the development, deployment and management of know-how.

Accordingly, the challenge for the Community is two-fold:

- how to develop the requisite know-how

- how to deploy it in a way that will continuously enhance its productivity, thereby shifting the Community's GDP growth on to a higher trajectory.

The completion of the single market provides a valuable opportunity to face these challenges which have become more daunting as the Second Industrial Revolution has progressed. Indeed, the single market will achieve even more in the process if it has a well defined vision of the Community's position in the world economy. At present, the Community ranks second to the USA in terms of income (Figure 18.3). It can regain the supremacy it lost to the USA at the beginning of this 'American century'. Until about 1970, the USA enjoyed a dominant position, but since then the economic 'centre of gravity' has shifted to the Pacific Basin in general and Japan in particular. However, as a recent study has shown, the new-found importance of Japan in trade, GDP and capital flows

Figure 18.3   Shares of world income: 1988

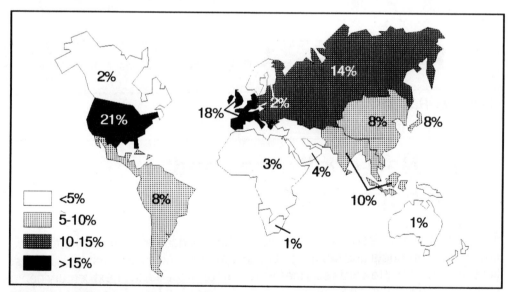

Source: Employment in Europe, 1989

is unlikely to grow beyond 1995 for several reasons: the high value of the yen affecting exports; rising social aspirations and reducing national savings; and a changing work ethos, raising corporate costs and improving efficiency [1]. Long-range forecasting is notoriously difficult in this area: for example, the USA's current foreign debt would have seemed inconceivable ten years ago.

Be that as it may, it seems unlikely that Japan can prolong its period of economic ascendancy for as long as America did, so the Community stands a good chance of altering the economic power base in favour of Europe. After all, it has all the requisite advantages: natural and physical resources, social and democratic traditions, and an innovative workforce. These advantages have remained compartmentalised to the extent that their collective achievements are less than the sum of individual parts. Hitherto, Europe has lacked a mechanism for orchestrating these advantages: the single market could be just the answer.

But as we have seen in the last four chapters, at present the 1992 programme suffers from a number of risks:

- it might not be implemented in time

- its objectives may be frustrated by vested interests

- it may be a zero sum game for the foreseeable future

- it may not revitalise the Community's economies in the long-run

- it may mean social hardship as market forces ensure survival of the fittest.

Given these risks, Chapters 15, 16 and 17 have also identified various actions that need to be taken to ensure that the single market not only rises above these risks but also enhances the Community's relative position in the world economy. Indeed, precisely because of these risks and the consequent need for actions, it is essential for the Community to develop a new vision for an integrated Europe.

18.3   The year 2000 and beyond

The Community is now in a position to adopt a new vision that has a high probability of realisation. A vision that aims to ensure that out of industrial restructuring a revitalised economic base will emerge that is capable of enhancing the Community's relative position abroad and living standards for all its citizens at home. This vision will turn what looks to be a zero sum game into a positive sum game in which everyone wins, some to a greater extent than others.

This new vision has already been described in a graphical form in Chapter 1. Quite simply, it sets the long-term aims, identifies the opportunities and challenges, and suggests the necessary actions. Although its aims are high, they are consistent with historical performance and the Community's current capabilities. Equally, although the necessary actions may look demanding, they are consistent with the art of the possible.

18.3.1   The vision

The proposed vision would shift the economic centre of gravity from the Pacific Basin to Europe over a twenty-five year period. This will not only involve raising the Community's share of world income but it will also mean raising its share of world trade and capital flows so that it has a decisive influence on the evolution of the global economy.

So much for the ends. The means to be deployed are those envisaged by the 1992 programme: namely, the elimination of physical, technical and financial barriers, leading to a new dynamism. There are two vital means of achieving this vision: the first is the competitive forces emerging from the frontier-free Europe, and the second is investment in skills and know-how, on a scale even larger than that implied by the Social Dimension. In particular, this investment should involve step-improvements in the quantity and quality of education and training, as described in Chapter 16.

Now that the vision is set and the key means identified, we move on to identify the opportunities and challenges, and then to discuss the nature of the further actions they call for.

18.3.2   Geo-politics

The momentous events in Eastern Europe in 1989 provide a major opportunity for more trade. Before then, however, the Community had already initiated talks with the COMECON countries of Eastern Europe and serious negotiations with the EFTA countries (Austria, Iceland, Norway, Sweden and Switzerland). The underlying object was to improve trade relations and have collaborative ventures, leading to the creation of the so-called Common European Economic Space.

Now the prospect of a disintegrating Iron Curtain and the emergence of social market democracies hold out hopes for new business opportunities and reduction in wasteful defence spending. The economic resources thus created or released offer a 'peace dividend' for socially worthwhile causes in Europe as well as the developing world.

Indeed, for the first time this century the geo-political outlook seems extremely favourable. Of course, much will depend on the nature of the political order that emerges out of the current turmoil in Eastern Europe. But there is little doubt that it will provide major trading opportunities on the one hand and greater political dialogue on the other. Of course, in the short-term there will be a lot of uncertainty about the status of a unified Germany as well as the political position of Mr Gorbachev. But this uncertainty does not detract from the fact that there is a real prospect of lasting peace in Europe, based on the greater economic integration of the former ideological factions.

18.3.3   The economy

The fresh impetus to trade arising first from the creation of the single market and then from the creation of the Common European Economic Space has the potential for providing a sound basis for sustained economic growth and new investment. Welcome though it may be, the new growth in trade will not necessarily be enough to minimise the adverse economic and social impact of industrial restructuring in the wake of renewed competitive forces. There will have to be greater harmonisation in monetary and fiscal policies between the member states, so as to eliminate the remaining significant obstacles in the allocation of resources.

The progress envisaged under the Delors Plan on monetary integration is rather slow because it touches on the sensitive issue of national sovereignty. Here again, the most vocal opposition comes from the UK. At economic level, there is no doubt at all that harmonisation is essential. If the UK Government persists with its opposition then one of two outcomes is likely: either the vision of Europe will be undermined; or other member states will press on through the creation of a two-speed Europe, in which some member states will proceed towards economic union without others. On present reckoning, the latter is the more likely outcome. In the meantime, it is essential for the UK to reflect on two issues: what does sovereignty mean in an integrated Europe; and should the UK once again limp along in the slow lane and fail to enjoy the benefits of the momentous changes occurring on its doorstep?

18.3.4   The environment

There are two sets of environmental challenges: physical and economic. On the physical side, there has been growing concern about waste and pollution to the extent that individual member states are now responding positively. The European Commission on its part needs to co-ordinate these actions as well as initiate some of its own. Against the background of sustained economic growth it is essential that quality of life issues remain at the fore. In this respect, the omens are good, as evidenced by the success of the Green Party in the 1989 Euro-elections. The neglect of environmental issues could well create a backlash against economic growth, as recent history has shown all too clearly.

On the economic side, the market environment will doubtless become more competitive, as we saw in Chapters 3 and 14. This will help to achieve a more efficient allocation of resources. But as is well known, economic competition creates inequalities in income and job opportunities. It also has the effect of rendering idle valuable human resources. Hence the major challenge here is to create a mechanism that tackles the adverse side-effects of greater competition. This brings us back to the Social Dimension.

18.3.5   The society

In the suggested vision of an integrated Europe, the Social Dimension has a key role in achieving an orderly management of change, as described in the last chapter. Unfettered operation of market forces will doubtless disadvantage various groups of individuals and regions. Various provisions on social protection and training will go a significant way towards alleviating the hardships arising from industrial restructuring.

However, for the new vision to materialise, there has to be large scale investment in education and training that goes well beyond that implied by the Social Dimension. The requisite investment has to face head-on the challenges identified in Chapter 13 and make provision that is at once comprehensive, responsive, motivative and integrative, as explained in that chapter. Specifically it means implementing those actions outlined in Chapter 16, involving companies as well as individual governments.

18.4   Concluding remarks

The foregoing is a suggested vision of an integrated Europe. In one sense it merely articulates and conceptualises the objectives of the European Commission when it first proposed the creation of the single market. But in another sense it goes further, by arguing that, while the gains from the present programme could be at best modest, it ought to be possible to enhance them by identifying further possible actions. The key areas for further action are policy harmonisation, the Social Dimension and large-scale investment in education and training.

Unless this vision, or a variant of it, is adopted, the 1992 programme will be a zero sum game. The programme arguably comes at the most favourable time in Europe's long and bloody history. It provides a springboard to a better future in the next millennium. The First Industrial Revolution started in Europe and paved the way for improvements over a wide area of human life. In the Second Industrial Revolution, however, the lead has come from Japan and the USA. The Community is well placed to overtake them through a better orchestration of its natural, physical, technological and human resources. It needs the will to do it and it needs the know-how to do it.

What Shakespeare wrote about human opportunity some five hundred years ago applies equally to the Community today:

There is a tide in the affairs of men
Which, taken at the flood, leads on to fortune;
Omitted, all the voyage of their life
Is bound in shallows and in miseries.
On such a full sea are we now afloat,
And we must take the current when it serves,
Or lose our ventures.

Julius Caesar, IV:3

Bibliography

Chapter 2   *Vision of a united Europe*

1. 'Europe without frontiers - Completing the internal market' (Commission of the European Communities, Brussels, 1988)

2. Dennis Swann, *The Economics of the Common Market* (Penguin, Sixth Edition, London, 1988)

3. Richard Owen and Michael Dynes, *THE TIMES Guide to 1992* (Times Books Ltd, London, 1989)

4. Paulo Cecchini, 'Research on the "cost of non-Europe", Basic Findings, Vol. 2' (Commission of the European Communities, Brussels, 1988)

Chapter 3   *Industrial impact*

1. Paulo Cecchini, 'Studies on the economic of integration: Research on the "cost of non-Europe", Basic Findings, Vol. 2' (Commission of the European Communities, Brussels, 1988)

Chapter 4   *Case studies: Static and dynamic effects*

1. Amin Rajan, *Services - The Second Industrial Revolution?* (Butterworths, Sevenoaks, 1987)

2. 'The structural, functional and technical future of the wholesale trade in Europe'. Preliminary report (Commission of the European Communities, Brussels, 1988)

Chapter 5   *Employment impact: An overview*

1. Victoria C. Price, '1992: Europe's last chance: From common market to single market' (Institute of Economic Affairs, London, 1988)

2.   *Financial Times* (London, 22 August 1988)

3.   W. S. Atkins, 'The cost of non-Europe in public sector procurement' (Commission of the European Communities, Brussels, 1988)

Chapter 6   *Labour force trends: A supply-side approach*

1.   R. P. Hagemann and G. Nicoletti, 'Ageing population: Economic effects and implications for public finance', OECD Working Paper No. 61 (OECD, Paris, January 1989)

2.   C. F. Hollander and H. A. Becker (eds), *Growing Old in the Future: Scenario on Health and Ageing: 1984 - 2000* (Bohn, Scheltema & Holkema bv, Utrecht, 1987)

3.   United Nations, 'Overall economic perspectives to the year 2000' (Economic Commission for Europe, Geneva, 1988)

4.   D. A. Wise (ed), *The Economics of Ageing* (National Bureau of Economic Research, New York, 1989)

5.   'Demographic and labour force analysis based on Eurostat data banks' (Eurostat, Luxembourg, 1988)

6.   'The labour market implications of international migration in selected OECD countries' in 'OECD Employment Outlook' September 1985 (OECD, Paris)

7.   Hugues de Jouvenel, *Europe's Aging Population: Trends and Challenges to 2025,* FUTURIBLES (Butterworths & Co Ltd, Paris, 1989)

8.   Giovanni Tarnburi, 'Commitments of national pension systems in OECD countries: Strategies for dealing with the future', paper presented at the joint Japanese - OECD Conference of High-level Experts on Health and Pensions Policies in the Context of Demographic Evolution and Economic Constraint, Tokyo, 25-28 November 1985 (OECD, Paris, 1985)

9. Martin Tracey, 'Retirement age practices in ten industrial societies 1960-76', Research Study No. 14 (International Social Security Association, Geneva, 1979)

10. Amin Rajan and Steven Beven (eds), 'Socio-economic trends in Britain: 1985-95 (Institute of Manpower Studies, Brighton, 1990)

Chapter 7   *Labour force trends: A demand-side approach*

1. Amin Rajan, 'Vocational training scenario for the member states of the European Community: A synthesis and evaluation' (CEDEFOP, Berlin, 1989)

2. Robert M. Lindley, 'New forms and new areas of employment growth: A comparative study' (Commission of the European Communities, Brussels, 1987)

3. 'Employment Outlook', September 1988 and September 1989 (OECD, Paris)

4. Amin Rajan, 'Vocational training scenarios for the member states of the European Community: Synthesis report for France, Greece, Italy, Portugal, Spain and the UK' (CEDEFOP, Berlin, 1989)

5. United Nations, 'Overall economic perspectives to the year 2000' (Economic Commission for Europe, Geneva, 1988)

6. Amin Rajan, 'Vocational training scenarios for the member states of the European Community: Country report for France, Italy and the UK' (CEDEFOP, Berlin, 1989)

7. Eduardo Grilo, 'Vocational training scenarios for the member states of the European Community: Country reports for Greece, Portugal and Spain' (CEDEFOP, Berlin, 1989)

8. Hugues de Jouvenel, *Europe's Ageing Population: Trends and Challenges to 2025,* FUTURIBLES (Butterworths and Co Ltd, Paris, 1989)

9.   Hilary Metcalf, 'Employer responses to the decline in school leavers in the 1990s' (Institute of Manpower Studies, Brighton, 1988)

10. Amin Rajan with Julie Fryatt, *Create or Abdicate: The City's human resource choice for the 90s* (Witherby & Co, London, 1988)

11. Paulo Cecchini, 'Studies on the economics of integration: Research of the "cost of non-Europe", Basic Findings, Vol. 2.' (Commission of the European Communities, Brussels, 1988)

Chapter 8   Solutions to imbalances

1.   Amin Rajan, 'Vocational training scenario for the member states of the European Community: A synthesis and evaluation' (CEDEFOP, Berlin, 1989)

2.   H. Franke, 'Der Arbeitsmarkt fur Fuhrrungskrafte bis zum Jahre 2000' in *Stellenjournal,* November 1984 (p.202)

3.   BIPE, 'Education standards in the year 2000: Consumers' needs and the response which state education can provide' (The Haut Comite Education-Economie, Paris, 1985)

4.   'The social dimension of the internal market', SOCIAL EUROPE, Special Edition, 1988 (Commission of the European Communities, Brussels)

5.   Amin Rajan, 'Vocational training scenarios for the member states of the European Community: Country report for France, Italy and the UK' (CEDEFOP, Berlin, 1989)

6.   Amin Rajan, 'Vocational training scenarios for the member states of the European Community: Synthesis report for France, Greece, Italy, Portugal, Spain and the UK' (CEDEFOP, Berlin, 1989)

7.   John Atkinson, 'Relocation and recruitment difficulties of employers in the South East' (Institute of Manpower Studies, Manpower Commentary No. 39, Brighton, 1988)

Chapter 9   Developments in the Community's labour markets

1.   Amin Rajan, 'Vocational training scenario for the member states of the European Community: A synthesis and evaluation' (CEDEFOP, Berlin, 1989)

2.   Amin Rajan, 'Vocational training scenarios for the member states of the European Community: Synthesis report for France, Greece, Italy, Portugal, Spain and the UK' (CEDEFOP, Berlin, 1989)

3.   'Panorama of European Commission industry, 1989' (Commission of the European Communities, Brussels, 1989)

4.   'Four scenarios for Denmark 10-15 years from now', Interview-survey Projects (CEDEFOP, Berlin, 1988)

5.   'Scenarios for vocational training systems for Ireland: 1986-92' (CEDEFOP, Berlin, 1988)

6.   Christopher V Rothkirth and Inge Weidig, 'Scenarios for the vocational training systems in the Federal Republic of Germany to 1995, and qualification structure of manpower requirements to the year 2000 (CEDEFOP, Berlin, 1988)

Chapter 10   Case study 1: France

1.   Ron Johnson, 'Vocational qualifications in the member states of the European Community and moves towards an open market' (NCVQ, London, 1990)

2.   'The conditions of teachers in the European Community' (Commission of the European Communities, Brussels, 1988)

3.   Patrice Sauvage, *Insertion des Jeunes et Modernisation* (Economica, Paris, 1988)

4.   Lucie Tanguy, *Lintrouvable relation formation/emploi* (Economica, Paris, 1986)

5.   'Enseignment technologique' *Journal Officiel Enseignement Technologique* (Paris, 1987)

6. 'L'enseignement superieur' (ADEP, Paris)

7. Pierre-Louis Marger, 'Les Enjeux de la formation professionelle face aux mutalions des tecniques industrielles' (ADEP, Paris, 1984)

8. Michel Godet, 'La maladie du diplome', Cadres CFDT No. 333 (December 1988 - January 1989)

9. Rene Monory, 'Plan pour l'avenir de l'education nationale', Le monde de l'education, No. 145 (Paris, 1987)

10. Pierre-Louis Marger, 'Les Enjeux de la formation professionelle face aux mutalions des tecniques industrielles' (ADEP, Paris, 1984)

11. 'Education standards in the year 2000: Consumers' needs and their response which state education can provide' (Haut Comite Education-Economie, June 1987)

12. Pascal Petit, *Slow Growth and the Service Economy*, (Frances Pinter, London, 1986)

13. Olivier Bertrand, 'The NIT revolution and educational strategies', *European Journal of Education,* Vol. 20 (1985)

14. Robert M Lindley, 'New forms and new areas of employment growth' (Commission of the European Communities, Brussels, 1987)

15. l'Avenir des qualifications dans les services (BIPE, Paris)

16. Olivier Bartrand, 'Evolution of the service occupations' (CEREQ-OECD, 1986)

17. Olivier Bartrand, 'Service employment in France' (CEREQ-OECD, 1988)

18. 'Delegation a la formation professionnelle', Continuing Vocational Training (Paris, 1987)

19. 'Employment Outlook' (OECD, September 1987)

20. 'Employment Outlook' (OECD, September 1988)

21. 'Training and the firm: A European challenge (ADEP, Paris, 1987)

Chapter 11   Case study 2: Italy

1. 'Demographic and labour force analysis' (Eurostat, Luxembourg, 1988)

2. B. Contini *et al*, 'New Forms and New Areas of Employment' (Commission of the European Communities, Brussels, 1987)

3. 'Labour force statistics, 1966-86' (OECD, Paris, 1988)

4. Amin Rajan and Christian A. Hansen, 'A provisional evaluation of the education, training and counselling measures in the European Community' (Commission of the European Communities, Brussels, 1987)

5. 'Employment Outlook' (OECD, Paris, 1988)

Chapter 12   Case study 3: United Kingdom

1. Amin Rajan, *Services - The Second Industrial Revolution?* (Butterworths, Sevenoaks, 1987)

2. Amin Rajan and Richard Pearson, *UK Occupation and Employment Trends to 1990* (Butterworths, Sevenoaks, 1986)

3. 'Review of the economy and employment', Institute of Employment Research (University of Warwick, 1988)

4. 'Employment Outlook' (OECD, Paris, September 1988)

5. 'Employment for the 1990s' (HMSO, London, 1988)

6. 'Employment Outlook' (OECD, Paris, September 1988

7. Amin Rajan with Julie Fryatt, *Create or Abdicate: The City's human resource choices for the 90s* (Witherby & Co, London, 1988)

8. 'The National Curriculum: From policy to practice' (Department of Education, London, 1989)

9. S Rassekh and G Vaidennu, 'The Contents of Education: A worldwide view of their development from the present to the year 2000' (UNESCO, Paris, 1987)

10. 'Demographic and labour force analysis' (Eurostat, Luxembourg, 1988)

Chapter 13 *New challenges to education and training policies*

1. Ron Johnson, 'Towards 1992: Vocational qualifications in the member states of the European Community and moves towards an open market' (NCVQ, London, 1990)

2. 'Continuing training for workers in the European Community' (Commission of the European Communities, Brussels, 1988)

3. 'The conditions of teachers in the European Community' (Commission of the European Communities, Brussels, 1988)

4. 'Vocational training systems in the member states of the European Community' (CEDEFOP, Berlin, 1984)

5. 'Evaluation of the education and training measures for the long-term unemployed' (Commission of the European Communities, Brussels, 1987)

6. 'Panorama of EC Industry: 1989' (Commission of the European Communities, Brussels, 1989)

7. W Ochel and M Oegner, 'Service economies in Europe' (Commission of the European Communities, Brussels, 1987)

8. Pascal Petit, *Slow Growth and the Service Economy* (Francis Pinter, 1986)

9. Amin Rajan, 'Vocational training scenarios for the member states of the European Community' (CEDEFOP, Berlin, 1988)

10. Amin Rajan with Julie Fryatt, *Create or Abdicate: The City's human resource choice for the 90s* (Witherby & Co, London, 1988)

11. Charles Handy, Colin Gordon, Ian Gow and Colin Randlesome, *Making Managers* (Pitman Publishing, London, 1988)

12. 'Demographic and labour force analysis', Theme 3, Series D (Eurostat, Luxembourg, 1988)

13. 'Employment Outlook' (OECD, Paris, September 1989)

Chapter 14   *A zero sum game*

1. Paulo Cecchini, 'The cost of non-Europe, Basic Findings, Vol. 1' (Commission of the European Communities, Brussels, 1989)

2. Evan Davis, P A Gerosk, John A Key, Alan Manning, Carol Smales, S R Smith and Stefan Szymanski, *1992: Myths and realities* (Centre for Business Strategy, London Business School, London, 1989)

3. F M Scherer, *Lessons for the EC from the US Experience* (*The Financial Times*, London, 24 January 1990)

Chapter 15   *Preconditions for success: A micro approach*

1. Rhiannon Chapman, *Personnel Management in the 1990s* (Personnel Management, London, January 1990)

2. Amin Rajan and Penny van Eupen, 'Good practices in the employment of women returners' (Institute of Manpower Studies, Brighton, January 1990)

3. Amin Rajan with Julie Fryatt, *Create or Abdicate: the City's human resource choice for the 90s* (Witherby & Co, London, 1988)

Chapter 16   Know-how development: Towards a new partnership

1. 'Vocational training systems in the member states of the European Community' (CEDEFOP, Berlin, 1987)

2. 'Continuing training for workers in the European Communities' (Commission for the European Communities, Brussels, 1988)

3. 'The conditions of teachers in the European Community' (Commission of the European Communities, Brussels, 1988)

4. 'Education and the economy in a changing society' (OECD, Paris, 1989)

5. Amin Rajan with Julie Fryatt, *Create or Abdicate: The City's human resource choice for the 90s* (Witherby & Co, London, 1988)

Chapter 17   The Social Dimension: A macro approach

1. 'Community Charter of Fundamental Social Rights' (Commission of the European Communities, Brussels, 1989)

2. Patrick Venturini, '1992: The European Social Dimension' (Commission of the European Commission, Brussels, 1989)

3. 'Employment in Europe, 1989' (Commission of the European Communities, Brussels, 1989)

4. 'Training in Britain: A study of funding, activity and attitudes' (Department of Employment, London, 1989)

Chapter 18   A new vision for the know-how century

1. Bill Emmott, *The Sun Also Sets: Why Japan Will Not Be Number One* (Simon & Schuster, London, 1989)

Appendix A   Discussion guide used in interviews relating to case studies in Part C

Set A: *Factors influencing the scale of training*

a. *Demand issues*

- What changes are taking place in the age structure of the population and how will education and training services respond to such changes?

- What are the expected effects of the internal market on manpower and skill requirements?

- What is the effect of emerging new occupations on the demand for education and training?

- Do you know of any recent studies on future training and qualification needs that have been carried out in your country?

b. *Social issues*

- What impact do rising social expectations have on the demand for education and training?

- What is the impact of changes in social values - i.e. an increasingly important role for women in the economy?

- What role is played by the social partners in determining the scale of supply and demand for training?

c. *Supply issues*

- What government training programmes are available to combat long-term unemployment, especially for disadvantaged groups?

- Are sufficient well-qualified teachers and trainers available to service the scale of training considered necessary?

d. Policy issues

- How are present and future skills shortages monitored?

- What funds are available for public body and private enterprise-financed training and are they regarded as adequate for their needs?

- Does the government of your country have a coherent and clear long-term strategy regarding the scale of training provision to meet the country's economic needs?

Set B: Factors influencing the content of training

a. Structural issues

- What impact do differences in regional and local needs have on training content as compared with national schemes?

- How does the spread of new technologies and new materials influence training content?

b. Target issues

- To what extent are new occupations affecting demand for multi/hybrid skills training programmes?

- How do the needs of small and medium enterprises affect training content?

- How do government schemes for unemployed persons affect training programmes?

c. Evaluation issues

- Are continuing general educational elements in training programmes seen as further or remedial education; and to what extent do poor basic education attainment levels pose problems for those responsible for training programmes?

- How are training programmes evaluated and how is training content altered as a result of such evaluations?

d. *Education system issues*

- To what extent does the trend towards rising demand for a more highly qualified labour force lead to the inclusion of further general education subjects in training programmes?

- How do national certification or credit systems affect the content of training programmes for good or ill?

- What role does computer-based training (CBT) play in training programmes and how does CBT affect training content?

- How do national certification of credit systems affect the content of training programmes for good or ill?

- What role does computer-based training (CBT) play in training programmes and how does CBT affect training content?

Appexdix B

Table B1   Employment indicators: Groups 1, 2 and 3

Relevant industries ISIC code	Employment as % of total manufacturing employment	Annual change 1975-83 (%)	1983-6	Wage costs per person (1,000 ECU)
Group 1: Competitively weak industries				
330 Computers	1.3	-1.2	4.1	28.7
344 Telecom equipment	4.2	-0.4	2.4	21.1
372 Medical equipment	0.5	10.5	2.5	19.2
Group 2: Industries facing rationalisation				
257 Pharmaceuticals	1.6	-0.4	-1.2	25.8
315 Boilermaking	1.1	-2.6	-2.3	20.7
362 Railway equipment	0.4	-2.4	-9.7	20.0
425 Wines and spirits	0.1	-1.2	-4.7	23.6
427 Brewing and malting	0.6	-4.3	-8.2	24.9
428 Soft drinks	0.3	-2.34	-4.8	21.3
Group 3: Industries facing some change				
341 Cables	0.4	-0.6	0.7	19.4
342 Electrical machinery	3.6	-1.7	-1.4	18.9
361 Shipbuilding	1.0	-4.7	-13.0	20.6
417 Pasta	0.1	-0.2	-1.0	23.5
421 Chocolate	0.7	-3.4	-6.8	20.2

Source: 'Employment in Europe, 1989' (European Commission, Brussels)

Table B2 Employment indicators: Group 4

Relevant industries ISIC code:	Employment as % of total manufacturing employment	Annual change 1975-83 1983-6 (%)		Wage costs per person (1,000 ECU)
Group 4: Industries affected directly				
247 Glass	1.0	-2.8	-6.5	20.9
248 Ceramics	1.1	-3.2	-2.6	17.4
251 Industrial chemicals	3.0	-2.0	-5.6	27.0
256 Other chemicals	0.7	-0.7	-5.8	24.0
321 Agric. machinery	0.8	0.1	-10.3	20.0
322 Machine tools	1.4	-4.3	-0.1	21.1
323 Textile machinery	0.5	-8.1	0.2	20.9
324 Food machinery	1.3	-2.4	-1.1	22.4
325 Mining machinery	1.9	-2.2	-3.3	21.8
326 Transmissions	0.9	-6.8	-2.6	20.5
327 Wood machinery	0.8	-2.0	1.1	21.6
345 Audiovisual	1.8	-3.2	-2.5	19.8
346 Consumer electricity	1.0	-3.4	-3.7	17.5
347 Electric lamps	0.4	-4.2	3.1	18.3
351 Motor vehicles	6.3	-1.5	-1.9	23.0
364 Aerospace	2.0	-0.1	-0.7	25.1
431 Wool	0.7	-6.4	-5.4	16.9
432 Cotton	1.0	-5.7	-9.1	16.7
438 Carpets	0.2	-3.2	-10.4	18.3
451 Footwear	1.2	-1.7	-6.6	14.4
453 Clothing	3.5	-4.1	-5.2	12.3
455 Household textiles	0.3	-2.3	-1.7	13.3
481 Rubber	1.6	-2.3	-5.7	19.7
491 Jewelry	0.2	-2.6	-8.4	17.4
493 Photography	0.2	1.5	-2.8	16.9
494 Toys	0.3	-4.8	-5.1	15.5

Source: 'Employment in Europe, 1989' (European Commission, Brussels)

Table B3   Community education and vocational training programmes

---

ERASMUS Programme

First phase on-going 1988-1900
Second phase planned for 1991-3

People involved:	Students in higher education. Participation of 43,000 students and 1,500 higher education institutions in the first phase.
Objective:	Increase the mobility of students in higher education in the Community and add a European dimension to their initial training.
Activities:	European network of inter-university co-operation. Grants for students to spend a period of training in another member state. Measures to develop the academic recognition of diploma.

COMETT Programme

First phase on-going 1987-9
Second phase planned for 1990-4

People involved:	Students in higher education and staff from enterprises participating in 1987-1988. 1,320 projects and 1,400 students.
Objective:	Stimulate university-industry co-operation in order to improve high level training linked to new technologies.
Activities:	University-industry partnerships. Transnational placements for students in enterprises. Joint continuing training projects.

Source: 'Employment in Europe, 1989' (European Commission, Brussels)

Table B4   Community education and vocational training programmes

---

Youth for Europe Programme

First phase on-going 1989-91
Second phase planned for 1992

People involved:	Young people from 15 to 25 years old. Participation in the first phase: 80,000 young people.
Objective:	Improve, develop and diversify young people's exchanges in the Community.
Activities:	Support for young people's exchanges of at least one week. National agencies for information and co-ordination of the programme. Study visits and assistance for training courses for the organisers of youth exchange.

Exchange of Young Workers Programme

Third phase on-going 1985-90
Forth phase planned for 1991

People involved:	Young workers or job seekers of 18 to 28 years old. Participation in 1987-88: 7000 young people.
Objective:	Offer training or work experience for young people in another Member State.
Activities:	Support for short (up to three months) or longer (up to 16 months) periods of work or training for young people in another member state. Exchange network.

Source: 'Employment in Europe, 1989' (European Commission, Brussels)

Table B5   Community education and vocational training programmes

---

PETRA Programme

First phase on-going 1989-92

People involved: Young people in vocational training following full-time
                        compulsory education. 154 training initiatives in 1989.
                        200 youth projects.

Objectives: Support, with a Community added-value, the
                        implementation of the Council Decision of the vocational
                        training of young people.

Activities: European network of vocational training initiatives in the
                        form of transnational partnerships. Initiatives and
                        information projects managed by young people
                        themselves. Co-operation in the research field.

IRIS Programme

First phase on-going 1988-92

People involved: Women in vocational training. 71 projects in 1989.

Objective: Develop the access of women to vocational training.

Activities: Network of innovative projects in vocational training for
                        women.

Source: 'Employment in Europe, 1989' (European Commission, Brussels)

Table B6   Community education and vocational training programmes

---

EUROTECNET Programme

First phase on-going 1985-89
Second phase planned for 1990-94

People involved: Young people and staff of enterprises in initial or
continuing training. 135 demonstration projects in 1989.

Objective: Dissemination throughout the Community of innovations
in the area of vocational training linked to new
technologies.

Activities: European network of demonstration projects in initial
and continuing training. Co-operation in the research
field.

ARION Programme

Activities began in 1978

People involved: Education policy-makers and experts. 3,200 study visits
since 1978.

Objective: Improve mutual understanding of the education systems.

Activities: Study visits of one week's duration.

Source: 'Employment in Europe, 1989' (European Commission, Brussels)

Table B7   Community education and vocational training programmes

---

LINGUA Programme

First phase planned for 1990-94

People involved:	Pupils and teachers from secondary and higher education. Whole of the current workforce.
Objective:	Improve the quantity and quality of language training for the citizens of the Community.
Activities:	Support for initial and continuing training of teachers (linked with ERASMUS). Drawing up of teaching materials. Pupil exchanges. Diagnosing the language needs of the business world.

Education of Migrant Workers' Children Programme

Activities began in 1977

People involved:	Primary and secondary schools with migrant children. 15 pilot projects in 1988.
Objective:	Improve the integration of migrant children at all levels of the education system.
Activities:	Pilot projects to the teaching of the mother tongue. Teacher training. Education for returning migrants.

Source: 'Employment in Europe, 1989' (European Commission, Brussels)

Index